LINCOLN'S PLANNER

A Unique Look at the Civil War Through the President's Daily Activities

LAMONT WOOD

Post Hill
PRESS

A POST HILL PRESS BOOK

ISBN: 978-1-68261-615-4

ISBN (eBook): 978-1-68261-616-1

Lincoln's Planner:

A Unique Look at the Civil War Through the President's Daily
Activities

© 2018 by Lamont Wood

All Rights Reserved

Cover art by Dan Pitts

Post Hill Press

New York • Nashville

posthillpress.com

Published in the United States of America

For Louise

&othable of&o
CONTENTS

❧INTRODUCTION☙

Knowing the outcome is one thing. Following along as it happens is another. Abraham Lincoln won a war, saved the Union, and freed the slaves. But, following along day by day, it is obvious that the outcome was not pre-ordained.

This book lets the reader follow Lincoln as he confronts each new day with no comforting knowledge of the eventual outcome. In the process, the reader can see Lincoln's mind at work. And his soul.

The author would like to thank his literary agent, Jeff Herman, for coming up with the idea for this book. Meanwhile, the author acknowledges that this book is based on the output of generations of Lincoln scholars, a vast body of researchers who share the same discovery: Abraham Lincoln is worth studying.

⮵KEYS TO⮳ USING THIS BOOK

Notes on the Text

Most histories do not follow serial timelines, preferring to explore the narratives of separate themes. This can allow for satisfying storytelling but does not demonstrate how events shaped the man or how the man shaped events. Nor does it acknowledge the fog of uncertainty that all adults confront.

This book's day-planner format confronts the reader with the evolving sequential events as Abraham Lincoln himself confronted them. Through this approach the reader can appreciate how Lincoln continually groped for the right thing to do next.

Many of the entries reflect accidental document survivals. Anyone (including myriads of office-seekers) could haunt the White House waiting room and eventually see Abraham Lincoln, who would send them to a department head with a memo or with an endorsement on whatever document they presented. We know of these encounters largely because (generations later) the documents showed up in the catalogs of autograph dealers. Inter-office paperwork had a somewhat better chance of ending up in official archives. Consequently, the entries in this book should be seen as representative rather than definitive. (See the Bibliography for a description of the source material.)

Omitted (reducing the text by a third) were:

- Duplications, as well as enigmatic or obscure items
- Routine administrative matters
- Routine diplomatic and treaty matters (including numerous Indian treaties)
- Petty job solicitations
- Most thank-you notes and solicitations for autographs
- Solicitations for military academy appointments that proved fruitless

- Formulaic refusals to petty congressional inquiries
- Interactions with inventors and would-be contractors that proved fruitless
- Lincoln's personal finances and purchases (which included numerous books) and library borrowings.

If there is no information for a particular day, it can mean the only items were like the above, or that no record of events survived from that day.

Daily entries are given in present tense, with editorial notes in square brackets. Any quotes are from Lincoln, unless stated otherwise. Editorial comments to establish context are in parentheses and are not in present tense.

In keeping with the overall effort to conceptualize Lincoln's activities as if he had a modern day-planner, spelling and some punctuation has been updated, to avoid any hint of "quaintness."

1860s Usages

Corps: A military force that could leave camp, march down a road, and camp again in a day—roughly 20,000 men. Corps were composed of divisions, divisions of brigades, and brigades of regiments.

Regiment: The basic administrative military unit. Commanded by a colonel, a regiment usually had ten companies of one hundred men, each commanded by a captain.

Volunteer army: Militia units raised at the state level for national service. Despite the name, it included draftees. The pre-war regular army being insignificant, the war was fought with a newly raised, entirely green volunteer army, for which the Union organized about 2,000 infantry regiments.

Generals: There were then, as now, four main grades of general: full general, lieutenant general, major general, and brigadier general. But at the time Congress only allowed for brigadier and major generals. Congress later revived the rank of lieutenant general specifically for

Ulysses S. Grant. For simplicity, the text makes no distinction between general ranks. Otherwise, officers are referred to by the rank they had on the day in question. (Confederate officers are not referred to by rank, in keeping with Lincoln's position that the Confederacy was not a real country with a real army.)

Brevets: Honorary promotions without increased pay or preferment, unless the officer was given a command at that grade. Many regular officers held separate ranks in the volunteer army and had brevets in both, giving them four different ranks.

Tariffs: Taxes on imports. Tariffs were the Federal Government's chief source of revenue before the war. That explains the attention that Lincoln paid to the management of customhouses in major seaports. An income tax was introduced during the war, but the war was mostly paid for through bonds and loans.

Cabinet: The Administration then had seven Cabinet-level departments, compared to the current sixteen.

Senators: They were then elected by state legislatures, an arrangement that framed the Lincoln-Douglas Debates of 1858. Since the 17th Amendment in 1913 senators are elected at large within their states.

Serenades: Restive crowds would clamor in front of the residence or hotel of a public figure, demanding a speech. The resulting speeches often appeared in newspapers.

Patronage: The engine that ran politics, also called the spoils system. Government jobs were handed out to campaign workers and party supporters. Lincoln had at least a thousand jobs at his disposal, and estimated that there were about 30,000 office-seekers. The system died with the creation of the U.S. Civil Service Commission in 1883.

Abbreviations Used

- AL=Abraham Lincoln of Illinois, 16th president the United States
- MTL=Mary Todd Lincoln, AL's wife
- RTL=Robert Todd Lincoln, adult son of AL and MTL
- Willie=child of AL and MTL
- Tad=child of AL and MTL
- Nicolay=Bavarian native John George Nicolay, personal secretary of AL
- Hay=John Hay, personal secretary of AL
- Browning=Orville H. Browning, AL's old friend and confidant, Illinois senator from June 26, 1861, to January 12, 1863, thereafter a lawyer and lobbyist in Washington.
- Buchanan=James Buchanan, fifteenth president of the United States
- Hamlin=Hannibal Hamlin of Maine, AL's first-term vice president
- Johnson=Andrew Johnson of Tennessee, senator, later military governor of Tennessee, later AL's second-term vice president
- Seward=William Seward, AL's Secretary of State
- Chase=Salmon Chase, AL's first Secretary of the Treasury
- Welles=Gideon Welles, Secretary of the Navy
- Cameron=Simon Cameron, AL's first Secretary of War
- Blair=Montgomery Blair, AL's first Postmaster General
- Smith=Caleb Smith, AL's first Secretary of the Interior
- Bates=Edward Bates, AL's first Attorney General
- Fox=Gustavus V. Fox, naval consultant, later Assistant Secretary of the Navy
- Stanton=Edwin Stanton, AL's second Secretary of War
- Usher=James P. Usher, AL's second Secretary of the Interior
- Fessenden=William Fessenden, AL's second Secretary of the Treasury
- Dennison=William Dennison, AL's second Postmaster General
- Speed=James Speed, AL's second Attorney General

- McCulloch=Hugh McCulloch, AL's third Secretary of the Treasury
- Gen. Scott=Gen. Winfield Scott
- Gen. McClellan=Gen. George McClellan
- Gen. Hooker=Gen. Joe Hooker
- Gen. Meade=Gen. George Meade
- Gen. Grant=Gen. Ulysses S. Grant
- Gen. Halleck=Gen. Henry Halleck
- Gen. Pope=Gen. John Pope
- Gen. Burnside=Gen. Ambrose Burnside
- Gen. Butler=Gen. Benjamin Butler
- Gen. Sherman=Gen. William T. Sherman (not Gen. T. W. Sherman)
- Gen. Frémont=Gen. John Frémont
- Gen. Meigs=Gen. Montgomery Meigs (starts book as a captain)
- Gen. Buell=Gen. Don Carlos Buell
- Gen. Rosecrans=Gen. William Rosecrans
- Comdr. Dahlgren=Commander (later Admiral) John Dahlgren
- Jefferson Davis=Confederate President Jefferson Davis (not Union Gen. Jefferson C. Davis)
- Alexander Stephens=Confederate Vice President Alexander Stephens
- Lee=Robert E. Lee, rebel commander
- Stonewall Jackson=Thomas J. Jackson, rebel general
- Longstreet=Pete Longstreet, rebel general
- Hood=John Bell Hood, late-war rebel commander in the Atlanta region
- J. E. B. Stuart=James Ewell Brown Stuart, rebel cavalry leader and Southern media darling

Note: All photos in the book are from the Library of Congress unless otherwise noted.

&ANTECEDENTS&
FEBRUARY 12, 1809,
THROUGH
FEBRUARY 22, 1861

Summary: Leadership is situational. When the hierarchy becomes invested in defending institutionalized human suffering (i.e., slavery) people might turn to a leader who understands suffering. But to understand suffering one must have suffered.

February 12, 1809

- ❖ Abraham Lincoln is born in Hodgenville, Kentucky, to subsistence farmers who drift westward to Illinois.
- ❖ AL later shows a preference for reading—which annoys his father.

October 5, 1818

- ❖ AL's mother, Nancy Hanks Lincoln, dies.
- ❖ His father, Thomas, thereafter leaves his son with an older sister and cousin in a log cabin for six months to find a new wife.
- ❖ AL's stepmother approves of literacy. He goes to school for about a year.
- ❖ His father hires AL to the neighbors for cash, in a form of slavery then allowed by law, until his twenty-first birthday.

January 20, 1828

❖ AL's older sister Sarah, having married, dies in childbirth.

February 12, 1830

❖ After his 21st birthday AL leaves his father and has little to do with him thereafter.

1831

❖ AL moves to the hamlet of New Salem in central Illinois and pursues a number of avocations: boatman, shopkeeper, soldier in the Black Hawk War (during which he helps bury bodies but sees no combat), owner of a general store that eventually fails, land surveyor, postmaster, and odd jobs that include splitting tree trunks into fence rails.

1832

❖ AL runs unsuccessfully for the Illinois state legislature.

1834

❖ AL is elected to the Illinois state legislature.
❖ He remains in office for four sessions (eight years) as a Whig, in opposition to the majority Democrats in Illinois.
❖ AL finds his passion in politics.

August 25, 1835

❖ AL's girlfriend Ann Rutledge dies of typhoid fever.

1836

❖ AL is admitted to the bar in Illinois, having studied law on his own.

- ❖ AL moves to Springfield, Illinois, a larger town in the same electoral district, which soon became the state capital.
- ❖ AL becomes a circuit court rider.
- ❖ They call him "Honest Abe" because of his guileless, open demeanor. His opinions are stated in fresh ways, indicative of his sincerity. He often tells humorous (sometimes off-color) stories that deflect tensions and can carry parable-like messages.

November 4, 1842

- ❖ AL marries Mary Todd, a politically attuned woman almost ten years his junior. She is a child of wealth, raised by a slave-owning family in Lexington, KY. (She later had relatives who fought for the Confederacy.) She had moved to Springfield to get away from her imperious stepmother. Unlike AL, she has a formal education and social polish. He broke the engagement a year prior and appeared to suffer a nervous breakdown. They later reunited.

Thereafter

- ❖ MTL proves to be neurotic, willful, spiteful, and at moments unethical, reacting to stress or perceived slights with hysterical outbursts, including physical tantrums. AL relies on calming words to ground her—or leaving the house.
- ❖ AL rides the entire court circuit and is gone half the time.

August 1, 1843

- ❖ Birth of RTL.

1844

- ❖ After two law partnerships AL sets up his own practice with William Herndon, another self-taught lawyer nine years his junior who shares AL's interests, albeit needing some prompting to stay sober.

❖ AL runs for Congress unsuccessfully.

March 10, 1846

❖ Birth of Edward Baker "Eddie" Lincoln.

1846

❖ AL runs for Congress and wins.

1847–1849

❖ AL serves in the U.S. House of Representatives. As a Whig congressman he is opposed to the policies of President James Polk (a Democrat) and Polk's entry into the Mexican–American War.
❖ He works dutifully for the Whig party, including the Zachary Taylor presidential campaign.
❖ After his term is over, he returns to his law practice and drops out of politics.

February 1, 1850

❖ Death of Eddie Lincoln, from cancer or tuberculosis.

December 21, 1850

❖ Birth of William Wallace "Willie" Lincoln.

January 17, 1851

❖ AL's father dies. AL had provided him with financial help but never invited him to AL's home.

April 4, 1853

❖ Birth of Thomas "Tad" Lincoln III. He has a speech impediment and is homeschooled by tutors.

1849–1854

❖ AL experiences a midlife crisis—cause unknown.

❖ Previously he had mostly functioned as a partisan hack, content to heap insult and satire on his opponents.

❖ The new AL is motivated by principles, avoids personal attacks, and sees enemies as friends that he has not yet won over. His ego-free approach to politics later allows him to transcend the theater of narcissism that characterizes Washington (as today), subtly manipulate its ego-driven hacks, and dominate events through the psychological ascendency of his personality.

❖ But, once invested in someone, he has trouble dropping them, even when they connive against him. And anyone who attacks one of his friends is in deep trouble.

❖ His distaste for slavery has become visceral hatred.

May 30, 1854

❖ Congress passes the Kansas-Nebraska Act, sponsored by AL's fellow Illinois politician and personal and professional rival Sen. Stephen A. Douglas.

❖ The law replaces the 1820 Missouri Compromise (under which Kansas and Nebraska would both have been non-slave territories) with "popularity sovereignty" meaning the settlers will decide the issue after settling there—and potentially tip the balance of power between the slave and non-slaves states in favor of the former.

❖ AL returns to politics.

1854–1856

❖ AL runs for U.S. Senate but is defeated.

- ❖ The Whig party disintegrates over the Kansas-Nebraska issue.
- ❖ AL helps establish the Illinois branch of the new Republican Party in 1856.
- ❖ The party nominates frontier celebrity John Frémont for president. AL campaigns for him in Illinois, but victory goes to the Democrat, James Buchanan.

1857

- ❖ The U.S. Supreme Court issues the "Dred Scott Decision" stating that black people have no rights and that the Federal Government cannot prohibit slavery in the territories.

June 16, 1858

- ❖ AL accepts the Republican nomination to run for the Senate against Sen. Douglas, who is up for reelection, famously saying, "A house divided against itself cannot stand."

Summer and Fall, 1858

- ❖ Sen. Douglas campaigns for reelection, arriving in towns on a special train festooned with banners, including a flatcar with a cannon to alert the public to his coming. His speeches are well-lubricated demagogic performances replete with imagined facts and racist rhetoric.
- ❖ AL arrives in each town the day of Douglas's performance or the next. AL draws a crowd and makes his own speech, calmly (and soberly) dismantling whatever Sen. Douglas said. The newspapers report his speech as they did Douglas's.
- ❖ AL agrees to stop haunting Douglas in exchange for a series of formal debates. Seven are held. Douglas stays sober. Their speeches are reprinted nationwide. AL becomes a national celebrity.

- ❖ AL maneuvers Douglas into claiming that his popular sovereignty doctrine was not rendered moot by the Dred Scott Decision because local legislatures could still pass laws unfriendly to slavery. This destroys Douglas with Southerners.
- ❖ The Democrats (who outspent the Republicans twenty to one) retain control of the Illinois legislature, and Douglas is reelected.

February 27, 1860

- ❖ To thunderous applause, AL gives his Cooper Union speech in New York, analyzing the Founding Fathers' voting records on slavery to show that they sincerely believed that "all men are created equal."

His address at Cooper Union arguably put Lincoln on the national political map.

May 18, 1860

❖ The Republican National Convention convenes in Chicago. AL sends a dedicated team of floor managers.

❖ AL's team finds the other candidates have powerful enemies. Not so with AL, and he is nominated on the third ballot.

Thereafter

❖ Sen. Douglas becomes the Democratic Party candidate, as expected. But the party splits into Northern and Southern factions. The Southern Democrats nominate their own ticket, led by Vice President John Breckinridge.

❖ A third party, the Constitutional Union Party, tries to avoid the slavery issue altogether. They pose John Bell of Tennessee for President and Edward Everett of Massachusetts for Vice President.

November 6, 1860

❖ AL carries the North and West, winning decisively with 180 electoral votes vs. 123 for all his opponents. Sen. Douglas only wins Missouri. Breckinridge wins most of the South, the rest going to the Constitutional Union Party.

December 20, 1860

❖ South Carolina secedes. The rest of the Deep South soon follows: Florida, Mississippi, Alabama, Georgia, Louisiana, and Texas. They begin forming the Confederate States of America, which neither Buchanan nor AL recognize.

❖ Secession is initially rejected in the rest of the South and the Border States.

❖ AL choses a Cabinet. Instead of snubbing the men who had been his rivals he incorporates them into his administration, leaving them invested in his success.

❖ AL visits his aged stepmother.

❖ He holds a party. He sells much of his furniture and rents his house. He tells Herndon to keep their law office going.

February 11, 1861

❖ Amid reports of threats to his life, AL boards a train for an eleven-city speaking tour, scheduled to arrive in Washington on February 23, 1861, for his inauguration on March 4, 1861.

His suffering has only begun.

ൠ1861 ൠ

FEBRUARY 23
THROUGH DECEMBER 31

FEBRUARY 1861

Summary: AL spends his first days in Washington meeting and greeting.

February 23, Saturday

Texas voters approve secession.

❖ AL arrives from Philadelphia at about 6 a.m., accompanied by aide and bodyguard Ward Hill Lamon and detective Allan Pinkerton. He is surprised to be greeted by his friend and supporter, Illinois Rep. Elihu Washburne, who drives him to Willard's Hotel.

❖ AL telegraphs MTL (still in Harrisburg, Pennsylvania) concerning his safe arrival despite reported assassination plots.

❖ AL has breakfast with New York Sen. William H. Seward. (Seward vainly hoped to dominate AL, as he did political novice Zachary Taylor in 1849.)

❖ The two then call on Buchanan at the White House, and meet Cabinet members.

❖ AL calls on Gen. Scott, seventy-four-year-old commanding general of the U.S. Army. He's not home. Scott returns AL's visit several hours later.

❖ AL visits with future Cabinet member Montgomery Blair and Blair's father, Francis P. Blair Sr., one of the founders of the Republican Party.

❖ MTL arrives via train at about 4 p.m. and is driven to the hotel by Seward and Washburne.

❖ AL later receives a delegation from Illinois headed by Illinois Sen. Stephen A. Douglas, AL's former rival.

❖ AL dines privately at Seward's residence at about 7 p.m.

❖ Back at his hotel room, AL finds a crowd waiting for him, and shakes hands.

❖ AL is called on by peace conference delegates, led by Ohio Senator-elect Salmon Chase, and Vermont Republican and banker Lucius Chittenden.

❖ AL is called on even later by members of the Buchanan Cabinet, and by a group of New York businessmen hoping for a compromise to assure commerce with the South.

February 24, Sunday

❖ AL and MTL attends worship services at St. John's Episcopal Church.

❖ After church AL spends two hours at Seward's home.

❖ AL then reads newspapers and receives callers, including Kentucky Sen. John Crittenden, Massachusetts Rep. Francis Adams, and Vice President John C. Breckinridge.

❖ AL poses at Matthew Brady's photography studio.

February 25, Monday

❖ AL and Seward attend informal receptions at both houses of Congress and then visits with Supreme Court justices in the afternoon.

❖ In the evening AL and MTL receive visitors at their hotel parlor.

February 26, Tuesday

❖ AL goes for a dawn walk with RTL and Nicolay.

❖ AL hears from two delegations urging the appointment of Massachusetts Gov. Nathaniel Banks as Secretary of War.

❖ AL hears from two other delegations urging the appointment of Indiana Rep. Schuyler Colfax as Postmaster General.

❖ AL visits the Senate to confer with Republican leaders,

❖ AL meets with Illinois Sen. Stephen A. Douglas and Maryland Gov. Thomas Hicks about the secession crisis.

❖ Writing a response to the congressional committee that reported the electoral college vote, AL formally acknowledges his election as President of the United States.

❖ MTL receives friends from 3 to 4 p.m. and from 8 to 10 p.m.

February 27, Wednesday

❖ AL walks two miles before breakfast and sees former Tennessee senator John Bell.

❖ Washington Mayor James Berret officially welcomes AL to the city. (AL would have Berret deposed and jailed in August for declining to take an oath of allegiance.)

❖ AL receives the clerks of various executive departments.

❖ In the afternoon, AL goes to the Capitol and receives Supreme Court justices.

❖ At 9 p.m., AL discusses sectional compromise with several politicians from Border States, including former treasury secretary James Guthrie of Kentucky, and Mexican— American War hero Alexander W. Doniphan of Missouri.

February 28, Thursday

North Carolina voters reject secession. Colorado Territory is organized in the Union.

❖ AL sees Kentucky Sen. John Crittenden, who urges compromise. (Compromise eventually failing, one of his sons became a general in the Union army, and another in the Confederate army. He also had a grandson who would die at the Little Bighorn.)

❖ AL sees Gen. John Wool, commander of the Department of the East.

❖ AL attends a private dinner at the National Hotel. Hearing of a Georgia resident who has sworn to wear no clothes produced under a Republican regime. AL says he'd like to see him wear only clothes from Georgia, limiting him to a shirt collar and a pair of spurs.

MARCH 1861

Summary: *AL is inaugurated. While the nation continues to disintegrate, AL must devote much of his time to patronage.*

March 1, Friday

* AL spends much of the time in private interviews with potential Cabinet appointees, and others.
* AL offers the War Department post to Pennsylvania Sen. Simon Cameron, who had backed AL's nomination. Cameron accepts.
* AL, Gen. Scott, British minister Lord Lyons, and other dignitaries attend a dinner hosted by the minister for the German city-state of Bremen.
* MTL tours the White House and visits with Harriet Lane, Buchanan's niece and acting First Lady.

March 2, Saturday

Nevada and Dakota territories are organized in the Union, and Congress adjourns.

* Seward, who had accepted the Secretary of State post in December, asks to withdraw, not wanting to serve in the Cabinet with Chase. AL successfully asks him to reconsider.
* AL goes for a carriage drive to avoid crowds.
* AL sees two delegations from Virginia.
* A delegation led by New York merchant and Seward supporter Simeon Draper protests the appointment of Chase as Secretary of the Treasury. AL offers to drop Seward's name, confusing them.
* AL dines with Gen Scott.

March 3, Sunday

Serfdom is abolished in Russia.

❖ AL attends the farewell speech in the Senate chamber of Kentucky Sen. John J. Crittenden.

❖ AL offers the navy cabinet post to Connecticut politician Gideon Welles, who accepts.

❖ AL hosts a dinner for his cabinet appointees: Seward (State), Chase (Treasury), Welles (Navy), Cameron (War), Blair (Postmaster), Smith (Interior), and Bates (Attorney General).

March 4, Monday

As many as 30,000 people gather for the Inauguration. Soldiers line the streets and rooftops. There are no disturbances.

❖ At noon, AL and Buchanan share an open carriage to the Capitol.

❖ The Senate is called into session. Hamlin is given the vice-presidential oath of office by outgoing Vice President (and future Confederate general) John Breckinridge.

❖ At 1 p.m., AL is introduced on the portico of the Capitol by long-time friend and former fellow Illinois politician, Oregon Sen. Edward D. Baker. (Baker was the namesake of AL's second son Eddie, who died in 1850. Baker moved to the Pacific Coast in 1852.)

❖ Reading from a manuscript he unfolds after adjusting his glasses, AL delivers his First Inaugural Address. He denounces secession but asserts he would use force against it only if necessary. He says he was not intent on abolishing slavery and lacks the power to do so anyway. He appeals for calm.

❖ Chief Justice Roger B. Taney administers the presidential oath of office to AL.

❖ After a procession to the White House, AL and Buchanan exchange farewells.

❖ AL appoints Nicolay as his private secretary.

❖ AL is handed a message from Major Robert Anderson, commander of Fort Sumter. He says he will run out of supplies before a relief expedition can reach him.

❖ The Inaugural Ball begins at 11 p.m. AL leaves before MTL.

March 5, Tuesday

❖ AL sees various parties and delegations.

❖ Seward officially accepts his Cabinet nomination.

❖ AL sends his Cabinet nominations to the Senate.

❖ AL receives more information about Fort Sumter's situation.

❖ RTL returns to Harvard.

❖ AL asks Cameron to give a War Department clerkship to AL's personal friend (and former law clerk) Elmer Ellsworth, who had organized a touring military-style drill team. (Ellsworth opts instead to raise an infantry regiment in New York.)

March 6, Wednesday

❖ Chase resigns his Senate seat to accept his Cabinet post, after prompting from AL.

❖ AL holds his first Cabinet meeting.

❖ AL sees various delegations and parties, including Welles.

March 7, Thursday

❖ AL confers with Cabinet members about the Fort Sumter situation, without deciding anything.

❖ AL confers with Virginia politician Lucius Chandler, concerning Union sentiment in Virginia.

❖ AL attends a reception for the Washington diplomatic corps.

March 8, Friday

❖ AL attends a formal reception for navy officers.

❖ A delegation of diplomats' wives calls on MTL.

❖ AL holds his first public reception in the White House, shaking hands for more than two hours.

March 9, Saturday

❖ AL sends written questions to Gen. Scott about options for Fort Sumter.

❖ AL later confers with the Cabinet on Fort Sumter.

❖ AL meets with a delegation from Oregon.

March 10, Sunday

❖ AL and family attend services at the New York Avenue Presbyterian Church, Dr. Phineas D. Gurley, pastor.

❖ Hay, on loan from a Department of the Interior clerkship, becomes Nicolay's assistant.

March 11, Monday

The Confederate government adopts a constitution enshrining slavery.

❖ AL attends a morning Cabinet meeting and discusses Fort Sumter.

❖ AL starts sending nominations to the Senate for various patronage jobs.

❖ AL invites Col. Ferguson of Memphis, Tennessee—for whom he once chopped wood—to the White House.

❖ MTL visits the Washington Navy Yard with friends.

March 12, Tuesday

❖ AL nominates Kentucky abolitionist Cassius Marcellus Clay as minister to Spain and names a minister for Mexico.

❖ AL attends an official reception for army officers.

❖ AL and MTL host a party with music and dancing.

March 13, Wednesday

- ❖ AL tells Seward to refuse to meet with Confederate commissioners as it would imply admission that their states had left the Union.
- ❖ A short Cabinet meeting considers other appointments.
- ❖ AL confers with former navy lieutenant (and brother-in-law of Blair) Fox on plans for getting supplies to Fort Sumter.

March 14, Thursday

- ❖ AL meets with the Cabinet about appointments and again discusses Fort Sumter.
- ❖ AL nominates a minister to Sweden.

March 15, Friday

- ❖ AL asks the Cabinet for their views on reinforcing Fort Sumter. Seward, Chase, Cameron, Welles, and Smith initially oppose the idea, feeling that a relief expedition is not practical or could spark war. Blair favors it.
- ❖ AL nominates a minister for Guatemala.

March 16, Saturday

- ❖ AL receives written opinions from four Cabinet members on a possible Fort Sumter expedition. They are lengthy and not decisive.
- ❖ AL sends a message to the Senate asking for its opinion on the idea of submitting the Vancouver Island boundary dispute to international arbitration.

March 17, Sunday

- ❖ AL attends church with Gen. Scott.
- ❖ AL discusses diplomatic appointments with Seward.

March 18, Monday

- ❖ AL nominates Massachusetts Rep. Charles Francis Adams (son of President John Quincy Adams and grandson of President John Adams) as minister to England and names others as ministers for Sardinia, Turkey, and France.
- ❖ AL meets with Horace Greeley, editor of the influential *New York Tribune* and one of the founders of the Republican Party.
- ❖ AL sends a proposal to Bates to make Elmer Ellsworth, now a lieutenant, the "Adjutant and Inspector General of Militia." (Bates later replied that it would involve setting up a new department, which would require an act of Congress, and the matter lapsed.)
- ❖ Chase reports that they could collect tariffs in the South offshore, given sufficient revenue cutters and naval escorts.
- ❖ AL asks Welles how many ships he could supply to the Revenue Service. (Welles later suggested twelve vessels.)

March 19, Tuesday

- ❖ AL confers with Fox about the Fort Sumter situation.
- ❖ Ohio Rep. James M. Ashley lobbies AL to appoint Ohioan Francis Case as surveyor general for Utah Territory.

March 20, Wednesday

- ❖ AL confers with two Colorado politicians about territorial office appointments.
- ❖ Willie and Tad develop measles.
- ❖ AL nominates ministers for Austria, Rome, and Denmark.

March 22, Friday

- ❖ AL and MTL greet guests at the second White House reception of the season.

March 23, Saturday

- ❖ AL attends a long Cabinet meeting.

March 25, Monday

- ❖ AL meets with a deputation of Baltimore citizens.
- ❖ AL attends a Cabinet meeting, apparently working on appointments before the Senate adjourns.

March 26, Tuesday

- ❖ AL hosts a Cabinet meeting for most of the morning, and later meets with Seward and Welles, plus New York Sens. Preston King and Ira Harris, about appointments.

March 27, Wednesday

- ❖ AL is interviewed by *London Times* correspondent William Russell.
- ❖ MTL and friends visit Mount Vernon, George Washington's home.

March 28, Thursday

- ❖ AL sees Cassius Clay, who declines his nomination as minister to Spain but then accepts a nomination as minister to Russia.
- ❖ German immigrant politician and Republican activist Carl Schurz calls at the White House and is nominated minister to Spain.
- ❖ The Senate adjourns.
- ❖ AL and MTL host their first state dinner, with Cabinet members and Gen. Scott.

March 29, Friday

- ❖ AL and Seward consult Capt. Meigs (an Army engineer) on the possibility of relieving Fort Pickens.
- ❖ AL, at a Cabinet meeting, announces his decision to reinforce both Fort Sumter and Fort Pickens.

❖ AL tells Cameron and Welles that he wants a naval expedition ready to leave by April 6.

❖ AL discusses California and Maryland patronage.

March 30, Saturday

❖ AL sets his visiting hours for the current season: 10 a.m. to 3 p.m.

❖ MTL sets White House Saturday visiting hours as 2 to 4 p.m.

❖ AL discusses California appointments with his old friend Oregon Sen. Edward D. Baker and with Baker's political opponent James W. Simonton, founder of the *San Francisco Bulletin*. Simonton makes personal remarks about Sen. Baker that offend AL, who tosses Simonton's list of appointments to the fireplace.

March 31, Sunday

❖ AL sees Capt. Meigs and Col. Erasmus Keyes, aide to Gen. Scott, on a plan to relieve Fort Pickens. He sends them to Scott with orders to proceed.

APRIL 1861

Summary: *The crisis becomes an actual war when the Confederates bombard Fort Sumter. The arrival of the Northern troops, and the failure of Maryland to secede, saves Washington.*

April 1, Monday

❖ AL writes a memo to Seward, rebuking Seward for a memo complaining that the administration has no national policy yet, pointing to AL's various policy statements. (He may not have sent this memo.)

❖ AL directs Gen. Scott to start making daily reports of troops movements and intelligence.

❖ Seward, Capt. Meigs, and navy Lt. David Porter launch an operation to relieve Fort Pickens, without consulting Welles, even though Welles is Secretary of the Navy.

April 2, Tuesday

❖ AL tells Seward to pay Capt. Meigs (about to leave for the Fort Pickens expedition) $10,000 "from the secret service fund."

❖ AL resets his visiting hours: 10 a.m. and 1 p.m.

❖ AL and family spend two hours visiting the Washington Navy Yard.

❖ AL visits military barracks during an afternoon drive.

April 3, Wednesday

❖ AL issues blanket orders to Col. Erasmus Keyes authorizing him to organize an expedition to Fort Pickens.

❖ AL tries to attend the wedding of the daughter of navy Capt. (and future Confederate admiral) Franklin Buchanan at the Navy Yard but gets there after the ceremony.

❖ AL sends an emissary to Richmond to arrange a consultation with Virginia Rep. George W. Summers, a Unionist. (His district later becomes part of pro-Union West Virginia.)

April 4, Thursday

In Virginia, a state convention votes down secession.

❖ AL sends a message to the besieged commander of Fort Sumter asking him to try to hold on until April 11 or 12 as relief is on the way. (The message can't be delivered.)

❖ Navy Comdr. Dahlgren, on duty at Navy Yard, confers with AL about what artillery to send to New York.

❖ At 11 a.m., AL confers secretly with Virginia Unionists John Baldwin and John Botts. (AL apparently considers, but rejects, a proposal to abandon Fort Sumter in return for a loyalty pledge from Virginia.)

April 5, Friday

❖ AL attends a Cabinet meeting for much of the morning.

❖ Comdr. Dahlgren is at White House and finds AL "ill at ease, and not self-possessed."

❖ The day's public reception is canceled due to the press of business.

❖ AL visits Matthew Brady's photography gallery.

April 6, Saturday

❖ AL confers with the governors of Indiana, Ohio, Maine, and Pennsylvania about the status of their militias.

❖ AL sees various Virginia Unionists, who want assurances that Forts Pickens and Sumter will be evacuated.

❖ AL sends messengers to South Carolina's governor saying that an attempt will be made to deliver supplies to Fort Sumter. If it is not resisted, no reinforcement or munitions will be sent.

❖ AL learns that his orders to reinforce Fort Pickens were not carried out as the Federal naval commander on the scene refused to let troops land. Welles sends a special messenger ordering a landing.

❖ AL attends MTL's second afternoon reception but only stays briefly.

❖ AL visits the Navy Yard

April 7, Sunday

❖ AL again confers with Virginia Unionist John Botts, about what could be done to prevent Virginia from seceding.

April 8, Monday

❖ AL hosts a public reception.

❖ AL gets a letter from Horace Greeley and several other New York Republicans urging him to name someone from their "wing of the party" to the position of surveyor of the Port of New York. AL has already named someone they nominated to the separate position of collector for the port, so he writes on the envelope that they want "two big puddings on the same side of the board."

April 9, Tuesday

❖ AL spends most of the day on minor appointments.

April 10, Wednesday

❖ AL confers with Ambrose Thompson, self-proclaimed major landowner in Chiriqui Province (on the Pacific Coast of what is now northwest Panama, adjacent to Costa Rica), concerning a proposed naval base there with Isthmus-crossing rights, and the possibility of colonizing the area with freed slaves.

April 11, Thursday

Confederate officials demand Fort Sumter's surrender. The commander refuses.

❖ AL confers for several hours with Maryland Gov. Thomas Hicks.
❖ AL confers with Carl Schurz about whom to appoint as commander of four different regiments.

April 12, Friday

The Confederates start bombarding Fort Sumter at 4:30 a.m.

❖ AL meets with the Cabinet on general matters.
❖ AL appoints his aide and bodyguard Ward Hill Lamon as a federal marshal.
❖ AL unofficially receives several Virginia commissioners.
❖ AL tells Massachusetts Sen. Charles Sumner that Fort Sumter will not be surrendered.

April 13, Saturday

Fires having broken out, Fort Sumter surrenders at about 2:30 p.m.

❖ AL receives no information regarding Fort Sumter except press reports.
❖ AL meets again with commissioners from the Virginia state convention, and tells them that, if Fort Sumter has been assaulted, he would stop mail service to seceded states but would not invade them to collect taxes. But military posts belong to the Federal Government and he reserves the right to use force to relieve them.

❖ AL converses for two hours about conditions in the South with Cameron, author James Gilmore, and former Kansas territorial governor Robert Walker.

❖ AL briefly attends MTL's reception.

April 14, Sunday

Fort Sumter is evacuated, the garrison leaving for the North on Union vessels.

❖ AL attends church.

❖ AL, Nicolay, Willie, and Tad take a carriage ride.

❖ Illinois Sen. Stephen A. Douglas sees AL and pledges to support AL's efforts to preserve the Union.

❖ AL meets with the Cabinet into the night. They call for the raising of a militia force of 75,000, and for a special session of Congress to convene July 4.

April 15, Monday

❖ AL issues an official proclamation calling for the rising of a militia force of 75,000.

❖ The Cabinet meets at 10 a.m. and remains in session most of the day.

❖ AL confers with Gen. Scott, and others concerning the defense of Washington.

❖ AL sees the mayor of Portsmouth, Virginia, a Unionist who urges AL to defend the naval shipyard there.

❖ AL writes to Col. Elmer Ellsworth, repeating his admiration, saying, "I have been, and still am anxious for you to have the best position in the military which can be given you."

April 16, Tuesday

North Carolina and Virginia refuse AL's call for troops. North Carolina begins seizing Federal installations.

❖ AL holds a patronage conference with a Pennsylvania delegation.

April 17, Wednesday

The Virginia state convention votes for secession. Missouri and Tennessee refuse the call for troops.

❖ AL confers with Gen. Scott on matters pertaining to the army depot in Harper's Ferry, Virginia, the Gosport Navy Yard in Portsmouth, and the defenses of Washington.
❖ A Maryland delegation asks AL to reinforce Fort McHenry (outside Baltimore).

April 18, Thursday

Union militia units begin arriving to defend Washington.

❖ AL hears an account from a New York traveler of the bombardment of Fort Sumter.
❖ Some arriving troops are housed in the East Room of the White House.
❖ Republican kingpin Francis Blair Sr. unsuccessfully offers the post of commanding general to Gen. Scott's selectee, Col. Robert E. Lee.
❖ AL confers with Welles and Gen. Scott on the defense of the Gosport Navy Yard and the fall of Harper's Ferry.

April 19, Friday

❖ AL proclaims a naval blockade of the seceded states.
❖ The Cabinet hears about conditions at the Gosport Navy Yard.
❖ AL drives out to inspect the forts around Washington.
❖ There, AL speaks with Col. John B. Magruder, a Southerner who expresses loyalty.

- ❖ Baltimore Mayor George Brown asks that Federal troops not pass through his city, as it will trigger violence. AL responds that he will have them go around.
- ❖ AL is then notified that the 6th Massachusetts Infantry was attacked by a mob while passing through Baltimore, with four soldiers and nine citizens killed.

April 20, Saturday

The Gosport Navy Yard at Portsmouth is abandoned, with about a thousand cannons and a salvageable warship, the USS Merrimack.

- ❖ AL confers with various parties about moving troops through Baltimore and Maryland, and preserving the peace in Maryland.

April 21, Sunday

- ❖ AL confers about conditions in New York.
- ❖ From late morning to early afternoon, AL confers again with Baltimore Mayor George Brown, Gen. Scott, and the Cabinet on moving troops through Maryland.

April 22, Monday

Arkansas refuses the call for troops.

- ❖ AL meets with a delegation from Baltimore demanding that he not bring troops through Maryland. AL is unsympathetic this time: "Go home and tell your people that if they will not attack us, we will not attack them; but if they do attack us, we will return it, and that severely."
- ❖ AL is surprised to hear that Col. John B. Magruder has resigned. (He becomes a general in the Confederate army.)
- ❖ The Cabinet meets at 3 p.m.

❖ AL is seen conferring with Gen. Scott in the White House driveway, so the old man won't have to climb the stairs.

April 23, Tuesday

❖ AL meets with the Cabinet.
❖ AL is seen pacing the floor, anxious for troops to reach Washington.

April 24, Wednesday

❖ AL talks to men wounded by the mob in Baltimore. Anxious for more troops to arrive, he says, "I begin to believe there is no North."
❖ AL writes that while he does not plan to invade either Maryland or Virginia, "I do not mean to let them invade us without striking back."

April 25, Thursday

❖ AL tells Gen. Scott that the Maryland legislature is about to meet and might secede, but arresting or dispersing the members is not justified or practical.
❖ AL, Seward, and Cameron review the 7th New York Militia.

April 26, Friday

❖ AL addresses troops quartered in the White House: "Whether the Union is to be broken in fragments and the liberties of the people lost, or blood be shed, you will probably make the choice, with which I shall not be dissatisfied."

April 27, Saturday

❖ AL authorizes Gen. Scott to suspend habeas corpus between Philadelphia and Washington.

❖ AL extends the blockade to North Carolina and Virginia.
❖ The 7th New York band performs on the south lawn of White House.
❖ AL confers with German immigrant and Republican activist Carl Schurz.

April 28, Sunday

❖ AL accompanies Seward and others visiting the 7th New York Militia, which is temporarily quartered in the House chamber of the Capitol.

April 29, Monday

The Maryland legislature votes against secession.

❖ AL hears from a New York delegation that, "The people were absolutely determined on maintaining their government."
❖ AL stands for a picture on the White House lawn with the new Cassius Clay Battalion.
❖ AL asks Welles to have a warship patrol the Potomac to prevent the construction of rebel artillery positions.

April 30, Tuesday

Union forces retreat from Indian Territory (modern Oklahoma).

❖ AL visits various regiments now stationed in Washington.
❖ AL approves enrolling loyal citizens in St. Louis to maintain Federal authority.
❖ In the afternoon, AL meets with Rufus King (named minister to the Papal States but on leave to be a general of Wisconsin volunteers) and New York Pvt. Robert Gould Shaw. Shaw leaves after a five-minute conversation, favorably impressed by AL.
❖ In the evening, AL meets with Carl Schurz, Blair, and Fox.

MAY 1861

Summary: *The situation stabilizes as more states take sides, but the throng of office-seekers never slows. The death of AL's friend Elmer Ellsworth is a reminder that this really is a war.*

May 1, Wednesday

- ❖ AL invites Major Robert Anderson (who had commanded Fort Sumter) to the White House for a social visit.
- ❖ AL confers with Kentucky politician Garrett Davis
- ❖ Massachusetts Sen. Henry Wilson and others urge AL and the Cabinet to adopt more aggressive war measures.
- ❖ Unionists from western Virginia ask AL for assistance.
- ❖ The band of the 7th New York Militia performs at the White House in the evening, and AL speaks briefly to them.

May 2, Thursday

- ❖ AL reviews the Rhode Island Marine Artillery.
- ❖ AL reviews the New York Fire Zouaves, a regiment commanded by his friend Col. Elmer Ellsworth.

May 3, Friday

- ❖ AL issues a proclamation calling for 42,034 three-year volunteers to bring the regular army to a total of 156,861 and the navy to 25,000.
- ❖ Capt. Meigs reports to AL concerning his expedition to Fort Pickens.

May 4, Saturday

❖ AL confers with Gen. Butler about the military situation at Baltimore.

❖ A committee from the Maryland legislature sees AL to protest the possible military occupation of the state by vengeful Federals. AL replies that troop dispositions will be guided by the public interest and not any spirit of revenge.

May 5, Sunday

❖ AL hears from a committee of Baltimore citizens who urge him to recognize the independence of the seceded states. AL rejects the idea.

❖ Connecticut Gov. William Buckingham assures AL of the support of the people of Connecticut.

❖ AL calls a meeting of government department heads 8 p.m. at the White House.

May 6, Monday

Tennessee and Arkansas secede.

❖ AL introduces Chase to James Gordon Bennett Jr., who is offering one or more yachts to the government for use as revenue cutters.

❖ AL tells another commission from the Maryland legislature that the movement of military units must "necessarily be contingent" on the situation.

❖ AL nominates a minister for Brazil.

May 7, Tuesday

❖ AL sends Col. Robert Anderson to recruit three-year troops in Kentucky and western Virginia.

❖ During the morning, Col. Elmer Ellsworth visits the White House.

❖ AL, Tad, and Hay attend exercises of Ellsworth's regiment.

❖ AL, Gen. Scott, and Cabinet members review New Jersey volunteer units.
❖ A committee representing the governors of Pennsylvania, Ohio, Indiana, Illinois, Michigan, and Wisconsin visit AL and pledge their full support.
❖ AL acknowledges a declaration from the Republic of San Marino (a tiny city-state in north Italy) granting him citizenship there.

May 8, Wednesday

❖ AL attends a flag-raising ceremony of the 69th New York on Georgetown Heights.
❖ AL writes to Chase about a patronage job in New York, where rival Republicans Horace Greeley and Thurlow Weed are backing the same person: "I suppose the like never happened before, and never will again."
❖ In afternoon AL goes for a drive in an open carriage with Seward.

May 9, Thursday

❖ AL joins an outing to the Navy Yard. He sees a dress parade of the 71st New York, attends a band concert, and boards the USS Pensacola to see its 11-inch guns fired.
❖ In the evening AL and MTL host a reception of commissioned officers. Finding Major Robert Anderson in the group, AL has Anderson stand with him.

May 10, Friday

Riots break out in St. Louis between Unionists and secessionists.

❖ AL authorizes the Union military commander in Florida to suspend habeas corpus.
❖ AL poses for photographs at Matthew Brady's studio.

- ❖ AL writes to Rhode Island Gov. William Sprague to say he will not appoint Sprague's nominee to a postmaster position, as most of the Rhode Island congressional delegation opposes the nominee.
- ❖ MTL arrives in Philadelphia with her entourage, on a shopping trip for White House fittings.

May 11, Saturday

Unionists prevail on the streets of St. Louis.

- ❖ AL sees someone whom Horace Greeley wants hired at the New York customhouse.
- ❖ AL and Carl Schurz watch the Marine band perform on the White House lawn.
- ❖ MTL leaves Philadelphia at 2 p.m. for New York.

May 12, Sunday

- ❖ AL joins Seward and Thurlow Weed for a three-hour cruise on the Potomac.

May 13, Monday

Union troops occupy Baltimore.

- ❖ AL, in the afternoon, reviews District of Columbia militia units on the White House grounds.
- ❖ Between 9 and 10 p.m., AL speaks to a serenading group.
- ❖ MTL, in New York, buys a carriage for $900.

May 14, Tuesday

- ❖ AL authorizes Col. Robert Anderson to distribute arms in Kentucky.

- ❖ AL asks Cameron to see what Blair is upset about. (Blair backs the wholesale promotion of volunteer officers, which the army bureaucracy opposes.)
- ❖ AL discusses military commissions with Cameron.
- ❖ AL attends a reception at Seward's house.

May 15, Wednesday

- ❖ AL reviews 4,000 troops from New York, Massachusetts, and Pennsylvania.
- ❖ Gen. Butler confers with AL.

May 16, Thursday

Kentucky declares its neutrality.

- ❖ AL attends the wedding of the son of Adjutant Gen. Lorenzo Thomas.
- ❖ AL sees a dress parade of the 7th New York Militia with Seward.
- ❖ Gen. Butler spends the evening conferring with AL, Gen. Scott, Blair, and Cameron.
- ❖ A delegation from Alexandria, Virginia, assures AL that the town opposes secession.
- ❖ MTL, in New York, orders a dinner service for the White House, plus mantel ornaments for the Blue and Green Rooms.

May 17, Friday

- ❖ The 1st Michigan and their band march to the White House to perform for AL.
- ❖ MTL leaves New York at 5 p.m. for Boston.

May 18, Saturday

- ❖ AL inspects outposts along the Potomac.

- ❖ AL sends a request to Missouri Rep. Francis Blair Jr. not to deliver an order (which he was hand-carrying) to Gen. William Harney removing him from command of the Department of the West, "unless in your judgment the necessity to the contrary is very urgent." (Gen. Harney was suspect because he was from Tennessee and had agreed to a truce in Missouri that let pro-South militias control most of the state. But he had already been dismissed and restored once. Blair later delivered the order.)
- ❖ AL and Seward inspect ordnance at the Navy Yard.
- ❖ AL attends an evening concert by the Marine band on the White House grounds.
- ❖ MTL arrives in Boston.

May 19, Sunday

- ❖ AL attends church.
- ❖ AL, Seward, and Gen. Meigs drive to Great Falls, Virginia, and return about dark.
- ❖ MTL visits RTL in Cambridge, Massachusetts.

May 20, Monday

North Carolina secedes. The Confederate capital moves to Richmond.

- ❖ AL writes to New York Gov. Edwin Morgan noting that Morgan is not justified in being upset that AL moved fourteen New York regiments to the front without consulting him: "We are in no condition to waste time on technicalities."
- ❖ AL talks with delegates from the "Pulaski's Legion," a Polish Battalion from New York, about the idea of mustering a Polish regiment from all states.
- ❖ MTL returns to New York.

May 21, Tuesday

- ❖ AL and Seward revise instructions for Charles Francis Adams, minister to England, emphasizing the need to oppose any move to recognize the Confederacy.
- ❖ MTL in New York spends $116.50 on carpeting.

May 22, Wednesday

- ❖ AL writes to New York Gov. Edwin Morgan suggesting a face-to-face meeting about Morgan's problem with the government's unilateral disposition of New York regiments. (Morgan declines.)

May 23, Thursday

Virginia voters approve secession.

- ❖ AL with MTL (returned from New York) attends a flag presentation ceremony for the 7th New York Militia.

May 24, Friday

Federal troops occupy Alexandria, where Col. Elmer Ellsworth is killed hauling down a secessionist flag flying over a hotel.

- ❖ AL weeps openly when he learns, through a War Department telegram, of the death of his friend Col. Ellsworth. AL calls a Cabinet meeting to discuss the incident, and then drives to the Navy Yard to view the body.
- ❖ AL later receives a reporter and Massachusetts Sen. Henry Wilson, but then excuses himself, being unable to talk.
- ❖ AL returns to the Navy Yard in the evening and arranges for Ellsworth's funeral.
- ❖ AL approves a bill for $952.48, for carpeting MTL purchased in New York.

May 25, Saturday

- ❖ AL and MTL attend funeral services for Ellsworth in the East Room. Tad and Willie join AL during the procession to the train depot to return the body to New York.
- ❖ AL writes condolences to Ellsworth's parents.
- ❖ AL and Cameron consider using the Rothschild organization to shape public opinion in Europe.

May 26, Sunday

Gen. McClellan enters western Virginia to protect the Baltimore & Ohio Railroad.

May 27, Monday

- ❖ AL talks to three members of a sixty-man artillery battery in Baltimore that is offering its services to the Union.
- ❖ Blair and Gen. Meigs discuss with AL the suggested appointment of a quartermaster general.
- ❖ Gen. Meigs confers with AL and Seward about Fort Pickens
- ❖ Carl Schurz calls on AL.
- ❖ RTL, on vacation from Harvard, is at the White House.

May 28, Tuesday

- ❖ AL and MTL host a levee in the East Room of the White House.

May 29, Wednesday

- ❖ AL and Blair decide Gen. Butler can employ fugitive slaves, and does not have to send them back.
- ❖ In afternoon, Seward and AL visit several army camps on the south side of Potomac.
- ❖ AL reviews the 14th New York.
- ❖ In the evening the 7th New York serenades AL.

May 30, Thursday

At Norfolk, Virginia, the Confederates raise the USS Merrimack.

❖ AL has Bates construct an argument supporting the suspension of habeas corpus, since Chief Justice Roger Taney has twice tried to get a writ executed for a man arrested for treason by the military.

❖ At 3 p.m., AL reviews four newly arrived New York regiments.

❖ At night, AL visits the Navy Yard where he boards the USS Monticello to see the damage it suffered exchanging fire with Confederate batteries at the mouth of the James River, May 18 and 19.

May 31, Friday

U.S. mail service to the Confederacy ends.

❖ AL limits interviews to matters of urgent importance.

❖ RTL, Nicolay, and Hay get passes to cross the river and visit Arlington House, the former home of Robert E. Lee, now a Confederate general.

JUNE 1861

Summary: *War fever sweeps the nation, and both sides begin parrying.*

June 1, Saturday

- ❖ AL reserves a family pew at the New York Avenue Presbyterian Church.
- ❖ AL sits for sketches by portraitist George Henry Story.
- ❖ AL and family listen to the Marine band from a White House balcony, but the performance is interrupted by the sound of brisk firing from the far side of the Potomac. It turns out to be target practice.

June 2, Sunday

- ❖ AL continues sitting for George Henry Story.
- ❖ At 6 p.m. AL and Seward, at the Navy Yard, tour the USS Thomas Freeborn, a patrol boat damaged the previous day by a Confederate battery at Aquia Creek, Virginia. The crew shows off a shell that hit the vessel.

June 3, Monday

Illinois Sen. Stephen A. Douglas dies in Chicago of typhoid fever, age forty-eight.

- ❖ AL continues sitting for George Henry Story.
- ❖ AL directs that government offices close for Douglas's funeral, and that White House and executive departments be draped in black for 30 days.

June 4, Tuesday

- ❖ AL, with the Cabinet, meets with several Baltimore shipbuilders and merchants.
- ❖ In the evening AL and MTL host a dinner for the diplomatic corps in a White House decorated by natural flowers, MTL having thrown out the artificial ones.

June 5, Wednesday

- ❖ AL lobbies Gen. Scott in favor of appointing Gen. Meigs as quartermaster general, although the War Department has a more senior nominee.
- ❖ Members of the Union Defense Committee of New York report to AL concerning troop movements and munitions.
- ❖ AL writes a testimonial backing Ward Hill Lamon's effort to organize a brigade of refugee Virginia Unionists.

June 6, Thursday

- ❖ AL agrees with the Cabinet that nearly all war expenses would be paid for by the Federal Government.

June 7, Friday

The government is closed to mark the funeral of Stephen A. Douglas.

- ❖ AL receives no visitors.

June 8, Saturday

Tennessee voters approve secession.

- ❖ AL meets with former Tennessee congressman Emerson Etheridge, who has been selected to hand out arms sent to Cairo, Illinois. (In late 1863 Etheridge attempted a coup against the government.)

- ❖ AL approves the roster of the governing board of the proposed U.S. Sanitary Commission, which is to promote the welfare of sick and wounded soldiers.
- ❖ AL reviews the newly arrived Garibaldi Guard (i.e., the 39th New York Infantry).

June 9, Sunday

- ❖ MTL attends church without AL.

June 10, Monday

- ❖ AL nominates ministers for Constantinople, Venezuela, and Costa Rica.
- ❖ AL writes to Cameron endorsing Gen. Meigs as quartermaster general.
- ❖ AL watches a demonstration of a new gun.
- ❖ At 5 p.m., AL and Gen. Scott review the 2nd Michigan at the White House.
- ❖ In evening, AL and MTL entertain a group of army chaplains.

June 11, Tuesday

Virginia Unionists begin organizing West Virginia. In Missouri, a truce breaks down and the secessionists are soon forced to retreat.

- ❖ AL informs Commissioner of Indian Affairs William Dole that AL cannot approve Dole's nominee as Indian superintendent for Washington Territory due to multiple complaints that the nominee is an immoral, bribe-offering influence peddler: "I presume you knew nothing of these things."
- ❖ AL meets balloonist Thaddeus Lowe.
- ❖ AL visits the Navy Yard where he receives an artillery salute and watches gun practice.
- ❖ AL, with Seward, reviews regiments from Michigan, Ohio, and New York.

❖ AL informs Gen. Meigs of his appointment as quartermaster general.

June 12, Wednesday

❖ AL meets with Gen. Meigs and with veteran Indian fighter Col. Erasmus D. Keyes, who wants a field command.

June 13, Thursday

❖ AL meets with wealthy inventor Hiram Berdan about forming a regiment of sharpshooters.
❖ AL meets with Hiram Barney, collector for the Port of New York, about patronage.
❖ AL, with Cameron, Chase, and a cavalry escort ride out to see fortifications on the Virginia side of the Potomac.

June 14, Friday

To restore discipline in the 21st Illinois Infantry, Illinois Gov. Richard Yates gives a colonel's commission to someone forced out of the army in 1854 for drinking: Ulysses S. Grant.

❖ AL makes a number of military appointments.
❖ AL, Tad, and Willie meet MTL in the afternoon at the railroad depot as she returns from a trip to Philadelphia.
❖ AL spends the evening at the Navy Yard.

June 15, Saturday

Mexico suspends foreign debt payments.

❖ AL attends a presentation of linen havelocks (service caps with a flap to protect the back of the neck) to three companies of the 2nd U.S. Cavalry at Arlington House (formerly the home of Robert E. Lee).

❖ AL authorizes payment for $7,500 worth of furniture and fittings that MTL bought for the White House in Philadelphia.

June 16, Sunday

❖ AL accompanies Seward visiting the camps of New York regiments.

June 17, Monday

❖ AL asks Cameron to furnish Navy revolvers and a sabre so MTL can send them to a friend who wants to take command of a militia company in Kentucky.

June 18, Tuesday

❖ AL receives a telegram from Prof. Thaddeus Lowe sent from a balloon above the grounds of the District of Columbia Armory.
❖ AL meets with Gen. Butler, a Democrat, who is upset with the lack of recognition he's gotten from Gen. Scott.
❖ A Cabinet meeting is devoted to regular Army promotions.
❖ AL confers with Kansas Sen. James Lane and other members of Congress about raising regiments in western states.

June 19, Wednesday

❖ AL announces that he will receive no visitors until the opening of the special session of Congress on July 4.
❖ In the morning, AL and Cameron review two Pennsylvania regiments.
❖ AL confers with Adjutant Gen. Lorenzo Thomas concerning military appointments.
❖ AL responds to Ninian Edwards, husband of Elizabeth Todd, MTL's sister, saying he is sorry to hear that Edwards

has gone broke but AL has not had time to find him a suitable government job.

❖ AL watches the 1st Massachusetts pass in review in front of the White House.

June 20, Thursday

❖ AL authorizes the suspension of the writ of habeas corpus in the case of a former Army engineer who has been charged with treason.

❖ AL writes to Cameron about additional New York regiments.

June 21, Friday

❖ MTL takes Tad and Willie on a carriage ride to visit the camp of the 25th New York south of the Potomac. On the return the horses bolt, throwing the driver, but nearby soldiers stop the carriage.

June 22, Saturday

❖ AL directs the heads of the various departments to submit reports showing the number of soldiers and seamen in service, and descriptions of the warships and other vessels in government service.

June 24, Monday

❖ AL confers with Commodore Silas Stringham about a possible expedition to the coast of North Carolina.

❖ Along with five generals and three Cabinet members, AL watches a demonstration of a "coffee mill gun" (i.e., a crude machine gun).

❖ AL reviews the 37th New York at White House.

❖ AL meets with the Cabinet.

❖ At 2 p.m. AL, Cameron, and others watch experiments with rifled cannon.

❖ In the evening AL sees the 1st and 2nd Rhode Island pass in review at the White House.

June 25, Tuesday

❖ AL and MTL attend a Hungarian funeral service for a private of the multi-national Garibaldi Guard. They then attend a review of the 37th New York.

❖ AL calls a conference concerning the military situation, saying he wants to "bag" the rebel force being organized in Virginia.

June 26, Wednesday

❖ AL receives an honorary Doctor of Laws from Columbia College (now Columbia University).

June 27, Thursday

❖ AL and Seward visit various infantry camps on the Virginia side of the Potomac.

June 29, Saturday

❖ AL at a Cabinet meeting, hears Gen. Irvin McDowell present a plan for attacking the Confederate forces massing at nearby Manassas, Virginia. But Gen. Scott prefers sending an expedition down the Mississippi to split the Confederacy while a naval blockade bankrupts the South, as the new regiments are too raw to fight battles. But AL and the Cabinet believe that the public wants immediate action. (Known as the Anaconda Plan, Scott's suggestions gradually became the main Union war strategy.)

June 30, Sunday

❖ AL, Seward, and Bates tour the USS Pawnee, which had been involved in the Battle of Mathias Point on Thursday.

JULY 1861

Summary: *AL's new army attempts to fight a decisive battle, but the result is a disaster. Fortunately, the Confederates are hardly better off. Meanwhile, the press of office-seekers never slackens.*

July 1, Monday

❖ AL is forced into temporary office space while MTL has new wallpaper, etc., applied to his office.

❖ AL meets in the evening with Illinois Sen. Lyman Trumbull, an old acquaintance. AL says he was not sure he had any legal authorization for increasing the size of the military and for using three-year enlistments. But it was better to err "than suffer all to be overthrown." He notes that everyone seems anxious for a forward movement (by the Union army).

July 2, Tuesday

❖ AL authorizes Gen. Scott to suspend habeas corpus from Washington to New York City.

❖ AL interviews Maryland Rep. Henry May, a Democrat. Then, suspiciously, May goes to Richmond. (He was arrested in September and held without charge until December. He then returned to his seat in Congress.)

❖ AL, with Cameron, reviews the 2nd New Hampshire and 11th Massachusetts.

July 3, Wednesday

❖ AL calls a noon Cabinet meeting to review his message to Congress.

❖ At 4 p.m., AL reviews the 1st Brigade of New Jersey Volunteers at the White House.

❖ In the evening AL discusses his message to Congress with Sen. Browning, an old friend who was appointed to replace Stephen A. Douglas. Speaking of the trials he experienced between his inauguration and the fall of Fort Sumter, "Could I have anticipated them, I would not have believed it possible to survive them."

July 4, Thursday

❖ AL presents his message to Congress as it opens in a special session, reviewing the state of the Union, the secession crisis, and the rise of the Confederacy. He denounces the secessionists' doctrines as sophistry. He recommends that Congress raise $400 million and 400,000 men.

❖ Joined by Gen. Scott and Cabinet members, AL reviews twenty-three New York regiments.

❖ AL adds his name to a temperance pledge previously signed by ten presidents, from Madison to Buchanan.

July 5, Friday

❖ AL, with family and friends, reviews the 26th and 27th Pennsylvania.

July 6, Saturday

❖ AL consults Smith and others concerning patronage appointments.

❖ AL and others see a demonstration of rifled cannons on the grounds of the (then unfinished) Washington Monument.

❖ AL and MTL hear opera singer Meda Blanchard at Willard's Hotel.

July 7, Sunday

* ❖ AL and Seward spend two hours at the Navy Yard.
* ❖ Gustave Koerner, a former lieutenant governor of Illinois, and other friends of AL spend three hours with AL in the evening. Koerner found AL "naively open-hearted."

July 8, Monday

* ❖ AL sees Sen. Browning and Paymaster Gen. Benjamin Larned in the morning. Sen. Browning returns by himself in the afternoon.
* ❖ AL interviews W. G. Terrell of Kentucky about the wisdom of enlisting troops in that state.
* ❖ A Rhode Island army band serenades AL.
* ❖ AL tells Cameron to supply arms and equipment for the defense of western Virginia.

July 9, Tuesday

* ❖ Sen. Browning again visits AL.
* ❖ AL and MTL host a White House reception in the evening.

July 10, Wednesday

* ❖ AL writes to (future Confederate general) Simon B. Buckner, whom Kentucky Governor Beriah Magoffin had sent to meet with AL to get support for Magoffin's policy of neutrality for Kentucky: "So far I have not sent an armed force into Kentucky; nor have I any present purpose to do so."
* ❖ MTL visits a Rhode Island regiment in the afternoon.

July 11, Thursday

* ❖ AL goes to Gen. Scott's office in the morning.
* ❖ AL meets briefly with Sen. Browning.

July 12, Friday

- ❖ AL is awakened by 4 a.m. to read a telegram announcing Gen. McClellan's victory at Rich Mountain, Virginia.

July 13, Saturday

- ❖ AL meets with Seward and others about James Harvey, minister to Portugal, caught communicating with the Confederates.
- ❖ AL dines with New York politician (and friend of Seward) Simeon Draper.
- ❖ AL signs legislation concerning import tariffs and other matters.

July 14, Sunday

- ❖ AL visits the Navy Yard at about 6 p.m.

July 15, Monday

- ❖ AL meets with Illinois Sen. Lyman Trumbull about patronage.

July 16, Tuesday

Gen. Irwin McDowell begins moving the 35,000-man Union army at Washington toward Manassas, Virginia.

- ❖ AL confers in the morning with Gen. Meigs concerning possible naval expeditions against Southern ports.
- ❖ AL hosts a reception in the evening.

July 17, Wednesday

- ❖ AL commissions William Stoddard as his secretary for signing land patents.

❖ AL approves legislation authorizing a $250 million national loan.

July 18, Thursday

In northern Virginia, Federal forces reach Centerville and begin probing toward Manassas.

❖ AL meets in the morning with New York Sen. Preston King and Pennsylvania Rep. Galusha Grow (who is also Speaker of the House) about patronage. AL writes to Cameron asking him to help find a position for each.

July 19, Friday

Probing continues in the Manassas area as Confederate reinforcements begin arriving.

❖ AL spends the evening with Sen. Browning and patronage seekers.
❖ A New York merchant submits a bill for $166 for chandeliers purchased by MTL.

July 20, Saturday

❖ Cameron returns from the headquarters of Gen. Irwin McDowell to report about preparations for an upcoming battle.

July 21, Sunday

The Federals cross Bull Run in the morning and attack toward Manassas, but succumb to a flank attack in the afternoon and retreat in disorder, losing the Battle of Bull Run. The Confederates are in the no shape to pursue.

- ❖ AL attends church.
- ❖ During the rest of the day, AL repeatedly visits the telegraph office of the War Department, reading dispatches from the front, some sent by young telegrapher Andrew Carnegie.
- ❖ AL dines at 3:30 p.m.
- ❖ On AL's return to the War Department, he finds that the Union troops are retreating.
- ❖ At 6 p.m., AL drives to the Navy Yard and talks with Comdr. Dahlgren.
- ❖ AL returns to the White House at 7 p.m. where Seward tells him the battle is lost.
- ❖ Various congressmen and senators show up later with eyewitness accounts.
- ❖ AL remains awake all night.

July 22, Monday

Remnants of the Union army pour into Washington.

- ❖ At 2 a.m., Gen. Scott insists that MTL, Tad, and Willie be sent north, out of danger. MTL refuses.
- ❖ At 3 a.m., AL has a long talk with Gen. Meigs, who had just returned from Bull Run.
- ❖ Gen. McClellan, newly famous for his western Virginia victories, is ordered to Washington to command the troops defending capital.
- ❖ AL talks with Sen. Browning from 5 to 7 p.m., going over reports from the battle.

July 23, Tuesday

- ❖ AL composes "Memoranda of Military Policy Suggested by the Bull Run Defeat." (AL wants to press the blockade, drill the army intensely, hold in place, then seize the railroads in northern Virginia, and then advance down the Mississippi and into Unionist eastern Tennessee.)

❖ AL and others visit various army camps on the Virginia side of the river. They are greeted with cheers and give rousing speeches.

❖ AL is unsympathetic to a captain who says Gen. Sherman threatened to shoot him: "Well, if I were you and he threatened to shoot [me], I would not trust him, for I believe he would do it."

❖ AL and Massachusetts Sen. Charles Sumner discuss emancipation until midnight.

❖ AL approves payment of bill for $1,500 for glassware cut with the U.S. coat of arms.

July 24, Wednesday

❖ AL and Seward visit the 71st New York at the Navy Yard.

July 25, Thursday

❖ AL receives Prof. Thaddeus Lowe, the balloonist.

July 26, Friday

❖ AL in the morning sees a delegation of Missouri office-seekers.

❖ AL attends a Cabinet meeting that lasts four hours.

❖ AL hears from a New York delegation urging him to recall New York native Gen. John Wool (age seventy-seven, but in better shape than seventy-five-year-old Gen. Scott) to active service.

❖ In the evening, AL and others the Navy Yard to observe experiments with a new (unspecified) weapon.

July 27, Saturday

❖ AL puts Gen. McClellan in command of all troops around Washington. McClellan is called to a Cabinet meeting but is tied up in a meeting with Gen. Scott.

- AL and MTL visit the 27th New York, chatting with the wounded.
- AL attends a White House levee.

July 28, Sunday

- AL attends church.
- AL and MTL meet Sen. Browning and invite him to dinner.

July 29, Monday

- AL advises New York Gov. Edwin Morgan to stop enlisting men for three months and to send 25,000 men for three years or the duration of war.
- AL receives a list of suggested brigadier general appointments from Sen. Browning.
- AL gets the Kentucky congressional delegation to endorse the idea of AL's friend Jesse Bayles raising a Kentucky cavalry regiment.
- AL receives the first of a series of letters from Horace Greeley advocating a negotiated peace.

July 30, Tuesday

- AL is visited by friend Hugh McCullough, an Indiana banker, who brings other friends.
- AL attends a White House levee and appears to be in good spirits.

July 31, Wednesday

- AL and Seward visit a hospital in Georgetown.
- AL confers with Sen. Browning, Rhode Island Rep. William Sheffield, and others, about patronage.
- The latest list of brigadier general appointments includes Ulysses S. Grant.

AUGUST 1861

Summary: *Outside of Missouri the situation stabilizes. The appointment of Gen. McClellan to command the troops in the east looks like a good idea—at first.*

August 1, Thursday

- ❖ AL responds to the Emperor of Japan, who is asking for more time to open certain ports and cities to foreign trade as required by treaty. AL requests that he consult with the U.S. minister.
- ❖ At 6 p.m., AL is seen by Illinois Sens. Lyman Trumbull and Browning, plus others, about patronage appointments.

August 2, Friday

- ❖ AL responds to a House resolution asking about loyal citizens imprisoned by the rebels. He reports several cases, including New York Rep. Alfred Ely.
- ❖ AL responds to a Senate resolution concerning the way seniority is determined between officers with the same appointment date. Some senators want it to be based on age, but AL prefers the existing lottery system.
- ❖ AL receives a memo from Gen. McClellan outlining his intentions.
- ❖ AL reviews the California Regiment commanded by his old friend, Col. (and Oregon Sen.) Edward D. Baker. (The troops were actually enlisted in New York.)

August 3, Saturday

- ❖ AL meets with the Cabinet at 10 a.m. to review Gen. McClellan's memo on his intentions.

❖ Prince Bonaparte (nephew of Napoleon Bonaparte) calls on AL at noon. Miffed that no one meets him at the door of the White House, he remains silent during the meeting.

❖ AL signs legislation concerning warship construction.

❖ AL, Seward, and Mrs. Seward visit a hospital in Georgetown.

❖ AL drafts a letter to Missouri Gov. Hamilton Gamble (i.e., the new Unionist governor) assuring Gamble that if he promises security to rebels who "voluntarily return to their allegiance" the government will respect his promise.

❖ AL and MTL host a 7 p.m. state dinner for Prince Napoleon, who is sociable this time.

August 5, Monday

❖ AL confers with Gen. Butler on military and slavery topics.

❖ AL approves a congressional resolution calling for the observation of a day of public humiliation, fasting, and prayer. (See September 26, 1861.)

August 6, Tuesday

❖ AL signs bills freeing slaves used by the Confederates for war-making; authorizing pay increases; setting penalties for recruiting for the enemy or for enlisting with the enemy; and legalizing AL's proclamations and orders since his inauguration. AL hesitates but then signs a bill authorizing the confiscation of property used for insurrectionary purposes.

❖ AL nominates a minister for Honduras.

❖ AL consults with Tennessee Sen. Andrew Johnson and Tennessee Rep. Horace Maynard about conditions in their state, and support for Gen. Robert Anderson.

❖ Congress adjourns.

August 7, Wednesday

* AL confers with the Illinois congressional delegation regarding a promotion for former Illinois businessman and ardent abolitionist Gen. David Hunter.
* Responding to a request from New York Gov. Edwin Morgan that a more experienced officer be sent to train the raw units at Fortress Monroe, AL authorizes Gen. Scott to send Gen. John Wool, replacing Gen. Butler, whose background is Massachusetts politics.

August 8, Thursday

* AL visits the Navy Yard with Blair to watch experiments with new guns.
* AL reviews two Wisconsin regiments, plus the Excelsior Brigade of four regiments, which were raised in New York by Col. Dan Sickles to repair his reputation. (Sickles, a New York politician, had left his pregnant wife at home when accompanying a diplomatic mission to London, taking instead his favorite madam and introducing her to various parties, including Queen Victoria, under the name of a political rival. Back home, finding his wife was having an affair with a lawyer, Sickles killed the man and then used the unheard-of "temporary insanity" defense to get acquitted. He then outraged the public by taking his wife back.)
* Tad and Willie, dressed in Zouave uniforms, camp out between the White House and the State Department.

August 9, Friday

* AL nominates a minister to Vienna.
* Sen. Browning visits AL at the White House.

August 10, Saturday

Union forces are defeated at Wilson's Creek, Missouri, the second major Confederate victory in a row.

❖ AL calls on Gen. Scott at home to settle differences between Scott and Gen. McClellan. (McClellan thinks Washington is in danger of an imminent attack by a powerful enemy force, and demands that all forces east of the Blue Ridge be placed under his command. Scott thinks Washington is safe behind its forts, and asks to be put on the retired list.)

August 11, Sunday

❖ AL confers with Gen. McClellan in the morning.

August 12, Monday

❖ AL proclaims the "last Thursday in September next, as a national day of humiliation, prayer and fasting."

August 13, Tuesday

❖ AL directs Cameron to appoint Gen. David Hunter to the rank of major general of volunteers, among other promotions.
❖ Gen. Robert Anderson, appointed to command in Kentucky but still convalescing, dines with AL.
❖ Gen. McClellan spends most of the evening at the White House.

August 14, Wednesday

❖ AL visits the Navy Yard.
❖ AL attends a Cabinet meeting.
❖ MTL leaves for the beach resort of Long Branch, New Jersey, accompanied by RTL, Hay, and Elizabeth Todd Grimsley (MTL's cousin).

August 15, Thursday

❖ AL visits the Navy Yard twice during the day, where he asks Comdr. Dahlgren about housing sixty-six prisoners from the 79th New York charged with mutiny. (They had three-year enlistments and rebelled when ninety-day volunteers were discharged and they weren't. About twenty ringleaders were later sent to prison.)

❖ AL telegraphs Gen. Frémont, who has been demanding reinforcements to counter Confederate advances: "Been answering your messages ever since day before yesterday. Do you receive the answers? The War Department has notified all the governors you designate to forward all available force."

❖ AL telegraphs Indiana Gov. Oliver Morton: "Start your four regiments to St. Louis at the earliest moment possible.... We shall endeavor to send you the arms this week."

❖ MTL is in New York.

August 16, Friday

❖ AL bans commercial intercourse with the rebels.

❖ AL is approached by William Darling about a West Point appointment for his son. But the son turns out to be only fourteen, and the minimum age was sixteen.

August 17, Saturday

❖ AL offers Simon B. Buckner a commission as brigadier general of volunteers. (Buckner would instead accept a commission of the same rank in the Confederate army.)

❖ On the recommendation of Gen. Scott, AL tells Cameron to make Henry Halleck a major general in the regular army.

❖ AL sees another demonstration of a "coffee mill gun." (presumably the Agar hand-cranked single-barrel machine gun) near the Washington Monument and offers to double the price if it is delivered within thirty days.

August 18, Sunday

❖ Ward Hill Lamon urges AL to adopt information security measures. Too many eavesdroppers and traitors are lurking about the White House, he says.

August 19, Monday

❖ AL orders newly appointed Gen. Halleck, in California, to report to Washington.
❖ Hay returns from traveling with MTL.

August 20, Tuesday

❖ AL confers with Mexican minister Matías Romero concerning possible European intervention in Mexico.
❖ AL asks Seward to find a job in England for Chicago abolitionist newspaper editor Zebina Eastman, as AL thinks he is "just the man to reach the sympathies of the English people."

August 21, Wednesday

❖ AL joins the Cabinet and Gen. McClellan reviewing nine Pennsylvania regiments and other units, in Georgetown.

August 22, Thursday

❖ AL confers with Kentucky Unionists concerning Kentucky's neutrality.
❖ At 10 a.m., AL reviews Col. (and Oregon Sen.) Edward D. Baker's California Regiment.
❖ AL tells Cameron, "Victor B. Bell, now of Colorado, is one of my most valued friends.... I would like for him to be an assistant quartermaster or commissary of subsistence of volunteers. Can you not fix it for me?"

❖ MTL and entourage attend a demonstration of lifesaving equipment at Long Branch, New Jersey, and later a "grand hop" in her honor.

August 23, Friday

❖ AL meets with the Cabinet.

August 24, Saturday

❖ AL replies to Kentucky Gov. Beriah Magoffin, who asked that a Federal force camped in the state leave. AL declines, noting that the force is small and composed entirely of Kentuckians. Additionally, "It is with regret search, and cannot find, in your not very short letter, any declaration, or intimation, that you entertain any desire for the preservation of the Federal Union." (The pro-Union state legislature later forced Magoffin out of office.)
❖ AL, Seward, and Gen. McClellan visit camps on the Virginia side of the Potomac.
❖ MTL and Tad are sick while in Long Branch, New Jersey.

August 25, Sunday

❖ AL, with Seward and Welles, joins the 2nd New Hampshire for worship services.

August 26, Monday

❖ AL attends a grand army review.
❖ Responding to multiples pleas, AL countermands an order from Gen. Frémont removing a regiment from St. Louis.

August 27, Tuesday

* AL directs Gen. Scott to supply qualified officers for New Jersey regiments, New Jersey's governor having not been able to find any.
* AL and Cameron sign an order authorizing the payment of eight dollars each for mules, despite complaints that the price was too high.
* AL listens to the band of the New York Second German Regiment.
* MTL travels to Auburn, New York, with Seward.

August 28, Wednesday

* MTL and party reach Niagara Falls, New York.

August 29, Thursday

* MTL stays with Mrs. Seward in Auburn. Later, she goes shopping in Niagara Falls.

August 30, Friday

* AL examines a "Prussian Needle Gun" (presumably a Dreyse breech-loading rifle with a long, narrow firing pin).

August 31, Saturday

* AL interviews Gen. John Reed, Massachusetts quartermaster, regarding military preparedness there.
* The Seward family calls on AL and he seems sick, with intermittent fever. But kittens that Seward gave AL are playing in the hall, and AL seems fond of them.
* Late at night Gen. Butler arrives to report his taking, Thursday, of Confederate Forts Hatteras and Clark on the North Carolina Outer Banks. (The victory ended that area's use by Confederate commerce raiders.)

SEPTEMBER 1861

Summary: *The Union's string of battlefield crises abates, but then Gen. Frémont becomes a major headache for AL.*

September 1, Sunday

- ❖ AL has Gen. Butler attend a Cabinet meeting to describe his recent capture of the Confederate forts guarding Hatteras Inlet, North Carolina.
- ❖ AL, Seward, Seward's family, and others review the 1st and 2nd New York. AL refers to an officer of short stature: "There's more in that colonel than you'd think at first. He begins low, but he goes high."

September 2, Monday

- ❖ AL responds to a recent proclamation by Gen. Frémont that seized the property and freed the slaves of all rebels and made carrying arms without authorization a capital offense. AL tells him to have no one shot without AL's consent, and that his threats to seize property and slaves must conform with recent legislation.
- ❖ AL and Seward review the 2nd and 5th Wisconsin.
- ❖ MTL spends $3,195 for a 190-piece double-gilt royal purple dining service with the coat of arms of the U.S. on each piece.

September 3, Tuesday

Confederate forces enter Kentucky, ending its neutrality.

- ❖ AL spends most of the morning inspecting the Washington Arsenal.

❖ AL inspects army installations in the afternoon near Falls Church, Virginia.
❖ AL visits the Navy Yard with Cameron and Gen. McClellan.
❖ AL rides in the evening with the Seward family.
❖ AL meets with Gen. Scott.

September 4, Wednesday

❖ AL meets with Missouri Gov. Hamilton Gamble regarding recruiting.

September 5, Thursday

Acting on his own initiative, Gen. Grant bloodlessly takes Paducah, Kentucky.

❖ AL confers with Gen. Scott about Gen. Frémont and other matters.
❖ AL is seen on Pennsylvania Avenue in the rain, carrying a parcel, with no umbrella.
❖ MTL and party return to Washington.

September 6, Friday

❖ AL confers with Commodore Silas Stringham, commander of the Atlantic Blockading Squadron.
❖ AL sees other callers at the White House, including ones from Ohio, New York, and Massachusetts.
❖ AL, MTL, and Seward visit the cavalry unit that Ward Hill Lamon raised.
❖ AL writes a check to "Master Tad" for one dollar.

September 7, Saturday

❖ The Russian minister, Baron de Stoeckl, has an audience with AL and presents a letter of friendship from the Czar.

September 8, Sunday

- ❖ AL pardons a soldier (Vermont Pvt. William Scott) who was to be shot for sleeping on guard duty. (The "Sleeping Sentinel" case was romanticized at the time. Pvt. Scott was killed in action the next April.)
- ❖ AL and MTL goes for a drive in their new open carriage.

September 9, Monday

- ❖ AL writes to Gen. David Hunter, recuperating from wounds, about AL's frustration with Gen. Frémont. "He needs to have, by his side, a man of large experience. Will you not, for me, take that place?" (Gen. Hunter is sent to him as a division commander.)
- ❖ AL discusses the problems involved in building ironclad warships with Connecticut industrialist Cornelius Bushnell.

September 10, Tuesday

- ❖ AL authorizes Gen. Butler to raise up to six regiments in the New England states (for a proposed expedition to New Orleans), assuming the governors there approve.
- ❖ AL meets with a delegation of Philadelphia citizens, introduced by Cameron, who express commitment to the war.
- ❖ AL meets with a delegation of prominent Kentuckians.
- ❖ AL meets with a navy board about Cornelius Bushnell's plans for ironclad warships.
- ❖ With Pennsylvania Gov. Andrew Curtin, AL attends a presentation of colors to Pennsylvania troops.
- ❖ With Curtin, Cameron, and Gen. McClellan, AL tours forts on the Virginia side of the Potomac.
- ❖ AL agrees to immediately see Jessie Benton Frémont (wife of Gen. Frémont) when she arrives at about midnight to lobby for more reinforcements for her husband—and to lodge various complaints.

September 11, Wednesday

- ❖ AL sends individual telegrams to the governors of the New England states asking them to consent to Gen. Butler's plan to raise six regiments in their jurisdictions.
- ❖ In response to a message from Gen. Frémont (brought by Mrs. Frémont Tuesday night) asking that AL state his September 2 request to Frémont (to change his recent proclamation to conform to Federal legislation) as a published order, AL does publish such an order.

September 12, Thursday

The Confederates besiege Lexington, Missouri, eliciting no response from Gen. Frémont.

With the Maryland legislature to convene in five days, Federal authorities begin arresting pro-Confederate members (about a third of the total) to prevent secession.

- ❖ AL responds Mrs. Frémont's complaints: "No impression has been made on my mind against the honor or integrity of Gen. Frémont; and I now enter my protest against being understood as acting in any hostility towards him."
- ❖ AL is seen walking through the White House garden during a band concert, on his way to the State Department, unnoticed by the crowd.

September 13, Friday

- ❖ AL confers with Gen. Scott about Gen. Frémont.
- ❖ AL confers about patronage in Kentucky.
- ❖ AL and Cameron meet with Prince Felix Salm-Salm, a Prussian officer with combat experience, offering his services to the Union. (He served through the war, married an American woman, rose to the rank of brigadier general, served in the Mexican army, returned to Germany, was

killed in action in the Franco-Prussian War, and inspired any number of German-language adventure novels.)
❖ AL approves government payment for the dinner service that MTL bought on September 2.

September 14, Saturday

❖ AL confers with Cameron about Gen. Frémont.
❖ AL has a long meeting with Welles.
❖ That night, AL steams down the Potomac to watch a test of electric lighting using glass containers of mercury vapor.

September 15, Sunday

❖ AL attends a Cabinet meeting where they discuss removing Gen. Frémont. They decide to wait for more information.
❖ AL, in the evening, has another long meeting with Welles.

September 16, Monday

❖ AL asks Gen. Scott to recruit loyal North Carolinians who make their way to the newly captured Fort Hatteras.
❖ AL hears that Gen. Frémont has arrested Col. (and Missouri Rep.) Francis Preston Blair Jr., the younger brother of a Cabinet member.

September 17, Tuesday

The Maryland legislature decides not to convene.

September 18, Wednesday

❖ AL attends Cabinet meetings in both the morning and afternoon to hear reports about conditions in Louisville under Gen. Frémont.
❖ AL appoints officers for a new Kentucky brigade.
❖ AL directs that a previously discussed expedition to seize Port Royal, South Carolina, as a base for blockading South Carolina and Georgia, "is in no wise to be abandoned."

September 19, Thursday

❖ AL attends a long Cabinet meeting where Blair reports about the arrest of his younger brother, apparently for criticizing Gen. Frémont's policies.

❖ MTL hosts an evening party at the White House for select friends, including Gen. and Mrs. Samuel Heintzelman.

September 20, Friday

Lexington, Missouri surrenders to the Confederates after a nine-day siege, there having been no intervention by Gen. Frémont.

❖ AL spends the afternoon observing a demonstration of Col. Hiram Berdan's sharpshooter regiment. AL takes part, and hits his target.

September 21, Saturday

❖ AL intervenes in the case of Isaac Miller, a long-time employee of the Washington Arsenal facing dismissal for alleged disloyalty, sending him to Seward. "I have seen him, and believe him to be loyal." (He was retained.)

❖ AL takes his long-time friend (and former roommate) Kentuckian Joshua Speed to see Adjutant Gen. Lorenzo Thomas about expediting arms and material to Gen. Robert Anderson's department.

September 22, Sunday

❖ AL writes to Sen. Browning that he opposed Gen. Frémont's original proclamation because it was based on an assumption that a general can do anything he wishes, whether demanded by military necessity or otherwise. "I cannot assume this reckless position; nor allow others to assume it on my responsibility."

September 23, Monday

❖ AL meets with Seward at 8 p.m. regarding Gen. Frémont.

September 24, Tuesday

❖ AL attends a 4 p.m. grand review of the army, with MTL and various officials.

September 25, Wednesday

❖ AL receives a message from Colorado Territory Gov. William Gilpin (dated August 26) asking for 10,000 muskets and other supplies.

❖ AL endorses permission for a Virginia Unionist to import salt through the Union lines to his home town, which he depicts as a Unionist enclave. (He got permission but was then arrested by the Confederates.)

September 26, Thursday

❖ AL attends church as the day is officially one of "humiliation, prayer and fasting."

❖ AL visits the War Department telegraph office and jokes with the staff: "Gentlemen, this is a fast day and I am pleased to observe that you are working as fast as you can."

❖ As part of the National Fast Day observances, AL attends a lecture on the U.S. Constitution at the House of Representatives by Prof. Amasa McCoy.

❖ AL responds to a message from Indiana Gov. Oliver Morton complaining that the state needs more arms to continue recruiting and that war in now on their borders, with enemy outposts in sight of Muldraugh's Hill, forty miles southeast of Louisville, Kentucky: "We are supplying all the demands for arms as fast as we can. We expect to order a lot to you tomorrow." As for the hill in question, the enemy held it last week and now are merely in sight of it.
"That is an improvement."

September 27, Friday

❖ AL invites Gen. McClellan to a Cabinet meeting in Gen. Scott's office, and the two generals apparently get into an argument.

❖ AL meets with Laura Redden, deaf journalist and poet from Missouri (pen name Howard Glyndon) about a book of poetry she is writing.

September 28, Saturday

❖ AL sees a delegation from Indiana seeking a general's commission for Thomas Morris of that state's militia. (It is later offered to him, but he declined.)

❖ AL talks to Charles Weston, a former military storekeeper (and whose brother is a newspaper publisher in Maine) who wants another storekeeper appointment, but his first attempt to get reinstated has failed. (Gen. James Ripley, chief or ordnance, didn't want him.) AL gets Cameron to help.

September 29, Sunday

❖ AL receives a letter from Col. (and Missouri Rep.) Francis Preston Blair Jr. with accusations of official misconduct against Gen. Frémont.

❖ AL sends a reassuring message to Indiana Gov. Oliver Morton: "You do not receive arms from us as fast as you need them; but it is because we have not near enough to meet all the pressing demands."

September 30, Monday

❖ AL hears from a Baltimore delegation concerning the arrest of that city's mayor two weeks earlier, for "complicity with those in armed rebellion." (AL does not immediately release him.)

OCTOBER 1861

Summary: Military threats seem less dire, but other headaches won't go away, especially Gen. Frémont. Then, one of AL's best friends is killed in action.

October 1, Tuesday

- ❖ Bates complains to AL in a Cabinet meeting that there is a "lack of system in running the government."
- ❖ AL writes a "Memorandum for a Plan of Campaign," envisioning the Port Royal, South Carolina, operation on the coast, plus taking the Cumberland Gap to permit access to Unionist eastern Tennessee.

October 2, Wednesday

- ❖ AL refers to Chase as being in despair and to Cameron as being unpopular, and mentions military and financial confusion in the Department of the West.
- ❖ AL approves a bill for $598.39 for goods bought by MTL to refurbish the White House.

Mrs. Lincoln's extravagant tastes at times brought undue embarrassment to her husband's presidency.

October 3, Thursday

❖ AL, MTL, and other officials attend a flag presentation ceremony for the 7th New Jersey.

October 4, Friday

* ❖ AL confers with Cameron and others about the situation in the Department of the West.
* ❖ AL witnesses a military balloon ascension. Untethered, it floats over Washington and lands twelve miles away in Maryland.
* ❖ AL meets with Welles, Fox, and various experts about ironclad warship construction. They agree to three projects. (One is the USS Monitor.)
* ❖ AL says he is agreeable to the release of former Kentucky governor Charles Morehead, as requested by the man's Unionist son-in-law, if local officials agree. (They did in January.)

October 6, Sunday

* ❖ AL goes to Rockville, Maryland, with Seward and Gen. McClellan to meet with Gen. Nathaniel Banks at the camp of the 19th New York.

October 7, Monday

* ❖ AL asks Gen. Samuel Curtis (formerly a Republican congressman from Iowa): "Ought Gen. Frémont to be relieved from, or retained in his present command?" ("It is only a question of manner and time," Curtis later replied.)
* ❖ AL calls a special meeting of selected Cabinet members and the assistant secretaries of War and the Navy.

October 8, Tuesday

Gen. Sherman replaces Gen. Robert Anderson at Louisville, Kentucky, the latter having collapsed from exhaustion. Gen. Sherman will also suffer a nervous breakdown at that post.

* ❖ AL attends with MTL a review of artillery and cavalry presented by Gen. McClellan.

October 9, Wednesday

❖ AL meets with the Cabinet in a special session to hear reports from Gen. McClellan.

October 10, Thursday

❖ AL visits Gen. McClellan's headquarters in the War Department, with Seward and Hay. They run across a pretender to the French throne, Count of Paris Philippe d'Orleans, now a captain in the Union army.

❖ AL meets with the Cabinet in the evening.

October 11, Friday

❖ AL sends Nicolay to St. Louis to examine conditions in Gen. Frémont's jurisdiction.

October 12, Saturday

❖ AL receives an estimate from Gen. McClellan that the enemy will not attack soon.

❖ AL inspects work at the Navy Yard in the afternoon.

❖ AL meets at Seward's house with the assistant secretaries of War and the Navy.

October 13, Sunday

❖ AL attends worship services with Seward at an army camp.

October 14, Monday

❖ AL authorizes Gen. Scott to suspend habeas corpus between Bangor, Maine, and Washington.

❖ AL directs the Chief of Ordnance to order 25,000 breechloaders.

October 15, Tuesday

- ❖ AL disposes of a list of routine pardon cases and patronage requests.

October 16, Wednesday

- ❖ AL has an informal meeting with Seward and Gen. McClellan.
- ❖ AL and Seward visit the Navy Yard.
- ❖ AL reviews the 4th Rhode Island.

October 17, Thursday

- ❖ AL refers an unnamed woman to the commander of the Washington Arsenal. "The lady—bearer of this—says she has two sons who want to work. Set them at it, if possible. Wanting to work is so rare a merit that it should be encouraged."
- ❖ AL meets with George Templeton Strong (New York lawyer and treasurer of the U.S. Sanitary Commission) and several others concerning prisoner exchanges and staff appointments.
- ❖ AL meets with Seward and Gen. McClellan.
- ❖ AL dines with Thomas Clay, son of Henry Clay, and several other Kentuckians.

October 18, Friday

- ❖ AL reviews the 8th Illinois Cavalry in the morning.
- ❖ At a Cabinet meeting AL reads the draft of a letter agreeing to Gen. Scott's retirement.
- ❖ AL and MTL participate in a flag presentation at the camp of the 2nd and 4th Rhode Island.

October 19, Saturday

- ❖ AL attends a Cabinet meeting at the Navy Yard. They then tour the USS Pensacola. They proceed down the river to inspect a fort, and return after sunset.

October 20, Sunday

❖ AL telegraphs congratulations to Utah Territory Acting Governor Frank Fuller on completion of the telegraph line to Salt Lake City. (Another line is being extended from California to Salt Lake City.)

October 21, Monday

Gen. Charles Stone probes toward Leesburg, Virginia, on the upper Potomac. His force includes Col. (and Sen.) Edward D. Baker's California Regiment. Resistance is strong, part of the force is trapped against the river at Balls Bluff, Virginia. Col. Baker is killed as are more than 200 others. Bodies float downstream past Washington.

❖ AL invites Archbishop John Hughes of New York to name Catholic chaplains for military hospitals, although no law authorizes such appointments.
❖ While visiting the War Department, AL reads a dispatch reporting the death of his friend, Col. (and Sen.) Edward D. Baker, at Balls Bluff. AL and MTL are distraught.
❖ AL hears that the Port Royal, South Carolina, expedition has sailed from Annapolis, Maryland.
❖ AL, the Cabinet, and a contingent of generals of local troops attend an evening conference.
❖ AL gets a message from Nicolay in Springfield, IL, saying there is no opposition in Illinois to the idea of removing Gen. Frémont.

October 22, Tuesday

❖ AL attends a Cabinet meeting mostly devoted to the Battle of Balls Bluff and to Gen. Frémont.
❖ AL and MTL, in mourning over Edward D. Baker, receive no visitors.
❖ AL spends the evening at the homes of Seward and Gen. McClellan.

October 23, Wednesday

❖ AL instructs U.S. Marshals of the Washington District to refuse to serve any writ of habeas corpus upon a military commander, having suspended the privilege in military cases.

October 24, Thursday

❖ AL does not hold a scheduled Cabinet meeting.
❖ In the evening the father, son, and nephew of the late Edward D. Baker call on AL, who is in conference with Thurlow Weed.
❖ AL receives a telegram directly from San Francisco over the newly completed transcontinental telegraph line.

October 25, Friday

The keel is laid for the USS Monitor in Brooklyn.

❖ AL goes with Hay to Seward's house in the evening, where they see Michigan Sen. Zachariah Chandler, Ohio Sen. Benjamin Wade, and Massachusetts Sen. Henry Wilson.

October 26, Saturday

❖ AL receives multiple messages over the now-operational transcontinental telegraph line.
❖ AL visits the Navy Yard in the evening.
❖ AL invites Gen. McClellan to join him examining repeating guns at the Navy Yard, but Gen. McClellan says he does not have time.
❖ With Hay, AL later visits Gen. McClellan's headquarters. They converse about the Jacobin Club, a factor in the French Revolution.

October 27, Sunday

❖ AL goes with Hay in the evening to Seward's house, where he also sees (as he did the previous Sunday) Michigan Sen. Zachariah Chandler, Ohio Sen. Benjamin Wade, and Massachusetts Sen. Henry Wilson.

October 28, Monday

❖ In the afternoon, AL watches the demonstration of a new gun at the Washington Arsenal.

❖ AL again asks Iowa Republican Gen. Samuel Curtis for advice on the Department of the West (although the contents of his letter are lost).

October 29, Tuesday

❖ AL discusses plans for the Army of the Potomac with Gen. McClellan.

October 30, Wednesday

❖ AL writes to the Rev. F. M. Magrath that he has no power to appoint chaplains for military hospitals, but if Rev. Magrath goes to a hospital and acts as a chaplain, "I will recommend that Congress make compensation therefor at the same rate as chaplains in the army are compensated." (AL is thought to have sent similar letters to at least seven people.)

❖ Gen. McClellan confers at the White House with AL.

❖ Willie writes a poem about the late Edward D. Baker.

October 31, Thursday

Spain, England, and France agree to intervene in Mexico to collect unpaid debts.

❖ AL receives Gen. Scott's official request for retirement status, forwarded by Cameron.

NOVEMBER 1861

Summary: AL finally relieves Gen. Frémont, although he stays in the army. Operations slow in the face of advancing winter. But then a major gaffe by the navy threatens war with England.

November 1, Friday

- ❖ AL attends a Cabinet meeting where Gen. Scott's retirement (at full pay) is made official. Gen. McClellan is appointed his successor.
- ❖ AL and Cabinet members later visit Gen. Scott at his home.
- ❖ AL issues an official notice to Gen. McClellan that he is now the Army's commanding general (except of Gen. John Wool's command, Gen. Wool having said he would resign if a younger officer were put over him).
- ❖ With Hay, AL visits the homes of Gen. McClellan and Seward.
- ❖ A messenger slips through Gen. Frémont's security network and delivers AL's order (dated October 24) relieving Gen. Frémont and replacing him with Gen. David Hunter.

November 2, Saturday

- ❖ Responding to the case of a captain demanding a court of inquiry, AL tells Cameron: "I think any officer who has been dismissed on suspicion of disloyalty, but does not go over to the enemy, continuing to protest his loyalty, entitles himself to a hearing."
- ❖ AL writes to Gen. Joseph Totten, Chief Engineer of the U.S. Army, telling him to remind AL to give a military academy appointment to the son of Prof. Dennis Mahan, assuming

both Totten and AL "are both alive, and in place in June 1862." (Prof. Mahan taught tactics at West Point. The son in question, Frederick August Mahan, waited until 1863 to enter West Point and was the younger brother of future naval theorist Admiral Alfred Thayer Mahan. Why AL was unsure about surviving another seven months was unaddressed.)

November 3, Sunday

❖ In response to a telegram from Gen. William Strong in St. Louis asking who is in charge, AL responds that Gen. McClellan is now commanding general overall.

November 4, Monday

❖ AL endorses plans for coastal fortifications in Maine.
❖ AL announced he can receive visitors only between 10 a.m. and noon, to make time to write his message to Congress for the upcoming session.
❖ AL spends an hour at Gen. McClellan's headquarters.
❖ AL approves a bill for $5,198 for MTL's purchase of French satin brocatelle curtains, tassels, fringes, cornices, hall carpets, and laces.
❖ *The National Republican* (a local newspaper) prints Willie's poem, "Lines on the Death of Colonel Edward Baker."

November 5, Tuesday

❖ AL attends a Cabinet meeting where they acquire two steam-powered fire engines for Washington.
❖ Gen. McClellan brings Gen. Halleck, newly arrived from California, to the White House to meet AL and the Cabinet. (The former army officer with a scholarly reputation had gotten wealthy in California, and Gen. Scott had gotten him reinstated and promoted.)

November 6, Wednesday

- ❖ AL meets in the morning for several hours with Gen. McClellan and Assistant Secretary of War Thomas Scott.
- ❖ AL approves a plan for Missouri State Militia to cooperate with U.S. troops in military operations within the state. (The governor will make the commander of the Department of the West the commander of the state militia.)
- ❖ AL gets word that a straight Union slate of candidates was elected to the Baltimore city council.
- ❖ AL receives Col. Rush Hawkins of Hawkins Zouaves.

November 7, Thursday

A naval expedition seizes the Port Royal and Hilton Head areas of South Carolina.

A raid on Belmont, Missouri, is the first major action commanded by Gen. Grant.

- ❖ In the evening AL entertains Col. Rush Hawkins of Hawkins Zouaves.

November 8, Friday

The USS San Jacinto stops the British-flagged Trent outbound from Cuba to arrest Confederate commissioners James Mason and John Slidell.

- ❖ Charles F. Havelock, British aide-de-camp to Gen. McClellan, calls on AL.
- ❖ In the afternoon, with Gen. McClellan, AL reviews Gen. Buell's division.

November 9, Saturday

- ❖ AL receives Gen. McClellan's apology for being unable to attend a meeting.

November 10, Sunday

❖ AL has a long meeting with Illinois Rep. Elihu Washburne about government contracts in the Department of the West.

❖ AL meets with Gen. McClellan about military matters in the evening.

❖ AL writes a social letter (i.e., not for publication) to Gen. John McClernand (a prominent Illinois Democrat married to a friend of MTL, who recruited his own brigade) to tell him that he is not forgotten. "Some of your forces are without arms, but the same is true here, and at every other place where we have considerable bodies of troops."

November 11, Monday

❖ AL meets with Augustus Bradford, newly elected governor of Maryland.

❖ Late in the evening AL, with Hay, visits McClellan's house.

November 12, Tuesday

❖ AL meets with a delegation from Baltimore and congratulates them on electing Unionists, as the Federal Government seeks "to save Baltimore and Maryland from the danger of complete ruin through an unnecessary and unnatural rebellion."

❖ AL corresponds with Joseph Holt, who AL has sent to Missouri to report on the controversies there.

❖ AL, with Hay, has tea in the evening with the Fox family.

November 13, Wednesday

❖ AL writes to Cameron seeking employment for Charles Todd of Kentucky, a distant relative of MTL who served in diplomatic positions under Presidents Monroe and Tyler.

❖ AL, Seward, and Hay wait at Gen. McClellan's residence to see him. Gen. McClellan returns home from a wedding—and goes straight to bed without speaking to AL.

November 14, Thursday

- ❖ AL gets a report on the Department of the West's situation from his friend and political operative Leonard Swett.
- ❖ AL consults with Gen. McClellan and Fox about a "big expedition" (presumably, the upcoming Peninsular Campaign.)
- ❖ AL calls on Seward's house and meets W. H. Russell, correspondent for the *London Times*, and Henry Raymond, editor at the *New York Times*.

November 15, Friday

The USS San Jacinto *arrives at Fortress Monroe with the diplomats taken from the* Trent *aboard, creating a sensation.*

- ❖ AL interviews Gen. Charles Stone, presumably about the Ball's Bluff disaster.
- ❖ Blair confers with AL about the Trent Affair.
- ❖ AL and several Cabinet members inspect the USS Pensacola.

November 16, Saturday

- ❖ AL with Gen. McClellan interviews Gen. Edwin Sumner, recently returned from commanding the Department of the Pacific in California.
- ❖ Massachusetts Sen. Charles Sumner and Blair urge AL to surrender Mason and Slidell at once.

November 18, Monday

- ❖ AL appoints the father of the late Col. Ellsworth as a military storekeeper.
- ❖ MTL visits the Washington Arsenal, escorted by Gen. Dan Sickles.

November 20, Wednesday

❖ AL drives six miles out of town with several Cabinet members to watch a grand review of 70,000 troops under Gen. McClellan. (It may have been the largest review held in North America to that time.)

November 21, Thursday

❖ AL watches the 15th New York demonstrate the construction of a pontoon bridge.

❖ AL authorizes Gen. McClellan to declare martial law in St. Louis, if necessary.

November 22, Friday

❖ AL attends a Cabinet meeting where they consider granting clearances to recaptured Southern ports.

November 23, Saturday

❖ AL steams down the Potomac at 1 p.m. for a naval review, accompanied by MTL, Hay, Seward, and Comdr. Dahlgren.

❖ In the evening the French illusionist "Hermann the Magician" performs at the White House for AL and family and as many as a hundred invited guests, pulling canaries from spectator's ears and so on.

November 24, Sunday

❖ AL calls a conference at the War Department with the Cabinet and several senators to discuss the Trent Affair.

❖ AL consults with Illinois Rep. Isaac Arnold about conditions in the Northwest.

November 25, Monday

❖ AL visits the Fox home in the evening.

❖ MTL visits the 65th New York Infantry.

November 26, Tuesday

❖ AL drafts a bill for compensated emancipation in Delaware. (It is never introduced.)
❖ AL responds to Mrs. Stephan A. Douglas, who has asked for advice. She has been urged to send her children south to avoid confiscation of their property there but fears their property in the North will then be confiscated: "I still do not expect the property of absent minor children will be confiscated."
❖ AL, Cameron, and Methodist Bishop Matthew Simpson discuss possible government bias against churches.
❖ MTL attends Gen. McClellan's morning review.

November 27, Wednesday

News of the Trent Affair reaches England, sparking outrage.

❖ AL orders the closing of government offices the next day, as it has been declared a day of thanksgiving.
❖ AL visits the Fox home in the evening.

November 28, Thursday

❖ AL hosts Thanksgiving dinner at the White House, attended by Joshua Speed and Speed's wife, among others.

November 29, Friday

❖ AL reads part of his annual message to the Cabinet.
❖ Seward introduces AL to a French admiral and a captain.
❖ AL tells a reporter he gets about fifty letters a week from European army officers offering their services to the Union.

November 30, Saturday

❖ AL examines a memo from pro-Union Maryland pamphleteer Anna Ella Carroll. After talking to Mississippi steamboat pilots, she urges the Administration to not launch an offensive down the Mississippi but instead advance into the South up the (less defensible) Tennessee and Cumberland rivers. (She thus predicted the Fort Henry and Fort Donelson campaigns.)

❖ AL meets with Seward, Comdr. Dahlgren, and others at Gen. McClellan's residence in the evening.

❖ AL endorses a request from former President Fillmore asking that his nephew be made a lieutenant in the regular army.

DECEMBER 1861

Summary: Lincoln avoids war with England over the Trent Affair.

December 1, Sunday

- ❖ AL completes his first annual message to Congress.
- ❖ AL consults with Massachusetts Sen. Charles Sumner on the Trent Affair.
- ❖ AL talks about the idea of compensated emancipation with Sen. Browning.
- ❖ AL asks Gen. McClellan how soon the Army of the Potomac could start advancing, and in what strength.

December 2, Monday

- ❖ AL attends a meeting of the Cabinet, which issues a blanket endorsement of his policies.
- ❖ Chief Justice Roger B. Taney, plus the associate justices of the Supreme Court, call on AL.
- ❖ The 37th Congress, second session, convenes.
- ❖ AL authorizes Gen. Halleck, commanding at St. Louis, to declare martial law and suspend habeas corpus in the area he commands, as needed.

December 3, Tuesday

- ❖ AL presents his annual message to Congress: "In the midst of unprecedented political troubles, we have cause of great gratitude to God for unusual good health, and most abundant harvests.... The Union must be preserved, and hence, all indispensable means must be employed.... The struggle of today, is not altogether for today—it is for a vast future also."

December 4, Wednesday

- ❖ AL confers with Iowa Sen. James Harlan and Sen. Browning about military appointments.
- ❖ AL meets with Alexander Galt, Canada's minister of finance, regarding uneasiness in Canada over the possibility of U.S. aggression.
- ❖ AL and MTL attend the flag presentation ceremony for a cavalry unit.
- ❖ AL in the evening visits the Fox home.

December 5, Thursday

The War Department reports that there are now 682,971 men in the army and navy.

- ❖ AL, Cameron and Seward review the 23rd Philadelphia Zouaves.

December 6, Friday

- ❖ With Seward, AL reviews an artillery company from Auburn, New York.
- ❖ AL sees Capt. Francis Young of the California Regiment and gives him a letter to take to Gen. McClellan, asking McClellan to help Capt. Young with a problem he's having. "I believe you know I was unfavorably impressed towards him because of apparently contradictory accounts he gave me of some matters at the Battle of Ball's Bluff," AL writes. (After reading it Capt. Young dared not show the letter to McClellan, went absent, and was cashiered.)

December 7, Saturday

❖ MTL holds a morning reception.

December 8, Sunday

❖ AL approves the idea of a submarine telegraph line linking Washington to Fortress Monroe. (They used cable left over from the 1858 trans-Atlantic cable, which failed after three weeks. The Fortress Monroe link also suffered periodic failures.)

December 9, Monday

Congress sets up the Joint Committee on the Conduct of the War, to investigate disasters like Balls Bluff. Mostly, it injects politics into military affairs.

December 10, Tuesday

❖ AL attends a Cabinet meeting where they hear from a New York delegation arguing for a prisoner exchange. They table a request from Gen. David Hunter (Gen. Frémont's replacement) to recruit a brigade of Indians. They discuss the organization of courts at retaken Beaufort, South Carolina.
❖ AL and MTL attend the evening wedding of a daughter of a Supreme Court clerk.

December 11, Wednesday

❖ AL, in New York, interviews Rabbi Arnold Fischel of New York regarding the appointment of Jewish army chaplains.
❖ AL visits the floor of the Senate to hear eulogies and proceedings marking the death of Oregon Sen. (and Col.) Edward D. Baker.
❖ AL receives telegraphed accounts of the Baker's funeral in San Francisco.

❖ AL restates for the *New York Times* the primary goals of his Administration: 1) to regard the Union as unbroken, 2) to restore national laws over the seceded states as rapidly as possible, 3) to protect the lives and property of all citizens in the seceded states who have not engaged in rebellion.

December 12, Thursday

❖ AL is introduced to historian George Bancroft.
❖ AL joins Gen. Joseph Totten, Chief Engineer of the U.S. Army, examining new gun carriages.
❖ AL writes to Gen. Samuel Curtis thanking for his help in the Gen. Frémont affair—and to apologize that a report on conditions in Missouri was published in a newspaper, although it contained a confidential interview with Gen. Curtis. (Curtis responded that he did not care.)

December 13, Friday

❖ AL meets with members of the New York Irish Brigade asking that their founder, Col. Thomas F. Meagher (an Irish revolutionary who escaped from exile in Tasmania) be promoted. (He was later made a brigadier general.)
❖ In the evening, AL sees Ohio Sen. John Sherman, who puts in the good word for his older brother, Gen. Sherman, who recently had a nervous breakdown while on assignment in Kentucky and is on leave.

December 14, Saturday

❖ AL writes to Rabbi Arnold Fischel, who he met with Wednesday, that he will have to get the law changed before he can appoint Jewish chaplains. (The law, which allowed only ordained Christian ministers, was changed three months later.)
❖ AL sends the Senate information about Col. Dixon Miles, who was accused of drunkenness at Bull Run. (He was

allowed to return to duty but then surrendered Harpers Ferry, Virginia, after a token defense during the Antietam Campaign.)

❖ MTL holds her first formal reception of the season, from 1 to 3 p.m.

December 15, Sunday

❖ Sen. Browning and Coleman C. Sympson, senate clerk, call on AL at about 5 p.m. Browning remains for tea.
❖ While they are having tea, Seward shows up, alarmed by a report that Great Britain considers the Trent Affair to be a violation of international law.

December 16, Monday

❖ New York Republican Hiram Barney confers with AL about the idea of AL appointing Chase to succeed Chief Justice Taney and appointing Barney to succeed Chase.
❖ AL drafts a letter for U.S. Marshall Ward Hill Lamon to send to the Senate in response to a Senate resolution asking how often he had jailed slaves at the request of their owners. (He'd done it three times, "based as I supposed upon some valid law.")
❖ On his way to Seward house AL meets Michigan Sen. Zachariah Chandler and Gen. Samuel Heintzelman. Gen. Heintzelman asks about getting his son into a military academy. Once they get to Seward's house, AL sends for Gen. McClellan.

December 17, Tuesday

In Mexico, France, England, and Spain seize Veracruz to collect debts.

❖ AL with Seward and Chase, consults with a committee from the New York Chamber of Commerce regarding naval protection for Union commerce in foreign waters.

- ❖ AL sends to Congress copies of correspondence with the governor of Maine concerning coastal fortifications.
- ❖ The first White House public reception of season is held from 8 to 10:30 p.m.

December 18, Wednesday

- ❖ AL and the Cabinet informally discuss the Trent Affair.
- ❖ Indiana Rep. Schuyler Colfax and New York Rep. Reuben Fenton urge AL to get the army into action.
- ❖ AL, with Seward, Cameron, and others, watch seamen drill at the Navy Yard.
- ❖ AL goes with Hay to the Seward house at 9:30 p.m., where they meet with Gen. McClellan and talk about the war until midnight.

December 19, Thursday

- ❖ AL orders the purchase of fifty "coffee-mill guns." (They are mostly installed in blockhouses rather than used in the field.)
- ❖ AL drafts a reply (never sent) to Lord John Russell, British Secretary for Foreign Affairs, concerning the Trent Affair, saying no offense was intended and offering reparations.
- ❖ In the evening AL converses with Sen. Browning, and they call on Gen. McClellan.

December 20, Friday

- ❖ A report shows that AL has made 650 army appointments of all kinds since August 27, 1861.

December 21, Saturday

- ❖ AL and others watch the 15th New York test a pontoon bridge. AL has his carriage driven across.

❖ Sen. Browning has a long talk with AL, covering the Trent Affair, a treaty with Mexico, and the Rothschild's offer of a loan. Later they call on Gen. McClellan.

December 22, Sunday

❖ AL and MTL attend church. Afterward they drive Sen. Browning home.

December 23, Monday

Lord Lyons officially presents the British demands in response to the Trent Affair.

❖ AL signs legislation to raise import taxes on tea, sugar, coffee, and molasses.
❖ Seward, Welles, and Chase call at White House to confer with AL on the Trent Affair. Massachusetts Sen. Charles Sumner again urges AL to surrender Mason and Slidell.

December 24, Tuesday

❖ AL endorses a letter to Cameron from the Rev. Robert Breckenridge of Kentucky asking for an aide-de-camp appointment for his son. (The son, Joseph Breckinridge, ended up becoming inspector general for the army and serving through the Spanish–American War.)

December 25, Wednesday

❖ AL attends a four-hour Cabinet meeting devoted to the Trent Affair. Massachusetts Sen. Charles Sumner reads letters from British Members of Parliament Richard Cobden and John Bright, and the French minister speaks to them, all urging them to release the Confederate envoys and avert war. They adjourn without an official decision.
❖ AL and MTL host a large Christmas dinner.

December 26, Thursday

❖ AL meets with the Cabinet again and they officially approve surrendering the Confederate envoys taken in the Trent Affair.

❖ AL orders the purchase of 10,000 Spencer seven-shot lever-action repeating rifles.

December 27, Friday

❖ AL signs legislation providing for three commissioners for each state to visit camps and expedite soldiers' pay.

❖ AL accompanies Comdr. Dahlgren on the second trial trip of the newly refitted USS Pensacola. He is quiet. They return after dark.

❖ AL tells Massachusetts Sen. Charles Sumner that he is preparing an emancipation doctrine.

December 28, Saturday

❖ AL sends a note to Seward asking if it time to release former Kentucky governor Charles Morehead, arrested for disloyalty in September. (He was released in January and fled abroad.)

❖ MTL holds an afternoon reception.

December 29, Sunday

❖ AL spends much of the day consulting with Gen. Burnside, returned from his ongoing expedition to seize the coast of North Carolina, and with Gen. McClellan.

❖ Sen. Browning visits AL in the evening.

❖ AL spends part of the evening with New York Rep. Alfred Ely, who was captured at Bull Run and released by the Confederates on Christmas Day in a prisoner exchange. (He was exchanged for James Faulkner, Buchanan's minister to France, arrested for negotiating Confederate arms deals while in Paris.)

December 30, Monday

- ❖ AL transmits to Congress correspondence between Seward and authorities in Great Britain and France, concerning the Trent Affair.
- ❖ AL attends parties at the homes of Chase and Cameron.

December 31, Tuesday

- ❖ AL sends a letter to Gen. David Hunter, rebuking him for his "ugly" letter complaining that his assignment to Fort Leavenworth is some kind of punishment: "I have been, and am sincerely your friend; and if, as such, I dare to make a suggestion, I would say you are adopting the best possible way to ruin yourself. 'Act well your part, there all the honor lies.'"
- ❖ AL confers for ninety minutes with the Joint Committee on the Conduct of the War.
- ❖ AL hears evening serenades from four bands.
- ❖ AL informs Gen. Halleck and Gen. Buell that Gen. McClellan is sick.

෮1862 ෨

JANUARY 1
THROUGH DECEMBER 31

JANUARY 1862

Summary: AL is frantic for his new armies to go into action. Meanwhile, politics never sleeps.

January 1, Wednesday

The Confederate officials captured in the Trent Affair board a British warship, ending the crisis.

❖ AL and MTL host a New Year's reception at the White House.
❖ AL telegraphs Gen. Halleck in St. Louis and Gen. Buell at Louisville, KY, that Gen. McClellan is sick and meanwhile he is worried that the Confederates will move against Gen. Buell with troops from Columbus, KY. He suggests a move against Columbus to keep them occupied. (Gen. Halleck replied that the Confederates have made no such move and the force at Columbus was too strong to attack.)
❖ AL writes to Gen. McClellan, telling him that he need not feel uneasy about the proceedings of the Congressional Joint Committee on the Conduct of the War.

January 2, Thursday

❖ AL visits Gen. McClellan and decides he is "very much better."
❖ AL drives to the Navy Yard with Fox to watch the firing of a heavy rifled cannon.

January 3, Friday

❖ At 8 p.m., AL attends a lecture at the Smithsonian by Horace Greeley entitled "The Nation." AL gets catcalls from pro-Frémont attendees.

January 4, Saturday

❖ AL reviews the 6th U.S. Cavalry in the morning.

❖ AL telegraphs Gen. Buell in Louisville, KY: "Have arms gone forward for East Tennessee?" (Gen. Buell replied that he can only get arms to the eastern Tennessee Unionists after the army occupies the area.)

January 5, Sunday

❖ AL talks to Blair at the White House about foreign affairs.

January 6, Monday

❖ AL visits Gen. McClellan again, and shows him the answer from Gen. Buell.

❖ He replies to Gen. Buell, saying he does not dare show Buell's answer to the east Tennessee congressional delegation. "They would despair—possibly resign to go and save their families somehow, or die with them."

❖ At 7:30 p.m., AL and the Cabinet meet with the Joint Committee on the Conduct of the War. Ohio Sen. Benjamin Wade demands the removal of Gen. McClellan for inaction.

January 7, Tuesday

❖ AL asks Gen. Halleck in St. Louis and Gen. Buell at Louisville, to set a date when they will start moving southward (to overrun Kentucky and afford access to eastern Tennessee.) (Gen. Halleck sends excuses. Gen. Buell does not respond.)

❖ AL hosts a levee from 8:30 to 10:30 p.m. AL appears in good health, albeit careworn.

January 8, Wednesday

❖ AL makes inquiries as to whether the telegraph connection to Louisville, Kentucky, is working. (The manager replied that Gen. Buell is out of town and so has not replied.)

❖ AL has a long conversation with Gen. James Shields, who nearly fought a duel with AL in 1842.

January 9, Thursday

❖ AL tells Gen. McClellan to meet with the Joint Committee on the Conduct of the War as soon as possible. (They don't think he's really sick.)
❖ AL complains to Gen. McClellan that neither Gen. Halleck nor Gen. Buell has named a day when they will be ready to move.

January 10, Friday

Gen. Grant, on his own initiative, launches a probe from Cairo, IL, toward Columbus, Kentucky.

❖ AL attends a Cabinet meeting where Bates complains that there is still too much confusion in the Administration.
❖ AL sends to Congress copies of correspondence with Austria, concerning the Trent Affair. (Austria had backed England.)
❖ AL interviews Thomas Beecher, brother of the better-known Henry Ward Beecher.
❖ AL consults with Thurlow Weed regarding Cameron's poor reputation and the possibility of removing Cameron from the Cabinet.
❖ AL tells Gen. Meigs: "The people are impatient; Chase has no money, and he tells me he can raise no money; the General of the Army has typhoid fever. The bottom is out of the tub. What shall I do?"
❖ AL comments on a letter from Gen. Halleck saying he is tied down in Missouri and cannot attack Columbus, Kentucky: "As everywhere else, nothing can be done."
❖ AL convenes an 8 p.m. "council of war" with Seward, Chase, Gen. Irwin McDowell, Gen. William Franklin, and others to discuss possible operations.

January 11, Saturday

❖ AL offers to make Cameron the minister to Russia since Cameron has expressed a desire to leave the Cabinet.

❖ AL asks Massachusetts Gov. John Andrew find officers for two regiments raised there.

❖ AL calls a second meeting of yesterday's "council of war" to discuss possible operations for the Army of the Potomac.

January 12, Sunday

❖ AL convenes another "council of war," with the addition of Blair and Gen. Meigs. They decide to adjourn until the next day, when Gen. McClellan can be present.

❖ Sen. Browning calls on AL in the evening and finds him full of plans and thinking about taking the field himself.

January 13, Monday

❖ AL attends a Cabinet meeting and names Edwin Stanton the new Secretary of War, and nominates Cameron as minister to Russia.

❖ AL, in the afternoon, convenes another "council of war." Gen. McClellan attends—but refuses to reveal his plans for security reasons.

❖ AL tells Gen. Buell that his suggestions are not orders but he would appreciate them being "respectfully considered."

January 14, Tuesday

❖ AL hosts an evening reception at the White House.

January 15, Wednesday

❖ AL asks Gen. Halleck to make AL's friend Gustave Koerner a brigadier general, as he could help ease the tensions among German-American soldiers who are upset over arrears in pay. (Halleck responded that it would be better to catch up on the arrears in pay, as planned. AL later nominated Koerner as minister to Spain.)

❖ District of Columbia Commissioner Charles Upton has an evening appointment with AL but never gets in to see him.

January 16, Thursday

❖ AL attends a public demonstration of "Greek fire" (i.e., incendiary) bombshells in Treasury Park at 8 p.m., but most of the material does not arrive in time.

January 17, Friday

❖ AL confers with leading New York Unionist Democrat Edwards Pierrepont.
❖ In the afternoon, AL talks with Kansas Sen. (and Gen.) James Lane about fugitive slaves being surrendered to loyal owners.
❖ AL confers with Bates about a pardon case.
❖ AL sends to Congress copies of documents that were exchanged with Prussia regarding the Trent Affair. (Prussia sided with England.)

January 18, Saturday

❖ MTL sends a carriage to bring Sen. Browning to the White House, where he has a long talk with AL, joined by Kentucky Sen. Garrett Davis.

January 20, Monday

❖ AL receives a protest from the veteran 14th New York State Militia (alternately, the 14th Brooklyn Chasseurs) against being renumbered as the 84th. (They would operate under both designations.)
❖ Pianist and composer Alexander Wolowski performs for MTL at the White House.

January 21, Tuesday

❖ AL attends a nighttime reception and appears to be in good spirits.

January 22, Wednesday

❖ A delegation of New York Germans calls on AL to protest the treatment of Gen. Franz Sigel. (He had been blamed for the defeat at Wilson's Creek.)

❖ In the evening AL sees a more successful exhibition of Greek fire.

January 23, Thursday

❖ AL confers about the progress of constructing mortar gunboats (for naval bombardments).

❖ AL discusses the issue of fugitive slaves with Kansas Sen. (and Gen.) James Lane and Kansas Sen. Samuel Pomeroy. They conclude that the government cannot return them.

❖ AL talks to Kentucky Sen. Lazarus Powell about measures to support homeless refugees.

❖ AL and MTL attend the Washington Theater to hear the New York Academy of Music perform operatic selections. Their appearance is greeted with applause.

January 24, Friday

❖ AL authorizes Stanton to effect unspecified measures "to secure more vigor and activity" in the Bureau of Ordnance.

❖ AL issues a stay of execution for convicted slave trader Nathaniel Gordon, to give Gordon time to contemplate his fate. (He was caught with a cargo of 897 slaves off the Congo River. Most were children. All were sent to Liberia. Gordon was hanged February 21, 1862.)

❖ AL asks for guidance from the Senate on the idea of a loan to Mexico. (The Senate turned down the idea.)

January 25, Saturday

- ❖ AL talks with William Schouler, the adjutant general of Massachusetts, regarding Gen. Butler's raising of troops in Massachusetts.
- ❖ Sen. Browning spends an hour with AL during the morning.
- ❖ Members of the Joint Committee on the Conduct of the War interview AL about Gen. Frémont's military administration.
- ❖ AL tells Ward Hill Lamon to refrain from arresting or jailing fugitive slaves.

January 26, Sunday

- ❖ AL expresses irritation about the slow progress in the production of mortars, and says he will take matters into his own hands. He consults with Stanton and an engineer.
- ❖ AL meets with several Cabinet members in the evening.
- ❖ MTL is not well enough to receive visitors.

January 28, Tuesday

Gen. Grant gets the permission of his superior, Gen. Halleck, to launch an offensive.

- ❖ AL interviews leaders of the U.S. Sanitary Commission about appointments to the medical bureau.
- ❖ AL meets with Gen. Nathaniel Banks.
- ❖ AL and MTL host an evening reception at the White House.

January 29, Wednesday

- ❖ AL meets with Ellen Sherman, wife of Gen. Sherman, accompanied by her father, former Ohio senator Thomas Ewing. She is anxious to counter rumors that her husband has gone insane. She has known him since he was 10, and he is the same now, she tells AL. (AL kept him in the army.)

January 30, Thursday

The hull of the USS Monitor is launched in Brooklyn.

❖ AL works in the morning at the War Department.

January 31, Friday

❖ Tired of merely urging, AL issues "Special War Order No. 1," saying that all Federal armies are to move forward on or before February 22.
❖ AL signs legislation authorizing him to take possession of railroads and telegraph lines as needed.
❖ AL assures Stanton that a planned expedition in Missouri would be small and not involve independent command for Gen. (and Sen.) James Lane.

FEBRUARY 1862

Summary: Finally, a Union general launches an offensive—but it's not Gen. McClellan. Then, at home, the unthinkable happens.

February 1, Saturday

- ❖ AL talks to Seward and former rebel prisoner New York Rep. Alfred Ely about whether crews of Confederate privateers should be held on the same footing as POWs. (The decision was to give them the same footing.)
- ❖ AL sends for Fox for an evening meeting.

February 2, Sunday

- ❖ AL is introduced to Ralph Waldo Emerson. They discuss the case of condemned slave trader Nathaniel Gordon.
- ❖ AL assures Kansas Rep. Martin Conway that Gen. James Lane does not have an independent command and serves under Gen. David Hunter.

February 3, Monday

- ❖ AL sends official thanks to the King of Siam (modern Thailand) for several gifts, but politely turns down his proposed gift of elephants.
- ❖ AL writes to Gen. McClellan asking him how McClellan's plan (to advance on Richmond from the coast of Chesapeake Bay) is better than AL's plan (to seize the railroads in northern Virginia).

February 4, Tuesday

Gen. Grant begins landing troops near Confederate Fort Henry on the Tennessee River.

❖ MTL cancels her weekly reception as she is planning a private party the next day.

February 5, Wednesday

❖ Having invited as many as 700 people, MTL hosts an elaborate party at the White House lasting past midnight.

February 6, Thursday

Confederate Fort Henry surrenders to Gen. Grant, opening the Tennessee River to Federal control as far south as Florence, Alabama.

❖ AL approves the withholding of pensions to Confederate sympathizers.

February 7, Friday

Gen. Grant moves his forces west to Confederate Fort Donelson on the nearby Cumberland River.

❖ AL spends much of his time with Willie, who is critically ill with typhoid fever.
❖ AL sees a Congressional delegation seeking to settle an ongoing argument between Gen. James Lane and Gen. David Hunter.
❖ AL sends to the Senate "correspondence relating to the presentation of American citizens to the Court of France." (The French Court would not present Americans at a ball because the American minister would not identify their "social quality." Seward subsequently sent the American minister in Paris guidance to the effect that the French could

do as they pleased and Americans with no better business than attending parties should return home.)

February 8, Saturday

- ❖ AL does not hold the usual Saturday reception due to Willie's illness.
- ❖ AL receives a petition from Colorado Territory citizens demanding the removal of territorial Gov. William Gilpin following the repudiation of government drafts issued by him to pay for military equipment.
- ❖ AL writes to Gen. McClellan asking about news from the west (He had none.), about the use of boats to form a pontoon bridge across the Potomac near Harper's Ferry (The boats could not get there, being too big for the canal locks.), and about his decision on a campaign plan (The roads were still being scouted.)

February 9, Sunday

Gen. Charles Stone is arrested.

- ❖ AL is at the War Department in the afternoon and hears Stanton accuse the superintendent of military telegraphs of neglecting his duty. AL defends the man.

February 10, Monday

- ❖ AL conducts minimal business due to Willie's illness. Tad also has fallen sick.

February 11, Tuesday

- ❖ AL again conducts minimal business due to Willie's and Tad's illness.
- ❖ AL meets with Seward, Ohio Sen. Benjamin Wade, and Michigan Sen. Zachariah Chandler to hear of testimony

relative to Gen. Charles Stone. (Unsupported gossip makes him sound like a turncoat.)

February 12, Wednesday

The siege of Fort Donelson begins.

❖ AL again conducts minimal business.

February 13, Thursday

❖ AL again conducts minimal business.
❖ AL appears before the House Judiciary Committee concerning the premature publication of his last annual message.

February 14, Friday

❖ AL meets with the Cabinet and hears a report on Gen. Burnside's coastal expedition.
❖ AL issues Executive Order No. 1, saying that all political prisoners in military custody will be released if they accept a parole, and swear not to give aid or comfort to the enemy.

February 15, Saturday

❖ There is no reception at the White House due to Willie's and Tad's illness.

February 16, Sunday

Fort Donelson surrenders, opening the Cumberland River to Nashville, Tennessee. Kentucky becomes largely untenable for the Confederates.

❖ AL sends suggestions to Gen. Halleck on various moves he might make to prevent the Confederates from retaking Fort Donelson. (Instead, the Confederates retreated toward the regional rail hub at Corinth, Mississippi.)

❖ AL announces that for reasons of public safety he cannot reveal the reasons for arresting members of the Maryland legislature.

February 17, Monday

❖ AL tells Stanton he wants to re-nominate Henry Judah as a brigadier general of volunteers, since the original nomination got lost. (The man had a drinking problem, so the loss might have been intentional. He got the promotion—and was then sacked after several foul-ups.)
❖ That night Stanton brings AL a nomination for Gen. Grant as a major general of volunteers. AL signs it immediately.

February 18, Tuesday

❖ AL cancels the evening reception at the White House because of the illness of Willie and Tad.

February 19, Wednesday

❖ AL signs a proclamation suggesting that the people celebrate Washington's Birthday (February 22) by listening to readings of his "Farewell Address."
❖ AL signs legislation prohibiting the so-called "coolie trade" (importing Asians under-slave like conditions).

February 20, Thursday

William Wallace "Willie" Lincoln, age 11, dies at 5 p.m.

The loss of Willie Lincoln devastated his family. He was the second of their sons to die from illness.

- ❖ AL weeps in his office.
- ❖ MTL is inconsolable.
- ❖ Sen. and Mrs. Browning spend the night at the White House.

February 21, Friday

- ❖ AL does not attend a Cabinet meeting.
- ❖ AL confers with Gen. Butler about an expedition to New Orleans.
- ❖ Cabinet members and their wives call at the White House.

February 22, Saturday

- ❖ AL does not attend the Washington's Birthday celebrations.
- ❖ Tad remains sick.
- ❖ Willie lies in state in the Green Room.

- ❖ AL's deadline for movement by Federal armies passes without notice.

February 23, Sunday

- ❖ AL is conferring with Stanton at the War Department when they are interrupted by Gen. Butler with his instructions from Gen. McClellan to proceed with an expedition to New Orleans.
- ❖ Tad appears to be recovering.

February 24, Monday

- ❖ Willie Lincoln's funeral is held at 2 p.m. in the East Room.
- ❖ AL, accompanied by RTL and Illinois Sens. Browning and Lyman Trumbull, follows the hearse to the Oak Hill Cemetery.
- ❖ Government offices are closed.
- ❖ Tad appears "decidedly better."

February 25, Tuesday

Union forces occupy Nashville, Tennessee.

- ❖ AL signs the Treasury Note (Legal Tender) Bill. "Greenbacks" are declared legal tender.
- ❖ The Cabinet discusses paroling prisoners of war.
- ❖ Gen. Butler calls on AL before leaving for his New Orleans expedition. AL says taking New Orleans will "break the back of the rebellion."
- ❖ AL hears a recommendation from the Joint Committee on the Conduct of the War that the Army of the Potomac be divided into corps.
- ❖ AL transmits to Congress copies of correspondence with the Russian government concerning the Trent Affair. (The Czar backed the U.S.)

February 26, Wednesday

- ❖ AL, pursuant to recent legislation, takes over all the nation's telegraph lines.
- ❖ AL interviews Gen. McClellan, who is about to leave town.
- ❖ Tad no longer appears to be in danger.
- ❖ MTL is still confined to her room.

February 27, Thursday

- ❖ AL appoints a commission to examine the cases of political prisoners who remain in military custody.
- ❖ Concerning Gen. McClellan, AL says: "The general impression is daily gaining ground that the general does not intend to do anything."
- ❖ MTL is described as ill.

February 28, Friday

- ❖ AL meets with the Cabinet about trade with seceded areas. He issues an order permitting such commerce as the Secretary of the Treasury feels fit to allow.
- ❖ AL visits the Navy Yard and the Washington Arsenal.
- ❖ AL has a talk with Gen. McClellan about his recent failures to act.
- ❖ AL has tea in the evening with Elizabeth Todd Edwards, sister of MTL.

MARCH 1862

Summary: Gen. McClellan finally puts his army in motion. Meanwhile, AL pushes the idea of compensated emancipation.

March 1, Saturday

The Confederates pull out of Columbus, Kentucky, basically abandoning the state.

March 2, Sunday

Gen. Grant begins moving up the Tennessee River to the vicinity of Eastport, Mississippi. The Confederates are retreating into the same area.

March 3, Monday

❖ AL sends Congress documents about the Portuguese government encouraging cotton cultivation in those parts of Africa it controls. (It might undercut the South's domination of the cotton trade.)
❖ AL sends Congress documents relating to the reaction of the Italian government to the Trent Affair. (They were simply happy that it did not lead to war.)
❖ In evening AL meets with an unspecified group of congressmen and holds a long conference concerning the state of the Union.

March 4, Tuesday

❖ AL appears before the Joint Committee on the Conduct of the War, along with Gen. David Hunter, to answer questions about events in Kansas.

❖ Fox notifies AL that the newly launched, and untried, USS Monitor is on its way to Hampton Roads.

❖ The Senate confirms AL's appointment of Johnson as the military governor of Tennessee.

March 5, Wednesday

❖ AL summons the Cabinet to a special 7 p.m. meeting about compensated emancipation.

March 6, Thursday

❖ AL urges Congress to provide aid to any state that adopts gradual compensated emancipation. (Congress merely endorsed the idea.)

❖ AL discusses compensated emancipation with Massachusetts Sen. Charles Sumner.

❖ AL signs legislation requiring that American sea captains take an oath of allegiance.

March 7, Friday

❖ AL consults with Gen. McClellan about his plan for capturing Richmond.

March 8, Saturday, First-Quarter

The salvaged USS Merrimack, now the ironclad CSS Virginia, steams out of Norfolk, Virginia, and destroys two large conventional wooden U.S. warships in Hampton Roads. A third is driven helplessly aground. The underpowered ironclad retreats as the tide falls. Barely noticed, the much smaller USS Monitor arrives at sunset and joins the third, grounded warship.

❖ AL summons Gen. McClellan to the White House at 7:30 a.m. to talk about rumors that McClellan intends to turn the capital and the government over to the enemy. AL denies any intent to accuse him.

❖ AL sends Fox to Hampton Roads.

❖ AL meets with Gen. McClellan's divisional commanders at the White House after they vote eight to four in favor of Gen. McClellan's plan for a peninsular campaign.

❖ AL issues a General War Order No. 2, dividing the Army of the Potomac into four corps. (Gen. McClellan balked, wanting to do it himself.)

❖ AL also issues General War Order No. 3, saying that during its upcoming offensive the Army of the Potomac must leave 50,000 troops around Washington.

❖ AL appoints eleven West Point cadets for 1862.

March 9, Sunday

The CSS Virginia attempts to destroy the grounded warship that it missed yesterday but encounters the USS Monitor. After a four-hour drawn firefight the CSS Virginia again retreats with the falling tide.

❖ The Cabinet meets in an emergency session to consider what to do if the *CSS Virginia* steams up the Potomac to Washington. Welles announces that a Union ironclad has been sent to the scene. Learning that it only has two guns, Stanton is furious.

❖ Stanton announces plans to block the river with obstructions.

❖ At about 4 p.m., AL learns of the retreat of the rebel ironclad.

❖ AL tells a journalist that cost-based objections to compensated emancipation miss the point. Assuming $450 per slave, the cost of emancipation for Delaware, Maryland, District of Columbia, Kentucky, and Missouri would be equal to eighty-seven days of war, but should shorten the war by at least that much.

March 10, Monday

AL and the Cabinet are still keyed-up by yesterday's brush with disaster. Meanwhile, the Confederates retreat from Manassas, Virginia. Gen. McClellan mounts no pursuit.

❖ AL attends a Cabinet meeting where they discuss the previous days' Battle of Hampton Roads.
❖ Carl Schurz meets with AL and talks about current events.
❖ AL consults with various Border State congressmen on his compensated emancipation idea.
❖ In the evening AL calls on the commander of the USS Monitor, in Washington for treatment of eye injuries suffered during yesterday's fight.

March 11, Tuesday

❖ AL issues War Order No. 3 revamping the chain of command. Gen. McClellan is removed from overall command and placed over the Department of the Potomac. Gen. Halleck is placed over the expanded Department of the Mississippi. A new Mountain Department (for the Alleghenies) is headed by Gen. Frémont. Department commanders report to Stanton.
❖ At a Cabinet meeting, a lot of dissatisfaction about Gen. McClellan and the conduct of the war is shared.
❖ AL goes for a ride with Comdr. Dahlgren.
❖ In the evening, AL summons several members of the Cabinet to the White House and reads War Order No. 3 to them.

March 12, Wednesday

❖ AL is introduced to Joseph Heco (Hikozo Hamada), the first Japanese subject to become a U.S. citizen. He had been an interpreter for the U.S. consul in Kanagawa (near Tokyo).

❖ Oregon Sen. James Nesmith expresses distrust of Gen. McClellan to AL, while former Ohio governor William Dennison expresses support.

March 13, Thursday

❖ AL approves a new military regulation forbidding the return of fugitive slaves.
❖ AL composes an official letter to Gen. McClellan telling him to leave a force to secure the Washington area, and take the rest to a new base or Fortress Monroe "in pursuit of the enemy."
❖ MTL is sick.

March 14, Friday

❖ AL shows California Sen. James McDougall that Border State compensated emancipation would cost the equivalent of eighty-seven days of war.
❖ AL again talks to former Ohio governor William Dennison about Gen. McClellan.
❖ AL sends Fox overnight to New York (presumably as part of a rush to build more monitors).

March 15, Saturday

Union forces begin massing at Pittsburg Landing/Shiloh on the Tennessee River, about twenty miles from the regional rail hub of Corinth, Mississippi, where the Confederates are likewise massing.

❖ AL has a private conversation with Bates, who warns him about extremists in Congress.
❖ AL confers with Vermont Sen. Solomon Foot about appropriations for the Capitol dome.

March 16, Sunday

❖ Blair wants to hear about the agitation to remove Gen. McClellan, but AL demurs.

March 17, Monday

Gen. McClellan begins embarking his command for Fortress Monroe, to begin the so-called Peninsula Campaign.

❖ AL meets with the Gen. Frémont, now head of the Mountain Department.
❖ AL meets with magnate Cornelius Vanderbilt and accepts a yacht for the government.

March 18, Tuesday

❖ AL meets with leading Massachusetts abolitionist Wendell Phillips.

March 19, Wednesday

❖ AL attends a Cabinet.
❖ In the evening AL confers with portraitist George Healy about placing a series of portraits of presidents in the White House, as ordered by Congress.

March 20, Thursday

❖ AL and Comdr. Dahlgren go to Alexandria, Virginia, to meet with Gen. McClellan, but miss him.
❖ MTL remains in seclusion.

March 21, Friday

❖ AL confers with Gen. Irwin McDowell about movements of the Army of the Potomac.

❖ After 3 p.m., AL embarks from the Navy Yard with Comdr. Dahlgren for a meeting with Gen. McClellan at Alexandria.

❖ AL continues meeting in the evening at the White House with Stanton, Welles, Fox, Gen. McDowell, and Comdr. Dahlgren.

❖ MTL, still in seclusion, receives a visit from Mrs. Irvin McDowell.

March 22, Saturday

❖ AL endorses a request from Gen. John Palmer to make John Condit Smith a quartermaster with the rank of captain, as he was personally acquainted with both men. (AL got his wish this time.)

March 23, Sunday

Fighting in Kernstown, Virginia, marks the opening of the Stonewall Jackson's Valley Campaign.

❖ AL meets with Carl Schurz and accepts his resignation as minister to Spain and nominates him as a brigadier general.

March 24, Monday

❖ AL writes to Horace Greeley that he would like to see Border State legislatures pass gradual compensated emancipation.

❖ Tad is reported as having recovered enough to play.

❖ MTL largely remains in seclusion.

March 25, Tuesday

❖ AL endorses a request from Hamlin that Hamlin's nephew be appointed a brigade surgeon.

❖ AL tours the Navy Yard.

❖ AL suspends the death sentence (for breach of parole) imposed on Ebenezer Magoffin, brother of (pro-South) former Kentucky governor Beriah Magoffin.

March 26, Wednesday

❖ AL meets with the Cabinet at Stanton's office in the War Department.
❖ AL asks Stanton why a requisition from Illinois Gov. Richard Yates (for fourteen batteries of artillery) has not been filled. (Stanton said it would cost too much and such requisitions should come from generals in the field.)

March 27, Thursday

❖ AL pardons two British subjects who have served three years of a seven-year sentence for resisting the master of an American vessel.
❖ AL replies to a letter from Henry Whipple, a Minnesota bishop concerned about the poor treatment of Indians there, referring the matter to Smith.

March 28, Friday

❖ AL takes a short trip down the Potomac with Comdr. Dahlgren.
❖ AL visits with Sen. Browning in the evening.
❖ AL asks that the appointment of a new governor of Colorado Territory be finalized immediately, replacing the incompetent William Gilpin.

March 29, Saturday

❖ Repeating a request that he originally made in December, AL asks Stanton to make Jesse Fell of Illinois a paymaster in the Regular Army. (He got his wish this time.)

March 30, Sunday

❖ AL meets in the evening with Gen. McClellan, who is leaving for Fortress Monroe to begin the so-called Peninsula Campaign.

March 31, Monday

❖ AL writes to Gen. McClellan apologizing for diverting a division to Gen. Frémont's department.

❖ MTL is visited by relatives from Springfield, Illinois.

APRIL 1862

Summary: *Gen. McClellan's offensive immediately stalls, but on other fronts the Confederates are not having things all their way. Meanwhile, AL whets his appetite for emancipation by freeing the slaves of the District of Columbia.*

April 1, Tuesday

❖ AL goes to Alexandria accompanied by Ninian Edwards (MTL's brother-in-law) and Comdr. Dahlgren to see Gen. McClellan, who was about to leave for the Fortress Monroe area.

April 2, Wednesday

❖ AL accompanies members of his extended family and Comdr. Dahlgren on a trip down the Potomac to visit Mount Vernon. AL, however, does not go ashore.
❖ Bates confers with AL on personnel matters.
❖ In the evening in AL talks about Gen. McClellan with Sen. Browning and Stanton.

April 3, Thursday

❖ AL discovers that Gen. McClellan has not left the agreed minimum garrison of 50,000 men in Washington. Stanton therefore retains Gen. McDowell's corps in Washington.

April 4, Friday

Gen. McClellan advances his huge force up the peninsula between the James and York Rivers, runs into a rebel

*trench line across the peninsula's neck at Yorktown,
Virginia, and stops.*

- AL meets with Ohio Sen. Benjamin Wade and agrees to meet again with the Joint Committee on the Conduct of the War.
- Sen. Browning talks during the night with AL.
- MTL instructs Hay to pay her (MTL) the salary of a dismissed White House steward.

April 5, Saturday

- Responding to a House resolution asking how other countries raise revenue, AL forwards a report from the U.S. minister in Holland summarizing the taxation methods used there.
- AL meets in the evening at the White House with Sen. Browning.

April 6, Sunday

*The Confederates attack Gen. Grant's unfortified force at
Pittsburg Landing/Shiloh. Surprised, the Federals are driven
back but then hold on.*

- AL telegraphs Gen. McClellan reminding him that he now has about 100,000 soldiers (McClellan says its 85,000) and urging him to break the enemy defense line at Yorktown, Virginia.

April 7, Monday

*Union reinforcements converge on the Shiloh battlefield and
drive the rebels away. Confederate fatalities include Samuel
B. Todd, half-brother of MTL.*

- AL signs a treaty with England to support the suppression of the African slave trade. (It placed arbitrators in New York, Sierra Leone, and South Africa.)

April 8, Tuesday

❖ AL attends a Cabinet meeting devoted to military concerns.

April 9, Wednesday

In Mexico, England and Spain pull out of the intervention force after realizing France intends to conquer the country.

❖ AL writes to Gen. McClellan about their disagreements: "Your dispatches complaining that you are not properly sustained, while they do not offend me, do pain me very much." McClellan still says he has 85,000 men but Stanton says he now has 108,000. Meanwhile, the 20,000 that McClellan left behind are not enough to defend Washington, AL complains. Finally: "I beg to assure you that I have never written you, or spoken to you, in greater kindness of feeling than now, nor with a fuller purpose to sustain you, so far as in my most anxious judgment, I consistently can. *But you must act.*"

❖ Sen. Browning visits AL at the White House in the evening and goes with him to the War Department for the latest news.

April 10, Thursday

❖ AL is confined to his bed with an unidentified illness. Sen. Browning visits him there for an hour in the evening.

❖ AL endorses an unidentified clemency appeal: "What possible injury can this lad work upon the cause of this great Union? I say let him go."

❖ AL issues a proclamation of thanksgiving for the Union's recent victories.

April 11, Friday

❖ AL has an evening meeting with Fox, Blair, and others.

April 13, Sunday

❖ AL hears from a delegation of Freedmen's Associations who urge him to provide African Americans with land from abandoned plantations at Port Royal, South Carolina.

April 14, Monday

❖ AL meets with the Cabinet in a special session to consider establishing a military government on the South Carolina coastal islands. AL meets with two paroled Southern prisoners.

❖ Sen. Browning meets with AL at the White House this evening to discuss a bill to end slavery in the District of Columbia and to plan patronage.

❖ AL meets with Bishop Daniel Payne of the African Methodist Episcopal Church and exchange good wishes.

April 16, Wednesday

The Confederacy begins conscription.

❖ AL signs legislation (long-sought by him) freeing the slaves of the District of Columbia, and appoints a three-man board to appraise the slaves of loyal owners for compensation.

❖ AL meets with Fox at the White House in the evening.

April 18, Friday

The Union navy begins bombarding the forts blocking the Mississippi River below New Orleans.

❖ AL transmits to Congress documents relating to the arrest of former secretary of war Simon Cameron, now minister to Russia, for assault and battery in Philadelphia at the residence of a Southern sympathizer whom Cameron had once ordered arrested. (The charges were later dropped.)

- ❖ Stanton confers with AL about the most recent dispatches from Gen. McClellan.
- ❖ AL confers with Sen. Browning about appointments to the District of Columbia slave-appraisal board.
- ❖ AL calls Fox to the White House for a conference.

April 19, Saturday

- ❖ AL in the afternoon boards a revenue cutter for a twenty-mile trip down the Potomac to Aquia Creek to meet with Gen. Irwin McDowell, whose force of 30,000 is camped at nearby Fredericksburg, Virginia. AL is accompanied by Stanton, Chase, Comdr. Dahlgren, and New York lawyer David Dudley Field II (brother of Cyrus Field, submarine cable entrepreneur).
- ❖ Gen. Irwin McDowell does not show up for the meeting.
- ❖ AL spends the night aboard the vessel.

April 20, Sunday

- ❖ Gen. Irwin McDowell shows up early in the morning and accompanies AL and his party back to Washington.
- ❖ The party arrives at 2:30 p.m. and dines at the home of Comdr. Dahlgren.
- ❖ In the evening AL discusses the ongoing operations against Yorktown, Virginia, and Corinth, Mississippi, with Sen. Browning.

April 21, Monday

- ❖ AL informs Gen. McClellan that Gen. Irwin McDowell will not be moving south from Fredericksburg, Virginia, to cooperate with McClellan's operations against Richmond, due to Stonewall Jackson's operations in the Shenandoah Valley.
- ❖ AL meets with Margarethe Schurz, wife of Carl Schurz and founder of the first kindergarten in the U.S.

April 22, Tuesday

Gen. McClellan remains stalled at Yorktown, Virginia.

❖ AL withdraws (at Berret's request) the nomination of former Washington mayor James Berret as a commissioner on the appraisal board for emancipated slaves. (Berret was still upset about being imprisoned and forced to resign on suspicion of disloyalty.)

April 23, Wednesday

❖ AL discusses troop movements with Stanton.
❖ AL affirms that a particular phrase in a purchasing contract does not mean that the seller can set a new price at will.

April 24, Thursday

The mortar boat bombardment having no visible effect, before dawn the Union fleet simply steams past the Confederate forts defending New Orleans. Fourteen of seventeen vessels get through.

❖ AL forwards to the Senate testimony of a court of inquiry in the case of navy Lt. Charles Fleming, who was found guilty of intemperance and incompetence.

April 25, Friday

❖ New Orleans, the South's largest city, surrenders to the Federal fleet, amidst riots and disorders.
❖ Welles rushes to the White House to tell AL about the taking of New Orleans.
❖ Sen. Browning visits AL in the evening and finds him alone and complaining of a headache. They discuss poetry, especially the works of English poet and humorist Thomas Hood. AL recites several of Hood's poems.

April 26, Saturday

* AL boards the French frigate *Gassendi* lying in the Potomac, becoming the first U.S. president to board a French warship.
* AL sends to the House a report concerning the operations of rebel privateers in foreign ports.

April 27, Sunday

* AL and several senators examine a sample hammock tent pitched in front of the Capital.
* AL attends a late Cabinet session where Stanton and Gen. James Wadsworth accuse Gen. McClellan of failing to protect Washington.

April 28, Monday

* AL responds to a Senate resolution inquiring into the arrest of Gen. Charles Stone, who was imprisoned in February: "I respectfully state that he was arrested and imprisoned under my authority and with my sanction, upon evidence which, whether he be guilty or innocent, required in my judgment such proceedings.... He will be tried without any unnecessary delay." (Stone was released in August, never having been charged with anything.)

April 29, Tuesday

Gen. Halleck begins operations from Pittsburg Landing toward Corinth, Mississippi.

* AL declines to provide the House with reasons for the Federal evacuation of Jacksonville, Florida. (Union naval forces had occupied it for a month, leaving April 9. There was apparently never any plan for a permanent occupation.)

MAY 1862

Summary: Gen. McClellan unenthusiastically gets his army in front of Richmond, convinced the enemy outnumbers him two to one. (The opposite is the case.) Reinforcements he begs for are diverted to confront Stonewall Jackson. Finally, an offensive is launched in front of Richmond—by the enemy.

May 1, Thursday

❖ AL tells Gen. Halleck that Missouri congressmen are pressing him to give Gen. John Schofield an independent command in Missouri. (Halleck opposed the idea.)

❖ AL writes to Gen. McClellan, still digging trenches in front of Yorktown, Virginia: "Your call for [heavy artillery] Parrott guns from Washington alarms me—chiefly because it argues indefinite procrastination." (McClellan replied that the idea was to speed up matters.)

May 2, Friday

❖ Illinois Sen. Browning finds that AL has a headache and spends an hour with him in the evening.

May 3, Saturday

With the Federal heavy artillery finally in place at Yorktown, Virginia, the Confederates abruptly retreat.

❖ AL sees a delegation of District of Columbia citizens concerning the appointment of a warden for the District of Columbia penitentiary.

❖ AL and MTL witness the demonstration of a breech-loading cannon at the Navy Yard. The demonstration is interrupted by "one of the president's stories."

May 4, Sunday

❖ AL writes to Dorothea Dix, Superintendent of Army Nurses, asking that nurse Rebecca Pomeroy be allowed to remain at the White House another two weeks to assist Mrs. Elizabeth Edwards (MTL's sister) as there is illness in Mrs. Edward's family. (Pomeroy assisted during the illness of Willie and Tad.)

May 5, Monday

The Union army advances from Yorktown, Virginia, clashing with the Confederate rear guard. AL decides to visit the front.

French efforts to conquer Mexico suffer a setback at Puebla.

❖ AL receives a visit from navy Lt. John Worden, who commanded the USS *Monitor* at the Battle of Hampton Roads. His eyesight is still impaired by wounds suffered during the battle.
❖ At sunset AL, Stanton, Chase, and several others leave the Navy Yard aboard a revenue cutter for an overnight trip to Fortress Monroe.

May 6, Tuesday

❖ AL arrives at Fortress Monroe at about 10 p.m. and has a brief conference with its commander, Gen. John Wool.
❖ At about midnight, AL visits the local navy flagship.

May 7, Wednesday

- ❖ AL tours various installations and facilities there, confers with the local navy commander, and boards the USS *Monitor*.
- ❖ AL goes ashore, views the ruins of Hampton, Virginia, (burned by retreating Confederates) and reviews troops.
- ❖ In the evening, AL holds a conference at the fortress and spends the night there.

May 8, Thursday

Stonewall Jackson defeats Gen. Frémont at the Battle of McDowell.

- ❖ AL watches Federal forces probe and bombard the Confederate fortifications of Norfolk, Virginia. The *CSS Virginia* stays out of range.

May 9, Friday

Gen. David Hunter, as commander of the Department of the South, issues an order freeing the slaves of South Carolina, Georgia, and Florida.

- ❖ AL tours the area in a revenue cutter and confers with Gen. John Wool about the possibility of taking Norfolk.
- ❖ AL goes ashore at a potential landing beach outside Norfolk. He returns to Fortress Monroe and sees troops embarking.
- ❖ When otherwise unoccupied AL reads aloud from Shakespeare.
- ❖ AL replies to Gen. McClellan, who is complaining that his corps commanders were not competent and wants to replace them or go back to using divisions. AL reminds McClellan that the adoption of corps was based on the unanimous advice of every military authority they consulted "excepting only you." (McClellan thereafter retained the corps echelon but set up two more corps commanded by his friends, Gen. Fitz-John Porter and Gen. William Franklin.)

May 10, Saturday

- ❖ AL, accompanied by Chase and Stanton, go with Gen. John Wool to the landing beach where Union troops have disembarked and are massing for the seizure of Norfolk, Virginia.
- ❖ AL and his party return to Fortress Monroe where AL learns that troops in the fortress and on the adjacent mainland have not been added to the force sent to Norfolk, Virginia. Angered, he issues written orders to Gen. John Wool to commit them.
- ❖ Gen. John Wool informs AL of the surrender of Norfolk, at about 11 p.m.

May 11, Sunday

The CSS Virginia *is scuttled outside Norfolk, Virginia.*

- ❖ AL has his vessel steam past the wreck of the *CSS Virginia* and then up the Elizabeth River, where he briefly visits newly captured Norfolk.
- ❖ AL telegraphs the news to Gen. Halleck at Pittsburg Landing, adding, "Be very sure to sustain no reverse in your department."

May 12, Monday

- ❖ AL arrives back in Washington in the morning.
- ❖ AL talks with Gen. Carl Schurz and predicts that he (AL) will lose support in the next Congressional election as he is not radical enough for the Republicans and too radical for the Democrats.

May 13, Tuesday

- ❖ AL makes a rare prepared speech to a regiment passing in review: "I assure you that the nation is more indebted to you, and such as you, than to me."

May 14, Wednesday

❖ In the evening AL talks about his trip to Fortress Monroe with Sen. Browning.

May 15, Thursday

In occupied New Orleans, Gen. Butler announces that any woman verbally assaulting Federal soldiers risks being treated as "a woman of the town plying her avocation."

❖ AL approves the establishment of the Department of Agriculture, although it is not given Cabinet status until 1889.
❖ AL writes to Gen. McClellan to say that despite recent military successes, "I am still unwilling to take all our force off the direct line between Richmond and here." (In other words, Gen. Irwin McDowell's force would remain in the Fredericksburg, Virginia, area, rather reinforce McClellan.)

May 16, Friday

Retreating in front of Gen. McClellan's force, the Confederates fall back to within three miles of Richmond.

❖ AL tells Gen. McClellan that he has received a petition signed by twenty-three senators and eighty-four representatives asking him to restore Gen. Charles Hamilton to the command of his division. McClellan had fired him April 30 without explanation. (McClellan replied that Hamilton was unfit to command a division. AL sent him to the western theater, where Gen. Grant eventually fired him for intriguing against other generals.)

May 17, Saturday

❖ AL, with Stanton, reviews the military situation in light of Gen. McClellan's repeated requests for reinforcements.

- ❖ AL tells Gen. Irwin McDowell to use his own judgment concerning the protection of Washington.

May 18, Sunday

- ❖ AL visits a hospital accompanied by Sen. Browning.

May 19, Monday

- ❖ AL voids Gen. David Hunter's May 9 proclamation freeing the slaves of the Department of the South. AL adds that such power is vested in himself alone. He also reiterates the Federal Government's willingness to provide financial assistance to any state that adopts gradual compensated emancipation.
- ❖ AL hears from a delegation of Marylanders concerned about Gen. James Wadsworth's enforcement of the Fugitive Slave Law, as he requires that owners prove their loyalty and even questions the slaves about it.

May 20, Tuesday

- ❖ AL signs the first Homestead Act, giving free land to settlers who will farm it for five years.
- ❖ At the Navy Yard, AL witnesses a demonstration of armor plate.
- ❖ In the evening AL goes horseback riding with Sen. Browning and others.
- ❖ At the request of British minister Lord Lyons, AL sends a signed letter to autograph hunter Sarah Sophia Child Villiers, Countess of Jersey: "I beg that her ladyship will accept the assurance of my sincere gratification at this opportunity of subscribing myself."

May 21, Wednesday

- ❖ AL signs legislation for educating "colored children" in Washington and Georgetown.

- ❖ AL assures James Gordon Bennett of the New York Herald that rescinding Gen. David Hunter's emancipation proclamation was not a source of friction in the Cabinet.
- ❖ AL again assures Gen. McClellan that he commands Gen. McDowell.
- ❖ AL writes to Massachusetts Sen. Charles Sumner regarding a soldier "subject to a lethargy" who was arrested for falling asleep on duty: "I should not knowingly let him be punished, if shown he has the infirmity." (The soldier was not court-martialed.)

May 22, Thursday

- ❖ AL reviews a cavalry regiment armed with repeating rifles.
- ❖ AL, Stanton, and Comdr. Dahlgren embark for Aquia Creek, Virginia, to visit the forces camped near Fredericksburg, Virginia.

May 23, Friday

A Union force at Front Royal, Virginia, is crushed by Stonewall Jackson, and his route to either Washington or the Potomac is open.

- ❖ AL, at Aquia Creek, Virginia, meets with Gen. Irwin McDowell and also with Col. Herman Haupt, chief of military railroads.
- ❖ AL reviews various divisions and rides along the line as the men cheer.
- ❖ AL leaves for Washington at about 10 p.m.

May 24, Saturday

Stonewall Jackson pursues retreating Federals toward the Potomac.

- ❖ AL arrives back in Washington at about 5 a.m. and spends much of the day in the War Department telegraph office with Stanton attempting to manage the deteriorating Shenandoah Valley situation.
- ❖ AL reverses himself concerning Gen. Irwin McDowell and tells him to send reinforcements west to the Shenandoah Valley.
- ❖ AL tells Gen. Frémont to move against Stonewall Jackson.
- ❖ AL turns down Gen. Halleck, who is also asking for reinforcements: "Each of our commanders along our line from Richmond to Corinth supposes himself to be confronted by numbers superior to his own."

May 25, Sunday

Stonewall Jackson catches up with the Federals at Winchester, Virginia, and crushes them again (despite religious scruples about fighting on Sunday).

- ❖ AL is visibly upset by the news from the Shenandoah Valley.
- ❖ AL telegraphs Gen. McClellan: "I think the time is near when you must either attack Richmond or give up the job and come to the defense of Washington."
- ❖ Sen. Browning drops by the White House in the evening.

May 26, Monday

- ❖ AL replies to a Congressional resolution of censure against former secretary of war Simon Cameron by reviewing the dire situation the government faced early in the war, stating that he himself, and all other heads of departments, were equally responsible for any errors.
- ❖ AL takes military possession of all railroads in the United States.

May 27, Tuesday

❖ AL telegraphs Gen. Frémont: "I see you are at Moorefield. You were expressly ordered to march to Harrisonburg. What does this mean?" (At Harrisonburg, Virginia, he would have been behind Stonewall Jackson. At Moorefield, Virginia, he was deep in the mountains and out of harm's way. Frémont said he went to Moorefield because his men were tired.)

May 28, Wednesday

❖ AL telegraphs Gen. Irwin McDowell, whose force is at Manassas Junction, Virginia, moving west toward the Shenandoah Valley: "For you [it is] a question of legs. Put in all the speed you can."

❖ AL and MTL hear opera singer Clara Louise Kellogg at Ford's Theater.

❖ AL telegraphs Gen. McClellan: "I am very glad of Gen. Porter's victory. Still, if it was a total rout of the enemy, I am puzzled to know why the Richmond and Fredericksburg Railroad was not seized." (Gen. McClellan's friend Gen. Fitz-John Porter had won a skirmish.)

May 29, Thursday

Stonewall Jackson reaches the Potomac and then begins retreating.

❖ AL tries to coordinate various forces to converge on Stonewall Jackson.

❖ AL warns Gen. McClellan that Stonewall Jackson may soon attack Harpers Ferry, Virginia.

❖ Sen. Browning goes with AL to the War Department in the evening.

May 30, Friday

Confederate forces evacuate Corinth, Mississippi, during the night, retreating south to Tupelo, Mississippi.

Gen. Irwin McDowell's force reaches the Shenandoah Valley, but Stonewall Jackson fights his way through.

❖ AL continues trying to coordinate forces to converge on Stonewall Jackson.

May 31, Saturday

Gen. McClellan splits his army across the Chickahominy River. The Confederates attack the isolated force on the south side but only dent the Union line.

❖ AL stays in the telegraph office much of the afternoon, waiting for news, and has operators send queries. The first dispatch from the Richmond front arrives at about 11 p.m.

JUNE 1862

Summary: *The stalemate in front of Richmond ends — with a successful Confederate offensive.*

June 1, Sunday

The fighting in front of Richmond ends. The Confederate commander is wounded, putting Lee in command.

❖ AL spends much of the day at the telegraph office waiting for news from Richmond.
❖ AL dispatches reinforcements to Gen. McClellan and suspends Gen. John Wool's independent command at Fortress Monroe, giving McClellan command of those forces.
❖ Joseph Kennedy, Superintendent of the Census, visits AL at the White House in the evening.
❖ Sen. Browning visits AL in the evening and returns with him to the War Department.

June 2, Monday

❖ AL sends to the Senate a report concerning the May 5 battle at Williamsburg, Virginia.
❖ Sen. Browning visits AL at the White House again.

June 3, Tuesday

❖ AL tells Gen. McClellan to be cautious about having his army athwart the Chickahominy River considering the recent heavy rains.
❖ AL asks Gen. Irwin McDowell if he knows where Stonewall Jackson is located in relation to the Union forces in the

Shenandoah Valley. (Gen. McDowell replied that he could only speculate.)

June 4, Wednesday

- ❖ AL tells Congress that the Administration knows nothing about the closing of schools for blacks in Union-occupied portions of North Carolina by the military governor there. (It turned out to be an effort to placate the local whites.)
- ❖ AL telegraphs congratulations to Gen. Halleck at Corinth, MS, after Halleck forwarded a report from Gen. John Pope saying he had captured 10,000 prisoners. (Gen. Pope later complained that he had reported no such thing.)

June 5, Thursday

- ❖ AL asks Stanton to reinstate West Point Cadet William Kellogg Jr., as AL knows the cadet's father: "I cannot be the instrument to crush his heart." (The cadet is reinstated but never managed to graduate.)
- ❖ AL signs legislation providing for commissioners to Liberia and Haiti, the first black governments to be recognized by Congress.
- ❖ Sen. Browning has tea with AL.

June 6, Friday

A Federal river squadron occupies Memphis, Tennessee.

- ❖ AL meets with Maryland Gov. Augustus Bradford and Col. John Kenly. The latter had been captured May 23 by Stonewall Jackson and paroled.

June 7, Saturday

- ❖ AL signs legislation requiring the direct collection of taxes in insurrectionary districts (i.e., taxes can't be paid through the mail or through intermediaries).

❖ The White House announces there'll be no more live music on the grounds for the rest of the season.

June 8, Sunday

With two Federal columns trying to converge on Stonewall Jackson, he turns on the one commanded by Gen. Frémont and defeats it at the Battle of Cross Keys, Virginia.

❖ AL examines the cases of court-martialed soldiers imprisoned in the District of Columbia penitentiary.

June 9, Monday

Stonewall Jackson turns on the other converging column and defeats it at the Battle of Port Republic, Virginia.

❖ AL receives two officers from the Danish Navy.
❖ AL sends reinforcements to the Shenandoah Valley but tells Gen. Frémont to go on the defensive.

June 10, Tuesday

❖ AL sends to Congress the completed treaty with England for the suppression of the African slave trade, asking that Congress enact certain legislation to support the treaty's execution.

June 11, Wednesday

❖ AL confers with Gen. Burnside, who is about to leave for Fortress Monroe.
❖ AL discusses the operation of the Fugitive Slave Law in the District of Columbia in the evening with Sen. Browning, Marshall Ward Hill Lamon, and Gen. James Wadsworth.

June 12, Thursday

Rebel cavalry leader J. E. B. Stuart begins a headline-grabbing three-day reconnaissance during which he rides entirely around Gen. McClellan's inert army outside Richmond.

❖ AL hears from a Kentucky congressional delegation upset that that previously captured Confederate general Simon Buckner (a Kentuckian) has been exchanged back to the South.

❖ AL tells Gen. Frémont that reinforcements are on the way and that he should fall back if pressed by Stonewall Jackson, but not farther than Harrisonburg, Virginia. (Gen. Frémont wanted to fall back an additional twenty miles.)

❖ MTL spends part of day visiting military hospitals. (She has done this often since leaving seclusion, but on this day a newspaper reporter noticed.)

June 13, Friday

❖ AL tells Gen. Frémont (still complaining that his men are exhausted) that he and Gen. Nathaniel Banks will have to take care of Stonewall Jackson between them as Gen. Irwin McDowell must be sent elsewhere.

❖ The Lincoln family moves to the (better ventilated) Soldiers' Home for the summer.

June 14, Saturday

❖ AL cancels a twenty-dollar fine imposed on a Washington restaurateur who sent brandy to a wounded soldier.

June 15, Sunday

❖ AL tells Gen. Frémont that he cannot expect significant reinforcements, as it has become clear that Stonewall Jackson's intention is to draw troops away from Richmond.

June 16, Monday

- ❖ AL orders that Lee's mansion on Arlington Heights be converted into a hospital.
- ❖ AL replies to Gen. Frémont, who is complaining that he has not received the 35,000 men he was promised when given command of the department. AL notes that at one point Gen. Frémont had that that many men but never used them to take eastern Tennessee as promised. Currently, facing Stonewall Jackson, "I am only asking of you to stand cautiously on the defensive."

June 17, Tuesday

Stonewall Jackson begins surreptitiously moving his forces from the Shenandoah Valley to Richmond.

June 18, Wednesday

- ❖ AL and Hamlin ride to the Soldiers' Home for dinner and then retire to the library. There, AL reads Hamlin a draft of the Emancipation Proclamation.
- ❖ AL responds to Gen. McClellan concerning (false) reports that the Confederates have sent significant reinforcements from Richmond to the Shenandoah Valley: "If this be true, it is as good as a reinforcement to you of an equal force."

June 19, Thursday

- ❖ Rendering moot the Dred Scott Decision, AL signs legislation freeing the slaves in all current and future territories of the United States.
- ❖ AL reviews a cavalry regiment, accompanied by Stanton and Gen. James Wadsworth.
- ❖ AL tells Gen. McClellan that recent reports of reinforcements being sent to Stonewall Jackson could be disinformation.

June 20, Friday

❖ AL receives a delegation of Progressive Friends (i.e., Quakers) with a petition against slavery. AL expresses relief that they are not office-seekers. But as far as a proclamation of emancipation, "Such a decree surely could be no more binding upon the South than the Constitution, and that cannot be enforced in that part of the country now."

June 21, Saturday

❖ AL responds to an offer by Gen. McClellan to come to Washington and brief AL on the military state of the nation by saying that neither of them have time for that.

June 22, Sunday

❖ AL signs a postal convention with Mexico.

June 23, Monday

❖ Accompanied by Gen. John Pope, AL leaves Washington at 4 p.m. on a special train and reaches New York at 1:30 a.m.

June 24, Tuesday

❖ AL arrives at a hotel near West Point, NY, at about 3 a.m.
❖ From breakfast until noon AL meets with (retired) Gen. Scott about the military situation.
❖ AL inspects West Point from noon to about 3 p.m.
❖ AL orders Gen. Butler in New Orleans to stop requiring foreigners to take loyalty oaths.
❖ After dinner AL visits the Parrott foundry nearby and watches cannon production.
❖ AL receives guests at the hotel from 9 to 11 p.m.

June 25, Wednesday

- ❖ AL, in West Point, NY, leaves by train at about 10 a.m.
- ❖ AL arrives in Washington at about 6:50 p.m.
- ❖ Sen. Browning and other friends visit AL in the evening at the Soldiers' Home.

June 26, Thursday

With Gen. McClellan's army still divided by the Chickahominy River, Lee attacks the northern wing with marginal help from newly arrived Stonewall Jackson, who's exhausted.

- ❖ AL orders that the Washington garrison and the commands of Gen. Frémont, Gen. Nathaniel Banks, and Gen. Irvin McDowell be combined into a new Army of Virginia under Gen. John Pope.

June 27, Friday

Under attack, Gen. McClellan pulls his army south of the Chickahominy River. Since his supply line runs north of the river he begins preparing a new base on the James River, to his south.

- ❖ AL accepts the resignation of Gen. Frémont and replaces him with Gen. Franz Sigel. (Gen. Frémont refused to serve under someone else, as was required when his force was made part of the new Army of Virginia.)

June 28, Saturday

Gen. McClellan telegraphs AL that he has been defeated by superior numbers. The telegraphers delete two passages where he bitterly blames AL and the Administration.

- ❖ AL responds to Gen. McClellan's edited message: "Save your Army at all events. Will send reinforcements as fast as we can…neither you nor the government is to blame."
- ❖ AL sends a statement to a conference of Union governors in New York hoping they will issue a call for more troops (without the Federal Government raising alarm by doing it), saying with 100,000 more they could take Richmond and end the war. (The governors didn't act.)
- ❖ AL writes to West Point Cadet Quintin Campbell, son of one of MTL's cousins, urging him to not be discouraged and quit. (He didn't, graduating in 1866.)

June 29, Sunday

Gen. McClellan continues retreating, his forces repelling Confederate attacks.

- ❖ AL talks to a war correspondent who was at the Richmond front twenty-four hours earlier, who reports that things there seemed under control. A report from Gen. McClellan's quartermaster agrees.

June 30, Monday

Gen. McClellan's retreating force masses at Malvern Hill, just north of his new base on the James River.

- ❖ AL asks Gen. Halleck in Corinth, Mississippi, if he can spare 25,000 men for the Richmond front. (He declined.)
- ❖ The Senate confirms AL's nomination of Isaac Newton to be a new Commissioner of Agriculture.
- ❖ Sen. Browning visits AL in the morning at the White House and in the evening at the Soldiers' Home.

JULY 1862

Summary: Gen. McClellan's army survives the crisis in front of Richmond. AL gets out of the generalship business. He promotes a more rigorous prosecution of the war. But he stops short of issuing an emancipation proclamation.

July 1, Tuesday

Gen. McClellan's army crushes uncoordinated Confederate attacks at Malvern Hill. Then it continues retreating.

❖ AL issues a proclamation calling for the raising of an additional 300,000 troops.

❖ AL signs legislation providing for a 3 percent income tax on annual income in excess of $600.

❖ AL also proclaims a 50 percent penalty on real-estate taxes due from rebellious states.

❖ After breakfast, AL discusses confiscation bills with Sen. Browning at the White House.

❖ In response to frantic calls for massive reinforcements from Gen. McClellan, AL responds: "If we had a million men we could not get them to you in time.... If you are not strong enough to face the enemy you must find a place of security, and wait, rest, and repair. Maintain your ground if you can; but save the army at all events."

July 2, Wednesday

Heavy rain ends heavy fighting in Virginia.

- ❖ AL signs legislation approving land grant colleges, setting up a transcontinental railroad (naming the eastern link Union Pacific), and banning polygamy.
- ❖ AL discusses the military situation with Indiana Rep. George Julian and with Sen. Browning.
- ❖ AL confers with Stanton on fugitive slaves. He decides that by law they cannot be sent back to their masters, but they should not be allowed to starve and therefore should be given work and paid reasonable wages.
- ❖ AL asks Gen. Halleck to visit him.
- ❖ In response to Gen. McClellan's demand for 50,000 more men immediately, AL replies: "I only beg that in like manner, you will not ask impossibilities of me. If you think you are not strong enough to take Richmond just now, I do not ask you to try just now."

July 3, Thursday

- ❖ AL sends telegrams to all Union governors asking for immediate reinforcements: "If I had fifty thousand additional troops here now, I believe I could substantially close the war in two weeks."
- ❖ AL responds to Gen. McClellan, who reports that his army is now safe: "I am satisfied that yourself, officers and men have done the best you could."

July 4, Friday

The Union navy captures a Confederate gunboat on the James River carrying an observation balloon made from ladies' silk undergarments.

- ❖ AL tells Gen. McClellan he can send no more than 30,000 reinforcements in the near future: "Under these circumstances the defensive, for the present, must be your only care. Save the army—first, where you are, if you can; and secondly, by removal, if you must."

❖ On his way to the Soldiers' Home, AL meets a column of ambulances on the road and rides along for some distance, talking to the men.
❖ At the Soldiers' Home in the evening, AL talks about the military situation with Gen. Meigs and others.

July 5, Saturday

❖ AL sends thanks to Gen. McClellan for his recent dispatches, which express confidence.
❖ AL confers with Stanton at the telegraph office in the afternoon.
❖ AL talks with Sen. Browning and others in the evening.
❖ AL retires early, too exhausted to keep any appointments.
❖ MTL tells a friend that AL often can't sleep at night.

July 6, Sunday

❖ AL allows Gov. William Sprague of Rhode Island to go to Gen. Halleck in Corinth, Mississippi, to try to convince him to send substantial reinforcements for the Richmond area.

July 7, Monday

❖ AL boards a vessel early in the morning to visit Gen. McClellan.

July 8, Tuesday

❖ AL arrives at Fortress Monroe in the morning and confers with several generals.
❖ AL arrives at Gen. McClellan's new base on the James River at Harrison's Landing at 6 p.m. and reviews troops until about 9 p.m.
❖ McClellan presents AL with his so-called "Harrison Bar Letter" spelling out his views of not only the military but the

political situation, saying that military operations should not interfere with slavery. AL reads it and makes no comment.

July 9, Wednesday

- ❖ AL, at Harrison's Landing, meets with various corps commanders who tell him the army is safe where it is, a withdrawal would be easy, but an advance would be tricky.
- ❖ AL stops for dinner at Fortress Monroe on the way back to Washington, departing at about 4:30 p.m.
- ❖ At nearby Hampton Roads, he makes a brief social call on a British warship.
- ❖ MTL arrives in New York in the evening and stays at the Metropolitan Hotel.

July 10, Thursday

- ❖ Steaming back to Washington, AL goes swimming when his vessel grounds for several hours.
- ❖ AL confers with Pennsylvania Gov. Andrew Curtain on to the appointment of a Commissioner of Internal Revenue.

July 11, Friday

- ❖ AL makes Gen. Halleck general-in-chief of Union land forces, removing himself from direct command.
- ❖ AL orders the completion of the southwest branch of the Pacific Railroad in Missouri, from Rolla to Lebanon, for military purposes.

July 12, Saturday

- ❖ AL urges a delegation of Border State congressman to adopt gradual compensated emancipation. He argues that otherwise the war could destroy slavery, "and you will have nothing valuable in lieu of it."

- ❖ AL signs legislation creating the Congressional Medal of Honor.
- ❖ AL authorizes a direct prisoner exchange with the Confederates.
- ❖ MTL and RTL and leave New York for West Point.

July 13, Sunday

- ❖ AL asks Gen. McClellan to account for the 50,000-man discrepancy between AL's tabulation of the number of men sent to McClellan, and McClellan's latest headcount. (McClellan sent a lengthy explanation of the difference between paper and actual strength.)
- ❖ AL writes to Gen. John Wool: "Two ladies are here now representing that there are four hundred sick soldiers in Baltimore, without shelter or any accommodations. Please have this looked into."
- ❖ AL attends the funeral of Stanton's small child James, who died of smallpox. AL rides in a carriage with Welles. He explains to Welles that, after much thought, he is convinced that it is a military necessity to issue a proclamation emancipating the slaves.

July 15, Tuesday

- ❖ AL asks the Senate to delay adjournment for a day while he considers a late bill.
- ❖ Sen. Browning visits AL in the morning and thinks he looks weary, care-worn, and troubled.

July 17, Thursday

In the west, Gen. Halleck is replaced by Gen. Grant.

- ❖ AL visits the Capitol at 10 a.m. and remains there until the Senate adjourns at 2 p.m.

- ❖ AL signs the Second Confiscation Act after it was amended to say that slaves of rebels would be confiscated and then freed, rather than emancipated. It also gave the president the power to pardon and grant amnesty to rebels.
- ❖ Congress then adjourns.
- ❖ MTL, RTL, and Tad leave New York for Washington.

July 18, Friday

- ❖ AL confers with Illinois and Wisconsin congressmen concerning patronage.
- ❖ MTL, RTL, and Tad return to Washington.

July 19, Saturday

- ❖ AL meets with the Cabinet and a delegation of senators and endorses a policy of troops subsisting on the enemy, making unrestricted employment of slaves, and prosecuting the war without delay, negotiation, or parlay.

July 21, Monday

- ❖ AL discusses the military events and slavery with the Cabinet.
- ❖ AL issues a general order stating that foreigners cannot be required to take an oath of allegiance to the government.

July 22, Tuesday

- ❖ AL reads the first draft of the Emancipation Proclamation to the Cabinet. Seward suggests that it not be proclaimed until the Union has had a military victory, so it will not look like an act of desperation. AL agrees.

A depiction of Lincoln reading the Emancipation Proclamation to his cabinet.

- ❖ The Cabinet also discusses Gen. McClellan. Chase favors his removal.
- ❖ AL approves an executive order allowing military commanders to seize real or personal property in rebel states for military purposes (while maintaining accounts for potential future compensation) and allowing them to employ persons of African descent, giving them reasonable wages.
- ❖ AL grants Stanton the power to draft man from state militia units to fill up existing regiments.

July 23, Wednesday

The Confederates begin massing at Chattanooga, for a counter-offensive into Kentucky.

- ❖ AL hold a lengthy conference with Stanton and Gen. Halleck at the War Department. Other generals attend parts of it.

July 24, Thursday

- ❖ AL spends part of the morning looking at maps with Sen. Browning, pointing out that opening the Mississippi River would be a good thing.
- ❖ AL attends a school program at the Smithsonian Institution, where he hands out awards.
- ❖ AL receives word of the death of former president Martin Van Buren in New York.

July 25, Friday

- ❖ AL discusses the idea of opening the Mississippi with Stanton, Chase, and Gen. (and astronomer) Ormsby Mitchel.
- ❖ AL proclaims the new Confiscation Act and calls on the rebels to return to their proper allegiance, on pain of confiscation.
- ❖ AL orders the government to go into mourning for Martin Van Buren.
- ❖ In the evening AL talks to Sen. Browning about public affairs.

July 26, Saturday

- ❖ AL replies to Maryland Sen. Reverdy Johnson, who reports that the residents of Louisiana resent attempts to organize black troops: "I shall not surrender this game leaving any available card unplayed."
- ❖ AL studies a plan presented by Gen. Ormsby Mitchel for opening the Mississippi.

July 27, Sunday

- ❖ AL confers with Chase, who presents financial arguments for removing Gen. McClellan, and discusses patronage and other matters.

July 28, Monday

❖ AL attends a conference on whether Gen. McClellan's army should be withdrawn from its current position on the James River.

❖ AL composes an open letter to Louisiana Unionist Cuthbert Bullitt: "What would you do in my position? ...I shall do all I can to save the government, which is my sworn duty as well as my personal inclination. I shall do nothing in malice. What I deal with is too vast for malicious dealing."

❖ AL replies to Missouri Gov. Hamilton Gamble: "You ask four regiments for Gen. Schofield, and he asks the same of the Secretary of War. Please raise them for me..."

❖ On behalf of RTL, AL asks Stanton to locate a soldier from Cambridge, Massachusetts. (He was found to have deserted.)

July 29, Tuesday

Defying efforts by U.S. authorities, the CSS Alabama leaves Liverpool, England, to raid U.S. commerce on the high seas.

July 30, Wednesday

❖ AL confers with a delegation from New York regarding recruitment for existing regiments.

July 31, Thursday

❖ AL responds to a letter forwarded by New York financier August Belmont accusing AL of having vacillating policies. AL responds that his policies are manifested in everything he has written and done since his inauguration.

AUGUST 1862

Summary: With the ebbing of Gen. McClellan's crisis, the focus returns to politics. AL considers an emancipation proclamation and makes a famous policy statement to Horace Greeley. But then the Confederates strike back.

August 1, Friday

- ❖ AL expresses astonishment at a recent speech by Kentucky Rep. Charles Wickliffe, calling for the suppression of both the rebels and the abolitionists.
- ❖ AL attends a Cabinet meeting.

August 2, Saturday

- ❖ AL attends a Cabinet meeting.
- ❖ AL asks Welles to grant a leave of absence to a navy officer who wishes to get married. "From evidence now before me, I believe there is a young lady who sympathizes with him in that wish."
- ❖ AL pardons about ninety soldiers who have been imprisoned by court-martials.

August 3, Sunday

Gen. McClellan is told to move his army to northern Virginia to oppose the developing Confederate offensive there.

- ❖ AL hears Chase at a Cabinet meeting urge a policy of assuring freedom to slaves in seceded states on condition of loyalty, organizing suitable freedmen into military units, and using the rest to cultivate plantations.

August 4, Monday

- ❖ AL meets with an (unnamed) delegation of "Western men" who offer him two black regiments from Indiana. AL says he would prefer to use them as labor troops as arming blacks would alienate the Border States.
- ❖ AL writes to French author Agénor-Etienne de Gasparin, who wrote a book about the war advocating the Union cause, urging him to be patient with the absence of victory so far: "I can only say that I have acted upon my best convictions without selfishness or malice."

August 5, Tuesday

A Confederate attack on Baton Rouge, Louisiana, is driven off.

- ❖ AL and Seward inspect forts and camps on the south side of the Potomac.
- ❖ AL meets with Theodore Fay, the recently retired U.S. minister to Switzerland, who tells AL that the Union is suffering "on account of a poorly defined policy." (Fay then moved to Berlin.)

August 6, Wednesday

- ❖ AL addresses a pro-Union rally on the east side of the Capitol. He tries to stifle rumors that Gen. McClellan and Stanton are feuding.
- ❖ AL consults with Stanton, Gen. Halleck, and others on the problem of drafting army replacements.
- ❖ AL has dinner with Illinois Republican activist and AL supporter James Conkling.

August 7, Thursday

- ❖ AL, Seward, and Stanton spend two hours at the Navy Yard watching experiments with the "Rafael" improved coffee-mill gun. They then take a river excursion to cool off.

August 8, Friday

❖ AL attends a Cabinet meeting.

❖ AL tells Stanton to order the arrest of anyone engaged in discouraging enlistments.

❖ AL confers with Connecticut Sen. James Dixon about Connecticut politics.

❖ AL assures Russian minster Baron de Stoeckl that although enlistments are slow, two or three million men would respond in an emergency.

August 9, Saturday

Stonewall Jackson having reappeared in northern Virginia, Gen. John Pope clashes with him at Cedar Mountain.

❖ AL tells Stanton that the Ordinance Bureau ought to examine the "Rafael" gun he saw demonstrated Thursday. (Later field trials were favorable, but the government never bought any.)

August 10, Sunday

❖ AL confers with "Judge Wright," who offers to lead black regiments.

August 11, Monday

❖ AL confers with Louisiana Unionist Christian Roselius, Seward, Stanton, and Blair about conditions in Louisiana and the conduct of Gen. John Phelps, who has been trying to organize black troops in the state. (Phelps soon resigned.)

❖ AL tells Stanton that Indiana Gov. Oliver Morton would not be a good choice as the military governor of Kentucky. (They keep the incumbent, Gen. Jeremiah Boyle.)

August 12, Tuesday

Stonewall Jackson retreats from the Cedar Mountain position.

- ❖ AL attends a Cabinet meeting.
- ❖ Judge David Noggle of Wisconsin confers with AL regarding the court-martial of his son, Lt. Charles Noggle. (He and two others were cashiered for "misconduct in battle," but AL thought the case "slight" and later reinstated all three.)
- ❖ AL tells a newspaper editor that Gen. Nathaniel Banks is one of the best men in the army: "He makes me no trouble."
- ❖ AL tells Cassius Clay that he would be willing to reappoint him minister to Russia if Simon Cameron quits.
- ❖ MTL receives a $1,000 donation from a Boston merchant for relief work in military hospitals.

August 13, Wednesday

The rest of Lee's army begins moving north from the Richmond area.

- ❖ AL meets with a Delaware delegation to discuss the impact of the draft there and the general military situation.

August 14, Thursday

- ❖ AL meets with a "committee of colored men" and proposes that blacks voluntarily relocate to an (unspecified) country in Central America.
- ❖ AL sends a telegram to the commander of a POW camp in Ohio: "It is believed that a Dr. J. J. Williams is a prisoner in your charge, and if so, tell him his wife is here, and allow him to telegraph to her." (They connected.)

August 15, Friday

- ❖ AL discusses patronage issues related to Connecticut with Welles and Chase.

❖ AL nominates a minister for Rome.

August 16, Saturday

Gen. McClellan's army completes its relocation to Aquia Creek, Virginia, and Alexandria, Virginia.

❖ AL confers with Welles for two hours to select Naval Academy candidates.
❖ AL asks Hiram Barney, the Collector of the Port of New York City, to send "two hundred dollars' worth of good lemons, and one hundred dollars' worth of good oranges" to MTL, which she will pay for with her hospital relief contributions.

August 17, Sunday

The Sioux Indians rise in Minnesota.

August 18, Monday

❖ AL dines with four officers recently exchanged from Confederate imprisonment.
❖ AL meets again with E. M. Thomas, chairman of the committee he met on Thursday.
❖ AL makes Michigan patronage decisions with Michigan Gov. Austin Blair and Michigan Sen. Zachariah Chandler.

August 19, Tuesday

❖ AL visits two Pennsylvania units.
❖ AL confers with Seward and Stanton about conditions in Louisiana.
❖ AL attends a Cabinet meeting and says he is uneasy about Gen. Pope's forward deployment.
❖ New York Rep. John Steele discusses patronage with AL.

❖ AL consults with Capt. Dahlgren on gunpowder and other
military matters.

❖ AL receives Horace Greeley's anti-slavery editorial, "The
Prayer of Twenty Millions," complaining that AL has shown
"deference to Rebel slavery."

❖ Word arrives that Alexander H. Todd, a Confederate colonel
and half-brother of MTL, died of wounds suffered in the
recent fighting at Baton Rouge.

August 20, Wednesday

Fighting breaks out at fords on the Rappahannock River.

❖ AL reviews Chase's patronage nominees with New York
Sen. Ira Harris.

❖ AL confers his friend Gustavus Koerner before Koerner
leaves for his new job as minister to Spain.

❖ AL discusses sending freed slaves to colonize Chiriqui
Province (on the West Coast of northern Panama) with an
agent for Chiriqui Real Estate Company.

August 21, Thursday

Confederate forces begin a new offensive into Kentucky.

❖ AL authorizes the governor of Union-occupied coastal
North Carolina to order elections in two Union-controlled
congressional districts.

❖ AL announces a list of seven appointees to the Naval
Academy. (Five went on to graduate.)

❖ AL refuses to issue a pass to Mrs. Margaret Preston, who
wants to transit Union lines into the south, presumably to
join her husband, a rebel general.

August 22, Friday

❖ AL writes an answer to Horace Greeley's anti-slavery
editorial, "The Prayer of Twenty Millions": "If I could save

the Union without freeing any slave I would do it, and if
I could save it by freeing all the slaves I would do it; and
if I could save it by freeing some and leaving others alone
I would also do that....I intend no modification of my oft-
expressed personal wish that all men everywhere could be
free."

August 23, Saturday

❖ Concerning Mrs. Gabriel Paul, who is urging AL to promote
   her husband, a career officer in the regular army, to brigadier
   general, AL writes: "She is a saucy woman and I am afraid
   she will keep tormenting till I may have to do it." (Her
   husband got the promotion but was blinded at Gettysburg.)
❖ Gen. Charles Stone applies to AL for an explanation of
   his arrest. (He apparently never got one. He was released
   August 16 without trial because a California congressman
   slipped a rider onto another bill, requiring that imprisoned
   officers be tried within thirty days. He was eventually
   reemployed in the western theater, and the Joint Committee
   on the Conduct of the War cleared him after another hearing,
   but he resigned before the war ended. He later served as a
   mercenary in Egypt, and, after returning, built the pedestal
   of the Statue of Liberty. Before his death in 1887, he wrote a
   magazine article about his work in Washington at the start of
   the war. He did not mention his imprisonment.)

August 24, Sunday

❖ AL discusses emancipation and colonization with
   transcendentalist Orestes Brownson.

August 25, Monday

*Stonewall Jackson crosses the Rappahannock unnoticed
beyond the Union west flank, reaching the Manassas Gap
Railroad by dark.*

August 26, Tuesday

Stonewall Jackson blocks the railroad behind Gen. Pope's force. Another corps of Lee's army, under Longstreet, follows.

❖ AL attends a Cabinet meeting where the atmosphere is upbeat.
❖ AL makes repeated trips to the telegraph office hoping for news.

August 27, Wednesday

Gen. Pope retreats, hoping to defeat Stonewall Jackson before Longstreet arrives. Jackson's men loot huge Union supply depots.

❖ AL telegraphs various commanders in the region asking whether they are in contact with Gen. Pope, whether they have spotted the enemy, and so on.

August 28, Thursday

Stonewall Jackson occupies a ridge near the old Bull Run battlefield. Gen. Pope masses against him, assuming (wrongly) that Longstreet has been stopped at Thorough-fare Gap.

❖ AL has an early morning conference with Chase and Stanton about the military situation.
❖ AL confers with Gen. Halleck about troop movements in Virginia.

August 29, Friday

Gen. Pope assaults Stonewall Jackson's position, still assuming Longstreet is a day's march away. Actually, he's half a mile away.

❖ AL meets with the Cabinet and discusses the Chiriqui colonization project. They decide to abandon it.
❖ AL telegraphs local commanders, asking for news and learning little.
❖ MTL visits soldiers at a hospital.

August 30, Saturday

Longstreet rolls up Gen. Pope's flank.

❖ AL dismisses twelve officers of the 71st Ohio for surrendering Clarksville, Tennessee, August 18 without a fight.
❖ AL remarks that Gen. McClellan seems to want Gen. Pope to be defeated.
❖ AL decides not to dismiss Gen. McClellan, although Stanton, Chase, Smith, and Bates favor it.

August 31, Sunday

Gen. Pope withdraws his army across Bull Run, and heavy rains mire the pursuit.

❖ AL at about 8 a.m. at the Soldiers' Home, tells Hay: "Well John we are whipped again, I am afraid. The enemy reinforced on Pope and drove back his left wing and he has retired to Centerville where he says he will be able to hold his men. I don't like that expression. I don't like to hear him admit that his men need holding."
❖ The Cabinet holds a Sunday meeting to discuss the situation.

SEPTEMBER 1862

Summary: The Union Army rebounds from Second Bull Run and stops Lee's invasion of the North. Finally able to point to a military victory, AL issues the preliminary Emancipation Proclamation.

September 1, Monday

The Union army continues retreating into Washington's fortifications.

- ❖ AL and Gen. Halleck confer until late in the evening. They put Gen. McClellan in command of the troops around Washington.
- ❖ AL hears a description of the Second Bull Run battlefield from two men who helped remove the wounded.

September 2, Tuesday

Lee's army begins massing at Chantilly, Virginia, and scouting toward Maryland. Invading Confederates occupy Lexington, Kentucky.

- ❖ AL goes with Gen. Halleck at 7 a.m. to Gen. McClellan's residence and informs him that he is now in command of the troops around Washington.
- ❖ AL meets with the Cabinet at noon and informs them he put Gen. McClellan in command of the Washington region. Stanton and Chase express heated disapproval.

September 3, Wednesday

Invading Confederates occupy the Kentucky state capital of Frankfort.

❖ AL orders Gen. Halleck to organize a field army "for active operations" separate from the Washington garrison.
❖ AL confers until midnight with Seward, who has returned from New York.

September 4, Thursday

Lee's army begins crossing the Potomac into Maryland in the Leesburg, Virginia, area.

❖ AL hears Gen. Pope's report on the Second Battle of Bull Run. (He is subsequently sent to Minnesota to fight the Sioux Indians.)
❖ AL attends a Cabinet meeting where they discuss the military outlook.
❖ In the evening, AL meets with Kentucky Sen. Garrett Davis, Tennessee Rep. Horace Maynard, and Tennessee newspaper editor William Brownlow.

September 5, Friday

❖ AL presents Gen. Pope's report on the recent fighting to the Cabinet. They decide not to publish it.

September 6, Saturday

Stonewall Jackson occupies Frederick, Maryland.

❖ AL reviews the military situation in the western theater with a delegation from Kentucky.
❖ AL consults with Chase concerning Gen. Irwin McDowell.

September 7, Sunday

Gen. McClellan begins moving his army slowly to the northwest from Washington to follow Lee.

❖ AL is at Gen. McClellan's headquarters in the morning before McClellan even wakes up.

September 8, Monday

❖ AL has various meetings at the War Department and at the Navy Department.

September 9, Tuesday

Although outnumbered by the slowly pursuing Federals, Lee divides his force into five columns: three to surround Harper's Ferry, Virginia, one to penetrate farther north, and one to guard the rear.

❖ AL attends a Cabinet meeting where the focus is on the trans-Mississippi theater.
❖ AL meets with a delegation from Baltimore and assures them that the government is adequately defending their city.
❖ AL learns that Gen. McClellan now has 95,000 men.

September 10, Wednesday

❖ AL hears from a delegation from New York representing the New England governors, who demand the dismissal of Seward and Blair.

September 11, Thursday

Lee's forces take Hagerstown, Maryland, as anxiety sweeps the North.

❖ AL discusses with Stanton, Chase, Gen. Halleck, and others the question of Pennsylvania Gov. Andrew Curtin calling up all able-bodied men.

❖ Although the colonization policy has been dropped, AL approves a provisional contract with the Chiriqui Improvement Company for a navy coaling station.

❖ AL sends assurances to Gen. McClellan: "I am for sending you all [reinforcements] that can be spared."

September 12, Friday

❖ AL, sleepless, queries Gen. McClellan about the situation at 4 a.m. and again later during the day. He gets the mistaken impression that Lee is retreating.

❖ AL meets at 9 a.m. with John Ross, chief of Cherokee Nation, about treaty relations. (Ross, a Unionist, was in Washington as a refugee from Confederate-dominated Indian Territory.)

❖ AL attends a brief Cabinet meeting devoted to military affairs.

❖ AL replies to Gen. Jeramiah Boyle, who complained that panic is breaking out in Louisville as the Confederates advance into Kentucky. AL refuses to interfere with the local commander.

❖ AL replies to Gov. Andrew Curtin of Pennsylvania, who had asked for 80,000 disciplined troops to be sent to his state: "We have not to exceed 80,000 disciplined troops, properly so called, this side of the mountains."

❖ AL replies to the mayor of Philadelphia, who had asked for military assistance: "Please do not be offended when I assure you that, in my confident belief, Philadelphia is in no danger."

September 13, Saturday

A copy of Lee's orders is found at a former Confederate camp site and Gen. McClellan comprehends how vulnerable the dispersed rebels are. But Lee soon learns of the leak.

❖ AL suffers sprains when his horse bolts during his morning commute from the Soldiers' Home to the White House.

❖ AL replies to a petition favoring national emancipation produced by a religious convention in Chicago, saying he would adopt the will of providence concerning slavery if he could ascertain it. Meanwhile, "I view the matter as a practical war measure, to be decided upon according to the advantages or disadvantages it may offer to the suppression of the rebellion."

September 14, Sunday

Gen. McClellan hits Lee's rear guard, but other Confederate columns surround Harper's Ferry, Virginia.

September 15, Monday

The Confederates take clumsily defended Harper's Ferry, Virginia, and 12,000 prisoners, while the rest of Lee's army concentrates at Sharpsburg, Maryland.

❖ AL responds to Gen. McClellan's exaggerated reports of yesterday's fighting with Lee's rearguard (claiming 15,000 rebel casualties): "God bless you, and all with you. Destroy the rebel army, if possible."

❖ AL tells Jesse Dubois, his former neighbor in Springfield, Illinois: "I now consider it safe to say that Gen. McClellan has gained a great victory.". (Celebrations erupted in Springfield, triggered by this message.)

❖ Gen. Franz Sigel (who was wounded at Second Bull Run) meets with AL and complains that his corps is not very big.

September 16, Tuesday

Lee gathers his army to face Gen. McClellan's force along Antietam Creek outside Sharpsburg, Maryland, on the north bank of the Potomac.

❖ AL telegraphs Pennsylvania Gov. Andrew Curtin at noon: "What do you hear from Gen. McClellan's army? We have nothing from him to-day."

❖ AL sends a follow-up message to Curtin at 2:25 p.m.: "Since telegraphing you, dispatch came from Gen. McClellan, dated 7 o'clock this morning. Nothing of importance happened with him yesterday. This morning he was up with the enemy at Sharpsburg, and was waiting for heavy fog to rise."

September 17, Wednesday

Although outnumbering Lee two to one, Gen. McClellan's clumsy assaults merely dent Lee's line in the bloodiest single day in U.S. history.

In the west, the invading Confederates take Munfordville, KY, and 4,000 prisoners.

❖ AL confers in Gen. Halleck's office with a Maryland politician and an army officer from Harper's Ferry, Virginia, presumably about the terrain that the armies are fighting over.

❖ AL completes the second draft of the Emancipation Proclamation.

September 18, Thursday

Lee retreats across the Potomac during the night.

❖ AL appoints Jacob Frankel as the first rabbi army chaplain.

September 19, Friday

Advancing from Corinth, Mississippi, the Federals take Luka, Mississippi.

❖ AL meets with the Cabinet and discusses recent military successes.

❖ Chase hands AL an open letter from social reformer and former Indiana congressman Robert Dale Owen calling for an end to slavery on moral grounds.

September 20, Saturday

Gen. McClellan mounts a half-hearted pursuit of Lee.

❖ AL works on the Emancipation Proclamation.
❖ AL urges Stanton to send paroled POWs to Minnesota to fight the Sioux. (They are not allowed to fight until exchanged, but the Sioux were not part of the agreement.)

September 21, Sunday

❖ AL is too busy to receive visitors.
❖ AL and Bates endorse a letter from Chase to Surgeon General of the Army William Hammond asking that Dr. S. W. Forsha be allowed to try out his "balm" on wounded soldiers. (Hammond avoided complying, later telling AL: "I have met with Dr. Forsha before, and am satisfied that he is an ignorant quack.")

September 22, Monday

❖ At a Cabinet meeting AL reads a passage by humorist Artemus Ward (Charles Farrar Brown).
❖ AL then reads the preliminary Emancipation Proclamation, stating that on January 1, 1863, all slaves in insurgent areas "shall be then, thenceforward, and forever free." The Cabinet favors publishing it.
❖ AL writes a testimonial for his podiatrist, Isachar Zacharie: "Dr. Zacharie has operated on my feet with great success, and considerable addition to my comfort." (The New York Herald later commented: "The president has been greatly blamed for not resisting the demands of the radicals; but

how could the president put his foot down firmly when he
was troubled with corns?")

September 24, Wednesday

- ❖ AL meets with the Cabinet about treaty complaints from
  the Cherokees, and the expediency of treaties regarding the
  voluntary colonization of freed slaves.
- ❖ AL proclaims martial law against rebels and insurgents, and
  suspends habeas corpus for them.
- ❖ AL responds to a serenade celebrating emancipation: "What
  I did, I did after very full deliberation, and under a very
  heavy and solemn sense of responsibility. I can only trust in
  God I have made no mistake."

September 25, Thursday

- ❖ AL confers with Chase about providing additional funding
  for the Missouri state government.
- ❖ AL's celebrity podiatrist, Isachar Zacharie, treats him for the
  sprain he suffered on September 13.

September 26, Friday

- ❖ AL attends a Cabinet meeting where they again discuss
  colonization.
- ❖ AL thanks the Union governors who recently met at
  Altoona, Pennsylvania, and approved emancipation.
- ❖ AL sends a note to Major John J. Key asking if he truly said
  (in response to the question of why the rebel army was
  not "bagged" at Sharpsburg), "The object is that neither
  army shall get much advantage of the other; that both shall
  be kept in the field till they are exhausted, when we will
  make a compromise and save slavery." (Key substantially
  confirmed it, and was cashiered the next day. AL reaffirmed
  the dismissal on November 24. Such attitudes were feared to
  permeate Gen. McClellan's army.)

September 27, Saturday

❖ AL confers with Edward Stanly, military governor of Union-occupied eastern North Carolina.

September 28, Sunday

❖ AL responds to Hamlin, who had written to AL praising the Emancipation Proclamation, noting that the North has responded with praise but that the stock market is down, and recruiting has slowed.

September 29, Monday

❖ AL talks with J. W. Forney, secretary of the Senate, about the probable impact of the Emancipation Proclamation and of the suspension of habeas corpus.
❖ AL reviews the 145th New York.

September 30, Tuesday

❖ AL attends a Cabinet meeting where they discuss trade regulations.

OCTOBER 1862

Summary: Gen. McClellan remains inert, apparently oblivious to the darkening tone of AL's messages. Out west, the armies of both sides are busy, with poor results for the Confederates. AL finds time to ponder Divine Will.

October 1, Wednesday

❖ AL leaves on a special train at 6 a.m. for Harpers Ferry, Virginia, to visit the headquarters of the Army of the Potomac, accompanied by various officials and congressmen.
❖ There, AL meets with Gen. McClellan in the afternoon and reviews troops.
❖ AL spends the night there.

October 2, Thursday

Gen. Buell moves his army out of Louisville, Kentucky, toward the invading Confederates.

❖ AL, in Harpers Ferry, reviews troops in the area in the morning and leaves at noon for the headquarters of Gen. McClellan.
❖ AL ascertains that Union troops in the area total 88,000.

October 3, Friday

❖ AL rises at dawn and walks up a nearby hill. Surveying the vast camp, AL complains: "This is Gen. McClellan's bodyguard."

❖ During the day AL reviews various units and poses for photographs.

Lincoln visited his army personally on several occasions, often putting himself in harm's way.

❖ AL is told that paroled POWs cannot be used to fight Indians, as parolees are not to "discharge any duties of a soldier."
❖ AL spends the night there.

❖ MTL finishes a weeklong effort to distribute 1,000 pounds of grapes to hospitalized soldiers.

October 4, Saturday

❖ AL returns to Washington.

October 6, Monday

❖ AL has Gen. Halleck order Gen. McClellan to "cross the Potomac and give battle to the enemy or drive him south."
❖ Chase and Indiana Gov. Oliver Morton ask AL to furlough Indiana soldiers so they can vote.
❖ AL's September salary is $2,022.33, or $61 less than previous months, thanks to the three percent income tax.

October 7, Tuesday

❖ AL meets with the Cabinet at noon and describes his visit to the Army of the Potomac. They also discuss Charleston, South Carolina, and Mississippi.

October 8, Wednesday

Union forces hit the invading Confederates outside Perryville, KY.

❖ AL responds to a Kentucky politician who asked that a particular Kentucky unit be sent home as it "suffered so much" in a recent march: "I sincerely wish war was an easier and pleasanter business than it is; but it does not admit of holidays."
❖ AL congratulates Gen. Grant on the October 3–4 Battle of Corinth and asks about AL's friend, Gen. Richard Oglesby of Illinois, who was wounded there. (Oglesby recovered.)

October 9, Thursday

The Confederates retreat from Perryville, Kentucky, signaling the end of their invasion. Rebel cavalry leader J. E. B. Stuart commences a four-day raid that (again) takes him entirely around Gen. McClellan's inert army.

❖ Gen. John Wool visits AL and successfully asks for an additional aide-de-camp.

October 10, Friday

❖ AL attends a Cabinet meeting that discusses trade through recaptured Norfolk, Virginia.

❖ AL meets again with Cherokee Chief John Ross regarding military protection for Unionist Cherokee Indians.

❖ AL approves the idea of forming a volunteer unit of Mississippi Unionists, if the volunteers are actually Southerners.

October 11, Saturday

❖ AL telegraphs Gen. Jeremiah Boyle at Louisville, Kentucky: "Please send any news you have from Gen. Buell today." (Reports had begun arriving of the Battle of Perryville.)

October 12, Sunday

❖ AL again prods Gen. Jeremiah Boyle at Louisville, Kentucky, for news: "We have had nothing since day-before-yesterday. Have you anything?"

October 13, Monday

❖ AL sends Gen. McClellan a long letter urging him to do something: "As I understand, you telegraphed Gen. Halleck that you cannot subsist your army at Winchester [i.e., if it were to advance thirty miles from Harpers Ferry, to Winchester, Virginia] unless the railroad from Harper's

Ferry to that point be put in working order. But the enemy does now subsist his army at Winchester at a distance nearly twice as great from railroad transportation as you would have to do."

❖ AL and Hamlin talk through the night at the Soldiers' Home about the military situation and about Gen. McClellan.

October 14, Tuesday

Congressional elections in Iowa, Indiana, Ohio, and Pennsylvania produce gains for the Democrats.

❖ AL orders the military authorities in Louisiana to cooperate with the resumption of elections.
❖ AL appoints his friend and former campaign manager David Davis to a Supreme Court vacancy.

October 16, Thursday

❖ AL meets with officers who were captured at Shiloh and paroled by the rebels.
❖ The Rev. William H. Channing, pastor of a church that has been converted into a hospital, talks to AL about being appointed a chaplain there. (He later got the appointment.)

October 17, Friday

❖ AL attends a Cabinet meeting where they again discuss trade through Norfolk, Virginia.
❖ Show business dwarf "Commodore Nutt," accompanied by P. T. Barnum, visits the White House.

October 18, Saturday

❖ AL, Chase, Stanton, and Gen. Halleck examine a "Confederate dispatch" purchased in England, but decide it's a forgery.

October 19, Sunday

❖ AL writes to his friend David Davis, and encloses Davis' Supreme Court nomination with the letter.

October 20, Monday

❖ AL endorses a plan by Gen. John McClernand to raise his own troops in Indiana, Illinois, and Iowa for an expedition to clear the Mississippi River.

❖ AL records that the Army of the Potomac has 231,997 troops of which 144,662 are fit for duty, while the Confederate Army has 89,563.

October 21, Tuesday

❖ AL orders Federal civil and military authorities in Tennessee to cooperate with the resumption of elections there.

❖ AL confers with Gen. Halleck about Gen. McClellan's inactivity.

October 22, Wednesday

❖ AL travels downstream to Alexandria, to review a division commanded by Gen. Dan Sickles, returning at sunset.

October 23, Thursday

The Confederates finish withdrawing from Kentucky into Tennessee.

❖ AL hears from a Pennsylvania delegation seeking a promotion for Col. Isaac Wistar, who had been wounded at Antietam. (He was later promoted.)

❖ AL hears from the New York State Colonization Society, urging colonization of freedmen in Liberia.

October 24, Friday

Having let the Confederates escape from Kentucky, Gen. Buell is replaced with Gen. Rosecrans.

October 25, Saturday

❖ AL attends a Cabinet meeting where they discuss Gen. Jefferson C. Davis, who in Louisville, Kentucky, killed his commander on September 29 following an ugly public reprimand. (No action was taken. Gen. Davis remained at the front, and was later sent to Alaska.)

❖ AL responds to a dispatch from Gen. McClellan complaining of his horses being worn out: "Will you pardon me for asking what the horses of your army have done since the battle of Antietam that fatigue anything?" (McClellan replied that the cavalry had been busy patrolling.)

❖ MTL is at the Metropolitan Hotel in New York.

October 26, Sunday

❖ AL has a prayer meeting in his office with Mrs. Eliza P. Gurney, widow of prominent English Quaker Joseph J. Gurney. He later writes to her: "If I had been allowed my way this war would have been ended before this, but we find it still continues; and we must believe that He permits it for some wise purpose of his own…yet we cannot but believe that he who made the world still governs it."

❖ AL elsewhere records his thoughts on Divine Will: "The will of God prevails. In great contests each party claims to act in accordance with the will of God. Both may be, and one must be wrong. God cannot be for and against the same thing at the same time…. By his mere quiet power on the minds of the now contestants He could have either saved or destroyed the Union without a human contest. Yet the contest began. And having begun He could give the final victory to either side any day. Yet the contest proceeds."

❖ AL writes again to Gen. McClellan about his tired horses, noting that the rebel horses seem fine. "But I am so rejoiced to learn from your dispatch to Gen. Halleck that you begin crossing the river this morning."

October 27, Monday

❖ AL returns to the tired horse subject, noting that Gen. McClellan was sent 7,918 fresh horses during the last five weeks, during which time the army did nothing. Meanwhile, concerning McClellan's plan to put draftees into existing regiments: "Is it your purpose not to go into action again until the men now being drafted in the states are incorporated into the old regiments?" (McClellan answered that it was not.)

October 29, Wednesday

❖ AL telegraphs Gen. McClellan: "I am much pleased with the movement of the Army. When you get entirely across the river let me know." (The crossing took a week.)
❖ MTL visits the Brooklyn Navy Yard and boards the USS North Carolina, accompanied by Gen. Winfield Scott.

October 30, Thursday

Astronomer Gen. Ormsby Mitchel dies of yellow fever in Beaufort, South Carolina.

October 31, Friday

❖ AL confers with local officials about building a railroad from Point of Rocks, Maryland, to Washington.

NOVEMBER 1862

Summary: AL finally dismisses Gen. McClellan. But there is no dramatic turnaround.

November 1, Saturday

❖ AL retains Capt. David Derickson and his Co. K, 150th Pennsylvania Volunteers, as the presidential guard. (The company remained his guard for the rest of the war.)

November 3, Monday

Gen. McClellan's army reaches Warrenton, Virginia.

❖ MTL, in New York, arranges for her dress designer, freedwoman Elizabeth Keckley, to receive $200 in government funds for her contraband aid association.

November 4, Tuesday

Republicans suffer in local elections in New York, New Jersey, Illinois, and Wisconsin, but retain control of the House, thanks to victories elsewhere.

❖ AL attends a Cabinet meeting where he reads the letter sent to Gen. McClellan on October 13, urging him to act.
❖ AL meets with Pennsylvania Gov. Andrew Curtin and Indiana Gov. Oliver Morton.

November 5, Wednesday

❖ AL orders Gen. Halleck to remove Gen. McClellan as commander of the Army of the Potomac and replace him with Gen. Burnside.

Lincoln had to regularly prod Gen McClellan to take action and finally had to relieve him of his command.

❖ AL replies to Col. William Morrison, who was wounded at Fort Donelson and recently elected to Congress as a Democrat, and who is complaining that he has not been promoted: "In considering military merit it seems to me the world has abundant evidence that I discard politics."

November 6, Thursday

❖ AL hears Chase report on the sugar industry in Louisiana converting from slave to wage labor.

November 7, Friday

❖ Gen. McClellan receives the order relieving him.
❖ AL asks Chase to acquire the latest New Orleans newspapers (presumably to follow election news).
❖ MTL arrives in Boston.

November 8, Saturday

❖ MTL, in Boston, is trapped indoors by bad weather.

November 9, Sunday

❖ AL telegraphs MTL in Boston to ask if nurse "Aunt Mary" and seamstress "Mrs. Cuthbert" should be allowed to move back to the White House as they complain that the Soldiers' Home is too cold.

❖ Gen. Burnside assumes command of the Army of the Potomac.

November 10, Monday

❖ AL replies to a letter from Carl Schurz dissecting the Republicans' recent election losses. (AL thinks the Republicans were busier with the war than with politics, and military setbacks gave the Democrats plenty of ammunition.)

❖ AL asks Gen. John Pope for the case records of 303 Sioux Indians recently condemned to death after their uprising was suppressed.

❖ MTL, in Boston, goes for a ride with RTL and Tad, and later meets with various celebrities, including Julia Ward Howe, who recently wrote the song "Battle Hymn of the Republic."

November 11, Tuesday

❖ AL confers with Gen. Halleck on troop movements in western Virginia and Tennessee.

❖ MTL leaves Boston in the morning.

November 13, Thursday

❖ AL orders that the Attorney General superintend the confiscation of rebel property.

❖ AL discusses with navy Capt. Dahlgren the possible promotion of his son, army Capt. Ulric Dahlgren. (He was made a colonel six months later.)

November 14, Friday

❖ AL telegraphs Gen. Francis Blair Jr., in St. Louis for Missouri election results. (Gen. Blair responded that the Administration did well.)

❖ AL approved Gen. Burnside's plans for an offensive.

❖ While walking to the War Department AL stops to watch telegraph operators practice a new flag code.

November 15, Saturday

Gen. Burnside begins moving the Army of the Potomac toward Fredericksburg, Virginia.

❖ AL joins Chase and Seward at the Navy Yard to see the test of a new rocket—which explodes. They are uninjured.

❖ MTL returns to New York from Boston.

November 16, Sunday

❖ AL discusses military strategy in the west with newly named Justice David Davis, who passes on a plan from a judge in St. Louis to concentrate the entire western army to clear the Mississippi. (AL later replied: "The country will not allow us to send our whole Western force down the Mississippi, while the enemy sacks Louisville and Cincinnati. Possibly it would be better if the country would allow this, but it will not.")

November 17, Monday

❖ AL replies to a telegram from habitual semi-coherent letter-writer Robert Maxwell of Philadelphia: "Your dispatch of today received. I do not at all understand it." (It included the phrase "Persevere in the sanctification of your material aims.")

November 18, Tuesday

❖ AL orders Federal civil and military authorities in Arkansas to cooperate with the resumption of elections there.

- ❖ AL asks Gen. John Dix, commander of Fortress Monroe, about Confederate strength in the Richmond area. (About 27,000, he later replied.)
- ❖ MTL remains in New York, receiving celebrities.

November 19, Wednesday

- ❖ AL confers with Pittsburgh businessman J. Wesley Greene, who claims to have had two recent conversation with Jefferson Davis, in which Davis said he was tired of the war and willing to restore the Union. AL concludes that Greene is a fraud.
- ❖ AL endorses a pardon for a Confederate officer who resigned and returned home to Missouri.

November 20, Thursday

Both sides continue a massive buildup in the Fredericksburg area.

- ❖ AL reviews a division commanded by Gen. Silas Casey.

November 21, Friday

- ❖ AL tells a delegation of Kentucky Unionists that he would die rather than take back a word of the Emancipation Proclamation.
- ❖ AL expresses his annoyance to the military governor of Louisiana that elections had not been organized there yet. (They would be held December 3.)

November 22, Saturday

Stanton releases nearly all political prisoners held by the military.

- ❖ AL rules that Union buyers cannot use Confederate money to buy cotton that they will then import into the Union.

❖ AL reacts with horror to Gen. Nathanial Banks' requisitions (presumably for the planned Red River Campaign): "If you had the articles of this requisition upon the wharf, with the necessary animals to make them of use, and forage for the animals, you could not get vessels together in two weeks to carry the whole, to say nothing of your twenty thousand men." (Banks replied that he was planning for the entire campaign, mostly just the start.)

November 23, Sunday

❖ AL reads a collection of newspaper editorials by Henry Ward Beecher criticizing the Administration.

November 24, Monday

❖ AL responds to a letter from Carl Schurz questioning the wisdom of appointing Democrat generals to high command positions: "I need success more than I need sympathy."
❖ AL responds to former Major. John J. Key, who was dismissed September 26 for defeatist's statements but who has since lost a son, killed in action at Perryville, Kentucky: "I had been brought to fear that there was a class of officers in the army…who were playing a game to not beat the enemy when they could, on some peculiar notion as to the proper way of saving the Union…. If there was any doubt of your having made the avowal, the case would be different…. I am really sorry for the pain the case gives you, but I do not see how, consistently with duty, I can change it."

November 26, Wednesday

❖ AL tries to intervene in the case of a loyal slave owner in Kentucky who is suing a Union officer for not returning a slave who reached Union lines. AL offers him $500 for the slave. (The owner persisted in court, and in 1871 the Federal Government paid a settlement of $924.46.)

❖ AL takes a boat trip to the Fredericksburg area to confer with Gen. Burnside.

❖ MTL leaves New York for Washington.

November 27, Thursday

❖ AL, aboard a steamer in Chesapeake Bay, confers with Gen. Burnside and Gen. Halleck about the anticipated offensive against Fredericksburg. Neither Burnside nor Halleck like AL's idea for a grand envelopment. Burnside prefers a direct assault.

❖ After returning, AL sees an Ohio congressional delegation seeking the release of former Ohio congressman Edson Olds, a Peace Democrat who was arrested in August for discouraging enlistments but was elected to the Ohio legislature while in prison. (He was released in mid-December.)

❖ MTL arrives in Washington.

November 29, Saturday

❖ AL asks Bates for advice on responding to Missouri Provisional Gov. Hamilton Gamble, who had asked AL if the state or the Federal Government controlled the troops that Gamble raised.

November 30, Sunday

❖ AL and MTL attend church.

DECEMBER 1862

Summary: AL finds a general who will fight, but the result is a bloody debacle. Despite the resulting gloom, AL presses on with the Emancipation Proclamation and the admission of West Virginia.

December 1, Monday

❖ Congress convenes, and AL sends his second annual message: Foreign relations are satisfactory and commercial relations with leading nations are undisturbed. Treasury receipts were $583 million, expenditures $570 million. The Department of Agriculture was organized, progress was made on the Pacific railroad, but the administration of Indian affairs may need revamping. Black colonists may soon be migrating to Haiti and Liberia. AL proposes three constitutional amendments. First, every State that abolishes slavery before January 1, 1900, shall receive compensation from the U.S. Second, all slaves who enjoyed actual freedom during the war shall be forever free. Third, Congress may provide for colonizing free colored persons, with their own consent, at places outside the U.S.

December 2, Tuesday

❖ AL issues an order specifying that Missouri Provisional Gov. Hamilton Gamble may remove or accept the resignation of officers in the Missouri state forces that he raised, although the actions must be confirmed by the War Department.

December 3, Wednesday

❖ The White House security detail arrests Francis X. Rabstock for annoying AL.

December 5, Friday

❖ Massachusetts Sen. Charles Sumner confers with AL about Gen. Butler (like Sumner, a Massachusetts politician), who has been relieved from duty in New Orleans.

December 6, Saturday

❖ Having read the case files, AL issues an order for the execution of thirty-nine of the 303 previously condemned Sioux Indians.

December 7, Sunday

❖ AL dines with Sen. Browning and New York Sen. Ira Harris.

December 8, Monday

❖ Wisconsin Sen. James Doolittle confers with AL on the case of Gen. Charles Hamilton, a Wisconsinite. (Gen. McClellan had dismissed him, apparently for intriguing against other generals, and after being transferred to the west he did it again, angering Gen. Grant.)

December 10, Wednesday

The House passes a bill creating the State of West Virginia.

❖ In response to a House resolution, AL forwards documents relating to the arrest of two Confederate naval officers in Morocco by the U.S. consul there last February.

December 11, Thursday

Union troops cross the Rappahannock River and seize Fredericksburg, Virginia. The Confederates retain the high ground beyond the town.

❖ AL refers to the Senate for ratification a treaty with the Republic of Liberia.

❖ AL endorses the promotion to captain of 2nd Lt. John Speed, son of James Speed, telling Stanton: "John Speed named within is a son of a particular friend of mine." (He later gets the promotion.)

December 12, Friday

❖ AL is at the War Department early seeking news from Fredericksburg.

❖ AL approves Welles' dismissal of navy Comdr. George Preble for failing to stop Confederate commerce raider CSS *Florida* at Mobile, Alabama. (He was reinstated after an investigation, and the CSS Florida outran him when he again encountered it.)

❖ AL sends Nicolay to Fredericksburg, Virginia, to look around.

❖ AL answers New York Mayor Fernando Wood's proposal for an armistice, saying the war will end when the Southerners cease resisting national authority.

December 13, Saturday

Gen. Burnside launches the Army of the Potomac against the Confederate positions outside Fredericksburg in massive, fruitless frontal assaults that cost 12,000 men.

❖ AL informs the Senate that the name of navy Capt. William Glendy has been withdrawn from the promotions list. (When he returned from overseas, it was found that he was past the retirement age that was imposed during his absence.)

December 14, Sunday

Gen. Burnside is talked out of resuming yesterday's futile bloodbath, and the Army of the Potomac withdraws across the river after sunset.

❖ AL hears a description of the Battle of Fredericksburg from correspondent Henry Villard.
❖ AL meets with several officers and advisors.
❖ MTL attends church with Sen. Browning.

December 15, Monday

Gen. Butler leaves New Orleans, to local jubilation.

❖ AL confers with Sen. Browning about the creation of the State of West Virginia.
❖ AL agrees to large-scale testing of a new formulation of gunpowder by Capt. Isaac R. Diller of Philadelphia.

December 16, Tuesday

❖ AL moves the execution date of the thirty-nine condemned Sioux Indians back one week, to the 26th, to leave time for security preparations. (One of the condemned was spared at the last minute.)

December 17, Wednesday

❖ AL suddenly receives, in the evening, the resignation of Seward and of his son, Assistant Secretary of State Frederick Seward. (The Republican Senatorial Caucus needed a scapegoat after recent disasters, especially the Battle of Fredericksburg, and the radicals had been poisoned against Seward by their friend Chase.)
❖ AL arranges a meeting with a senatorial delegation tomorrow.

December 18, Thursday

❖ AL meets in the morning with Kentucky Rep. John Crittenden, Maryland Rep. John Crisfield, and Missouri Rep. William Hall to discuss public opinion in the Border States.

❖ AL meets in the evening with nine Republican senators about the Cabinet crisis (i.e., the resignation of the two Sewards).
❖ AL talks with Sen. Browning late in the evening.

December 19, Friday

❖ AL spends most of the day on the Cabinet crisis, and has a joint meeting of the Cabinet (minus Seward) and the Republican Senate Caucus delegation.
❖ Blair offers to resign, but AL tells him that would not be helpful.
❖ AL invites Gen. Burnside to the White House.

December 20, Saturday

Gen. Grant abandons his overland offensive against Vicksburg but launches another through the swamps of the Yazoo Delta.

❖ AL receives Chase's sudden resignation. He tells Chase not to leave town.
❖ AL decides he cannot accept either resignation as "the public interest does not admit of it."
❖ Both Seward and Chase resume their duties.

December 21, Sunday

❖ MTL is in Philadelphia.

December 22, Monday

❖ AL confers with Stanton and Gen. Burnside.
❖ AL receives a proposal for Gen. William Franklin and Gen. William S. Smith for a campaign against Richmond via the James River.

December 23, Tuesday

- ❖ AL asks the Cabinet their opinion on whether West Virginia's admission to the Union is constitutional and expedient. (Unhelpfully, they split.)
- ❖ AL receives a proposal from Johnson and other Tennessee figures, that the Emancipation Proclamation not apply to Tennessee.
- ❖ MTL is involved in preparing Christmas dinners for hospitalized soldiers.
- ❖ AL writes to Fanny McCullough (age about 22) whose father Lt. Col. William McCullough was killed in action December 5. She has gone into seclusion. (McCullough had been a court clerk in Illinois and was well known to AL.) "In this sad world of ours, sorrow comes to all; and, to the young, it comes with bitterest agony, because it takes them unawares. The older have learned to ever expect it. I am anxious to afford some alleviation of your present distress. Perfect relief is not possible, except with time. You cannot now realize that you will ever feel better. Is not this so? And yet it is a mistake. You are sure to be happy again. To know this, which is certainly true, will make you some less miserable now. I have had experience enough to know what I say; and you need only to believe it to feel better at once. The memory of your dear Father, instead of an agony, will yet be a sad sweet feeling in your heart, of a purer, and holier sort than you have known before."

December 24, Wednesday

- ❖ Ohio Rep. Samuel Cox lobbies AL for the promotion to general of Col. Samuel Gilbert. (The Ohioan later got the promotion.)
- ❖ Massachusetts Sen. Charles Sumner spends the evening with AL discussing the Emancipation Proclamation.

December 25, Thursday

❖ AL and MTL visit multiple hospitals in the afternoon.

December 26, Friday

❖ AL attends a Cabinet meeting where they discuss the admission of West Virginia.

December 27, Saturday

❖ AL confers with Bates about Rev. Samuel McPheeters of St. Louis, who has been expelled from Missouri for rebel sympathies. AL suspends the order, complaining that McPheeters has not been accused of anything specific.

December 29, Monday

Gen. Grant's offensive against Vicksburg through the Yazoo Delta is turned back by Confederate fortifications on the high ground.

❖ AL reads the Emancipation Proclamation to the Cabinet for criticism. They also discuss West Virginia.
❖ Two generals from the staff of Gen. Burnside confer with AL about Burnside's plans—and about the demoralization of the army, and ask for Gen. Burnside's removal.
❖ Sen. Browning and others confer with AL in the evening and again unsuccessfully bring up the case of Major. John J. Key and his dismissal.

December 30, Tuesday

Gen. Rosecrans moves against the Confederates concentrated at Murfreesboro, Tennessee.

❖ AL hands out copies of the Emancipation Proclamation to the Cabinet, asking for suggestions.

❖ AL telegraphs Gen. Burnside: "I have good reason for saying you must not make a general movement of the army without letting me know."

December 31, Wednesday

In Tennessee, the Battle of Murfreesboro rages along the Nashville—Murfreesboro Turnpike on and off for the next three days.

❖ AL holds a Cabinet meeting at 10 a.m. for final revisions to the Emancipation Proclamation.
❖ AL signs legislation admitting West Virginia.
❖ Smith resigns as Secretary of the Interior, for health reasons.
❖ AL agrees to the plans of promoter Bernard Kock to colonize freed slaves on the twenty-square-mile Ile à Vache (Cow Island) off the southern coast of Haiti. But AL later tells Seward not to countersign the agreement, "but to retain the instrument under advisement." (Underfunded and starving, the resulting colony later had to be evacuated.)

ಬ1863 ಜ

JANUARY 1
THROUGH DECEMBER 31

JANUARY 1863

Summary: Despite winter weather, AL's armies maintain operations, but AL realizes he needs to find another commander in the east.

January 1, Thursday

- ❖ AL looks "buoyant" at the White House New Year's reception.
- ❖ Gen. Burnside offers to resign, AL complains that Gen. Halleck has not already looked into the matter, Halleck offers to resign, AL withdraws his complaint, so Halleck drops the matter, and nothing is resolved.
- ❖ AL signs the Emancipation Proclamation.

January 2, Friday

- ❖ Gen. Butler confers with AL, who asks him to go to Mississippi and organize black units.

January 3, Saturday

The Confederates withdraw from Murfreesboro, Tennessee.

- ❖ AL receives a delegation of thirty Jews concerned about Gen. Grant's December 17 "Order No. 11," which banished all Jews from his department. AL rescinds it. (Gen. Grant apparently had specific individuals in mind.)
- ❖ AL endorses an appeal for clemency: "Let this woman have her boy out of Old Capitol Prison." (Who she and the boy were is not known.)

January 4, Sunday

Gen. John McClernand takes what he apparently sees as his private army up the Arkansas River to take Fort Hindman, Arkansas.

❖ AL attends church.

January 5, Monday

❖ AL advices Gen. Samuel Curtis in Missouri to go easy on arrests, banishments, and assessments based on citizen denunciations, as they are often made for malice, revenge, and profit.
❖ Gen. Burnside again tries to resign.

January 6, Tuesday

❖ AL confers with two New York officers about organizing black troops in Louisiana.

January 7, Wednesday

❖ AL responds to Gen. John McClernand, who fears that the Emancipation Proclamation will make it hard to negotiate peace with the South: "I have issued the Emancipation Proclamation, and I cannot retract it."

January 8, Thursday

❖ AL turns down Gen. Burnside's resignation.
❖ The Senate confirms Usher as the new Secretary of the Interior.

January 9, Friday

❖ In the evening AL talks to Sen. Browning, New Hampshire Sen. John Hale, and Admiral Andrew Foote about compensated emancipation.

January 10, Saturday

- ❖ AL hosts a reception with MTL from 1 to 3 p.m.
- ❖ AL tells Gen. Samuel Curtis in St. Louis: "I understand there is considerable trouble with the slaves in Missouri. Please do your best to keep peace.". (Gen. Curtis replied that he knew of no trouble.)
- ❖ In the evening, AL attends patriotic readings delivered by elocutionist James Murdoch in the Senate chamber.

January 11, Sunday

Gen. John McClernand takes Fort Hindman. Gen. Grant orders him to return to base immediately.

January 12, Monday

- ❖ AL confers with Stanton on military affairs.
- ❖ AL asks the Army Judge Advocate General to report on the court-martial of Gen. Fitz John Porter.

January 13, Tuesday

- ❖ AL attends a Cabinet meeting where they examine intercepted mail in the possession of Welles.

January 14, Wednesday

- ❖ AL asks Gen. John Dix, commander of Fortress Monroe, if it would be practical to use black troops to defend the installation. (Gen. Dix said that the fortress was too important, and they would be better used at nearby Yorktown, Virginia.)
- ❖ Seward introduces AL to George-Etienne Cartier, recently Attorney General and Premier of Canada East.

January 15, Thursday

- ❖ AL confers in the morning at the Navy Yard with Capt. Dahlgren regarding Capt. Isaac R. Diller's supposedly revolutionary gunpowder.
- ❖ AL meets with Horace Greeley, editor of the *New York Tribune*.

January 16, Friday

- ❖ AL attends a Cabinet meeting.
- ❖ AL meets with Pennsylvania Rep. Robert McKnight and Gen. Samuel Heintzelman concerning the appointment of Heintzelman's son to West Point.

January 17, Saturday

- ❖ AL authorizes the Treasury to issue up to $100 million for military payrolls, and promises "judicious" measures to fight inflation.
- ❖ In the morning, AL discusses the state of Union with Horace Greeley.
- ❖ MTL holds a Saturday afternoon reception.

January 18, Sunday

- ❖ AL attends services at the Foundry Methodist Episcopal Church to hear a special sermon on the missionary cause.
- ❖ AL converses with Justice David Davis on general topics.

January 19, Monday

Gen. Burnside starts moving his army inland, hoping to launch a fresh offensive. The weather is clear.

- ❖ Elocutionist James E. Murdoch performs at the White House.

January 20, Tuesday

Rain sets in, miring Gen. Burnside's maneuvers.

❖ At a Cabinet meeting, AL queries the members on their preferred railroad gauge and decides that the Union Pacific will have a gauge of five feet. (He was later overridden by Congress, as eastern interests preferred the "standard" gauge of 4 feet 8.5 inches.)

❖ AL sends to the Senate a report concerning contraband and Mexico. (The Mexican army was not able to acquire guns through U.S. ports, but the French army was able to acquire mules and wagons, since those were not "arms.")

❖ A blizzard rattles the White House windows.

January 21, Wednesday

❖ AL approves the court-martial sentence cashiering Gen. Fitz John Porter for his failures at Second Bull Run. (After the war, Porter got the case reheard with testimony from former Confederate generals, and the findings were reversed.)

❖ AL endorses a letter from Gen. Halleck to Gen. Grant explaining that he (Gen. Grant) could not simply expel all Jews from his military department.

January 22, Thursday

Gen. Grant starts an attempt to dig a canal through a river switchback so his vessels can steam around Vicksburg, in another effort to take the city.

❖ AL responds to a letter from Gen. John McClernand, who had written to AL denouncing Gen. Halleck for not promoting or otherwise appreciating him: "Allow me to beg, that for your sake, for my sake, and for the country's sake, you give your whole attention to [your job]."

❖ AL tells Gen. Frederick Steele that his next promotion hinges on a satisfactory explanation of charges that he returned a fugitive slave while he was in Helena, Arkansas. (He explained that he rescued a girl from prostitution. AL promoted him.)

January 23, Friday

Gen. Burnside's "Mud March" is abandoned, amidst bickering among the generals.

- ❖ AL meets with the Cabinet (minus Stanton).
- ❖ AL sees the wife of Capt. John Green, who is seeking a promotion for her husband (to major) as had been recommended by Gen. McClellan. (AL has the matter looked into, but Green remained a captain until he got a field promotion at Gettysburg.)
- ❖ The widow of Col. Henry Kingsbury (killed in action at Antietam) asks that her husband's adopted son be appointed to West Point. (He was admitted but did not graduate.)
- ❖ AL tells Stanton to send Gen. Butler back to New Orleans (to organize black troops) even if he does not want to go, if he is not going to command a department. (Butler got himself a command on the east coast instead.)

January 24, Saturday

- ❖ AL poses for photographer Alexander Gardner.
- ❖ The day's White House reception is described as unusually well attended.

January 25, Sunday

- ❖ AL relieves Gen. Burnside of command of the Army of the Potomac and replaces him with Gen. Hooker.
- ❖ A Boston antislavery delegation meets with AL and complains that the Emancipation Proclamation has failed to accomplish its purpose.

January 26, Monday

- ❖ AL sends his congratulations to Gen. Hooker on being made commander of the Army of the Potomac. But, "I have heard, in such way as to believe it, of your recently saying that both the army and the government needed a dictator. Of course, it was not for this, but in spite of it, that I have given you the command. Only those generals who gain successes can set up dictators. What I now ask of you is military success, and I will risk the dictatorship."

❖ Cameron urges AL to not send Gen. Butler to New Orleans as he is a likely presidential candidate, and so must remain in Washington.

January 28, Wednesday

❖ AL meets with Gen. Andrews Humphreys, who complains he has not gotten the promotion that Gen. Burnside recommended for him. (He did get it, but it took more than a year.)

January 29, Thursday

❖ AL writes to Thurlow Weed: "Your valedictory to the patrons of the *Albany Evening Journal* brings me a good deal of uneasiness. What does it mean?" (Weed had denounced abolitionist fanatics. He replied to AL that he was talking about Horace Greely.)

January 30, Friday

❖ AL attends a Cabinet meeting.

January 31, Saturday

❖ AL endorses the request of Lt. Edward Baker, son on his deceased friend Col. Baker, to be made a captain in the Commissary Department. (He got it six weeks later.)
❖ AL endorses a list of more than a hundred people in Kentucky who have been fined by Union officers and whose fines should be refunded.

FEBRUARY 1863

Summary: *The winter weather interferes with major operations in most theaters, although Gen. Grant keeps probing toward Vicksburg.*

February 1, Sunday

❖ AL telegraphs Indiana Gov. Oliver Morton that he cannot meet with Morton secretly in Harrisburg, Pennsylvania, as Morton has requested, as word would leak out and the meeting would be misconstrued as a conspiracy. (Morton wanted to discuss various anti-war plots.)

February 2, Monday

❖ AL hears from a New York delegation seeking a West Point nomination for Eliphalet Nott Chester, of Buffalo, New York, currently a private in a New York regiment. (He got it and graduated in 1867.)

February 3, Tuesday

Gen. Grant has a levee opened at Yazoo Pass north of Vicksburg, to try to reach that city through the Yazoo River.

❖ AL attends a Cabinet meeting where they discuss shooting a deserter as an example to the army.
❖ Vermont Sen. Solomon Foot asks AL about getting his wife's nephew appointed to West Point. (He gets the appointment but does not graduate.)

February 4, Wednesday

❖ AL tries to get information on a riot in Baltimore. (Union army convalescents fought with blacks who worked at their facility.)

February 5, Thursday

❖ AL writes an apology to Gen. Franz Sigel for the tone of AL's response to an earlier complaint by Sigel: "If I do get up a little temper I have no sufficient time to keep it up."

❖ At 9 p.m., AL and MTL have Gen. and Mrs. Randolph Marcy as guests.

February 6, Friday

❖ AL attends a Cabinet meeting.

❖ AL reports to the Senate on arms transactions with the Japanese government. (They bought three warships, a field artillery battery of six guns, and a rifling machine.)

❖ AL sends the Senate available information on the death of U.S. citizen Frederick T. Ward in the military service of China. (The former filibusterer became a pro-government warlord and died in battle against the Tai-Ping rebellion.)

February 7, Saturday

❖ AL and MTL host an afternoon reception.

February 9, Monday

❖ Due to reports of anti-government political agitation, AL has Stanton raise four regiments in Illinois as home guards. (The idea was dropped six weeks later.)

February 10, Tuesday

❖ AL sends to the Senate Seward's report on the visit of Henri Mercier, the French minister, to Richmond the

previous April. (Seward said Mercier carried no message
from the Administration, nor had the Administration had
any communication with the insurgents beyond prisoner
exchanges.)

❖ Gen. Butler asks AL to appoint Philip Reade to West Point.
(He entered in 1865 but did not graduate.)

❖ MTL entertains Gen. and Mrs. Samuel Heintzelman in the
evening. (Gen. Heintzelman heads the newly reorganized
Department of Washington.)

February 12, Thursday

❖ AL meets with Gen. Thomas F. Meagher, commander of the
Irish Brigade, who complains that two officers in his brigade
have not received deserved promotions. (One was later
killed in action before he could be promoted, the other got
promoted in 1865.)

❖ AL sends to the Senate information on international offers to
mediate or arbitrate the war.

February 13, Friday

❖ AL, Stanton, and others watch the testing of a new electrical
firing mechanism.

❖ AL sends to Senate a report concerning the use by the French
of African troops in Mexico. (Reportedly, 450 were sent from
Egypt.)

❖ The Secretary of the Interior reports that the cause of
the recent Indian trouble in the Northwest cannot be
determined.

❖ At 8 p.m., AL and MTL host a reception for "General Tom
Thumb" (circus dwarf Charles S. Stratton) and his recent
bride, dwarf Lavinia Warren.

February 14, Saturday

❖ The day's reception at the White House is well attended.

February 15, Sunday

- ❖ AL examines a plan for attacking Charleston, South Carolina, with Stanton, Gen. Halleck, and others.
- ❖ Gen. Butler is the guest at an informal White House dinner.

February 16, Monday

The Senate passes the Conscription Act.

- ❖ AL has Bates pardon Nathan Darling, captain of the Capitol police force, who had been fined for the way he suppressed protestors in the House gallery the previous year. (There had been a disturbance when the House voted against accepting a gift of captured Confederate battle flags, as they were not the flags of a real nation.)

February 17, Tuesday

- ❖ AL attends a Cabinet meeting where they discuss Fernando Wood, former mayor of New York City who was recently elected to Congress. (He had wanted New York City to secede, but not join the Confederacy.)
- ❖ AL meets with Gen. Butler about his next command.
- ❖ AL hears from a New York delegation urging that establishment of "armed free labor colonies" in Florida.

February 18, Wednesday

- ❖ AL sends to the Senate an additional article for the treaty with Great Britain regarding suppression of the African slave trade. (It added Madagascar, Puerto Rico, and San Domingo to the patrol area, which was originally Africa and Cuba. The Senate ratified it.)

February 19, Thursday

- ❖ AL attends a special Cabinet meeting where they discuss calling a special session of the Senate.

❖ AL corresponds with Thurlow Weed about raising $15,000 from New York merchants, for Republican electioneering in New England.

February 20, Friday

❖ AL has a long conference with chiefs of the Chippewa Indians.

February 21, Saturday

❖ AL meets with New Mexico Territory Rep. John Watts and others and they appoint a Chicago man to be territorial surveyor general, later finding that he doesn't want the job.
❖ AL is described as looking haggard and careworn at the well-attended Saturday White House reception.

February 22, Sunday

❖ AL declines to preside at a meeting of the U.S. Christian Commission held that day in the House chambers.

February 23, Monday

❖ AL receives Simon Cameron's resignation as U.S. minister to Russia.

February 24, Tuesday

❖ AL meets with a delegation from West Virginia asking for more protection against Confederate guerrillas.
❖ AL hears Irish-American comedian Barney Williams at Grover's Theater.

February 25, Wednesday

❖ AL signs legislation establishing a national bank system.

February 26, Thursday

❖ AL consults with Bates about draft riots in Missouri.

February 27, Friday

❖ Pennsylvania Rep. Elijah Babbitt lobbies for a West Point appointment for the son of Pennsylvania Judge Garrick Mallery. (He got the appointment and graduated in 1867.)
❖ Barney Williams, the comedian AL watched on Tuesday, asks AL for a military academy appointment for his nephew. (The nephew was not identified in their correspondence, so the result is not known.)

February 28, Saturday

❖ As is customary at the close of a Congressional session, AL occupies a room at the Capitol so that enrolled bills do not have to be taken to the White House for his signature.
❖ AL does not attend the Saturday White House reception.

MARCH 1863

Summary: The armies mostly wait for spring, although Gen. Grant continues trying to get into Vicksburg. With Congress adjourning after passing a stack of new legislation, AL is absorbed with the tasks of governing.

March 1, Sunday

❖ AL confers about military appointments with Stanton, Gen. Halleck, Gen. Samuel Heintzelman, and Gen. Lorenzo Thomas.

❖ AL and MTL host a levee at the White House.

March 2, Monday

❖ AL sends to Congress the acceptance of the Legislative Assembly of the Territory of New Mexico of the benefits of the Federal higher education land grants program.

March 3, Tuesday

❖ AL signs legislation authorizing free mail delivery in forty-nine cities, authorizing the grant of public lands to Kansas for railroad and telegraph construction, establishing the National Academy of Sciences, making Idaho a territory, and setting up the nation's first draft.

❖ Fox thinks that AL looks depressed.

❖ Congress adjourns.

March 4, Wednesday

❖ AL provides a letter of introduction to the Commissioner of Patents for his friend Jonathan Haines, who has invented a harvesting machine.

❖ AL consults with Blair about colonization.

March 5, Thursday

❖ AL forwards to the Treasury $868 that he received from an anonymous letter-writer in Brooklyn who said he came into the money "in a dishonest manner."
❖ Welles confers with AL late into the evening.

March 6, Friday

❖ AL sees Gen. Frémont and says he should get definite information about a new command for him soon. (It never happened.)

March 7, Saturday

❖ AL discusses the recently passed "Marque and Reprisal Bill" with Seward. (Such laws allowed private armed vessels to prey on enemy merchant vessels.)

March 8, Sunday

❖ AL approves a memo from Seward for Lord Lyons suggesting that England allow the building of no further ships in her ports for Confederate service.

March 9, Monday

❖ AL is lobbied by Pennsylvania Rep. Thaddeus Stevens, who wants a Pennsylvania colonel to fill the vacancy created by the capture of a brigadier general by a Confederate raiding party at 2 a.m. that morning in nearby Fairfax, Virginia. (AL supposedly said he did not mind the loss of the brigadier general as much as he did the loss of the horses that the raiders also took. He could appoint a brigadier general, but horses cost $125 each.)

❖ AL sees a delegation seeking the promotion of a West Virginia officer.

March 10, Tuesday

❖ AL attends a Cabinet meeting where they discuss regulations for letters of marque.
❖ AL proclaims amnesty for soldiers who are absent without leave but who report back to their units by April 1.
❖ AL, Seward, Stanton, Gen. Samuel Heintzelman, and several senators discuss sending troops to Arizona.

March 11, Wednesday

Gen. Grant's effort to reach Vicksburg through the Yazoo River delta is thwarted by Confederates on the only dry land.

❖ AL meets with New Hampshire Sen. John Hale and Col. Edward Cross of that state. The latter is seeking a promotion after being wounded nine times. (He died at Gettysburg, still a colonel.)

March 13, Friday

❖ AL writes a note to the commander of a POW camp: "You will deliver to the bearer, Mrs. Winston, her son."
❖ AL attends a Cabinet meeting where they again discuss letters of marque.
❖ AL sees James Hackett as Falstaff in Shakespeare's *Henry IV* at Grover's Theater.

March 15, Sunday

❖ AL receives a delegation from New York with a list of ships being built in England supposedly for China, but which, they are convinced, are intended for the Confederacy.

❖ AL and Massachusetts Sen. Charles Sumner read aloud to each other from Theodore D. Woolsey's "Introduction to the Study of International Law."

March 16, Monday

❖ AL attends a Cabinet meeting where they again discuss letters of marque.
❖ An aide to the governor of West Virginia lobbies AL about promoting Col. Isaac Duval. (It took a year and a half to get the promotion.)

March 17, Tuesday

A Federal cavalry probe across the Rappahannock River triggers a battle.

❖ AL attends yet another Cabinet meeting where they again discuss letters of marque.
❖ In response to comments about the political makeup of the new House of Representatives, AL tells Maryland Rep. Henry Davis, "Let the friends of the government first save the government, and then administer it to their own liking."
❖ AL and MTL tour the Patent Office, which includes displays of gifts sent by foreign rulers.
❖ AL responds to Gen. Rosecrans, who had complained of not getting the date of rank he asked for: "The world will not forget that you fought the battle of Stones River and it will never care a fig whether you rank Gen. Grant on paper, or he so, ranks you."
❖ AL writes to his old friend Joshua Speed: "I understand a Danville, Illinoisan, by the name of Lyman Guinnip, is under an indictment at Louisville, something about slaves. I knew him slightly. He was not of bad character at home, and I scarcely think he is guilty of any real crime. Please try if you cannot slip him through." (Guinnip was indicted for helping a slave escape. He did not appear for trial and forfeited part of his bail.)

March 18, Wednesday

❖ AL proclaims a treaty of commerce and navigation with Liberia.

March 19, Thursday

❖ AL confers with two Arizona officials about posting troops there.

March 20, Friday

❖ AL conditionally revokes the court-martial sentence of *New York Herald* correspondent Thomas Knox, who was banned from Gen. Grant's army for questioning Gen. Sherman's sanity. The condition is that Grant must agree. (Gen. Grant deferred to Sherman, who refused.)

❖ AL again confers about sending troops to Arizona.

March 21, Saturday

❖ AL hears from his old friend Dr. Anson Henry, surveyor general of Washington Territory, who is seeking to remove from office the collector at Port Angeles.

March 23, Monday

❖ AL writes to Administration critic and Democrat Horatio Seymour, who was recently elected governor of New York, asking for his support for the war effort. (Seymour expressed full support.)

March 24, Tuesday

❖ AL asks Stanton if he can supply Kentucky with $250,000 for raising troops while auditors were looking at the state's accounts. (Stanton said Kentucky would have to wait.)

March 25, Wednesday

- ❖ AL commutes the death sentence of Maryland resident James Pleasants to imprisonment during the war. (He had harbored enemy soldiers.)
- ❖ AL authorizes Benjamin Gratz of Lexington, Kentucky, to shelter the wife of a Confederate cavalry officer "so long as you choose to be responsible for what she may do."
- ❖ AL meets six recently exchanged survivors of the eighty-seven-mile Great Locomotive Chase, which took place the previous April between Atlanta and Chattanooga.
- ❖ AL and Nicolay watch "Hamlet," starring Edward Loomis Davenport, at Grover's Theater.

March 26, Thursday

- ❖ AL writes to Johnson, saying that as a prominent citizen of a slave state, and himself a slave holder, he should set an example and raise black units. (Johnson neither replied nor acted.)

March 27, Friday

- ❖ AL meets with a contingent of Indian chiefs, including Lean Bear of the Cheyenne and Spotted Wolf of the Arapahoe. "You have asked for my advice. I really am not capable of advising you whether, in the providence of the Great Spirit, who is the great Father of us all, it is best for you to maintain the habits and customs of your race, or adopt a new mode of life. I can only say that I can see no way in which your race is to become as numerous and prosperous as the white race except by living as they do, by the cultivation of the earth."

March 28, Saturday

- ❖ Saturday White House receptions end for the season.

March 29, Sunday

❖ AL orders Gen. Nathaniel Banks to assist Gen. Daniel Ullmann to raise black units in the New Orleans area. (He raised five regiments.)

March 30, Monday

❖ AL designates April 30 as a "day of national humiliation, fasting and prayer."

March 31, Tuesday

❖ AL issues an order permitting the licensing of trade with insurrectionary areas by the Secretary of the Treasury when it "will favorably affect the public interests."

❖ AL, Seward, Chase, Usher, and Blair attend a pro-Union rally at the Capitol.

APRIL 1863

Summary: *An attempt to take Charleston, South Carolina, using ironclads fails. As spring weather arrives the Union army launches offensives on the Mississippi and in Virginia.*

April 1, Wednesday

❖ AL cautions Gen. David Hunter about the use of black troops: "The enemy will make extra efforts to destroy them; and we should do the same to preserve and increase them." (He had recently used black units to occupy Jacksonville, Florida.)

❖ AL discusses Missouri affairs with Bates and others.

April 2, Thursday

❖ AL issues a proclamation dropping all exceptions to previous bans against commerce with insurgent areas, except as licensed by the Treasury Department.

❖ AL goes to Welles' house in the evening to read a document he prepared concerning letters of marque.

April 3, Friday

❖ AL attends a Cabinet meeting where letters of marque are again discussed.

❖ AL begins sitting for a full-length portrait.

❖ AL arranges to meet with Gen. Hooker at Hooker's headquarters the next day.

April 4, Saturday

Gen. Grant begins moving his forces southward on the west side of the Mississippi River, entirely avoiding Vicksburg.

❖ AL meets with several members of the Joint Committee on the Conduct of the War.

❖ Welles and Fox confer with AL about an application they received for a letter of marque.

❖ AL endorses a request from "Miss Davis" for a West Point nomination for her brother, John M. K. Davis. (He graduated in 1867.)

❖ AL embarks on a steamship in the evening with MTL, Tad, Bates, journalist Noah Brooks, and others for Gen. Hooker's headquarters. A snowstorm hinders progress.

April 5, Sunday

❖ AL reaches the headquarters of Gen. Hooker near Falmouth, Virginia, at about noon, where his party occupies three hospital tents.

❖ AL scans Southern newspapers for news from Charleston.

April 6, Monday

❖ AL, in Falmouth, visits army hospitals with his party. A grand review is called off due to the weather.

April 7, Tuesday

Admiral Samuel Du Pont launches a long-planned attack on Charleston with nine ironclads, five of which are damaged before the attack is called off. The Confederates fire fourteen shells for every Union shell.

❖ AL visits the headquarters of Gen. Dan Sickles and gets a kiss from Princess Salm-Salm (wife of a German-born officer). MTL later throws a tantrum about this.

April 8, Wednesday

The USS Keokuk, an ironclad hit ninety times in yesterday's attack on Charleston, sinks without loss of life.

❖ AL attends a review representing four infantry corps. AL is seen to touch his hat in response to salutes from officers. For enlisted men, he uncovers.

April 9, Thursday

❖ AL attends a review representing three more corps.

April 10, Friday

❖ AL reviews two more corps.
❖ AL's party leaves after noon and reaches Washington at about midnight.

April 11, Saturday

❖ AL confers in the morning with Welles, Seward, Chase, Stanton, Fox, and Gen. Halleck about the military situation.
❖ Gen. Carl Schurz asks AL to make his command separate from the Army of the Potomac. AL declines.
❖ In the evening, AL watches British comedic actress Matilda Vining Wood portray Pocahontas at the Washington Theater.

April 12, Sunday

❖ News of the defeat at Charleston reaches AL.
❖ AL acknowledges a message from Gen. Hooker outlining his plans for an offensive.

April 13, Monday

❖ AL orders Admiral Samuel Du Pont to hold his position outside Charleston, but does not order him to renew the attack.

April 14, Tuesday

❖ AL tells Louisiana Unionist John Bouligny that no patronage position was found for him in Washington, contrary to an understanding they had, as AL had expected Bouligny to be elected to Congress.

April 15, Wednesday

❖ AL tells Gen. Hooker that he is uneasy that the cavalry that is supposed to be raiding Lee's rear has only covered twenty-five miles in three days. (Torrential rains inhibited progress.)

❖ Massachusetts Sen. Charles Sumner shows AL a draft of antislavery resolutions he hopes to get adopted at public meetings in England.

April 16, Thursday

A twelve-vessel convoy runs past Vicksburg to join Gen. Grant's infantry. Eleven make it.

❖ AL cancels the contract with Bernard Koch, provisionally signed on December 31, to colonize freed slaves on Ile à Vache (Cow Island), just south of Haiti. (Seward, skeptical of Koch, had opposed the plan. Koch later tried to proceed with private backing, but the project was a failure.)

❖ AL replies to a complaint about quarreling Republicans in Missouri: "I have stoutly tried to keep out of the quarrel, and so mean to do."

April 17, Friday

❖ AL attends a Cabinet meeting.

April 18, Saturday

❖ Gen. Samuel Heintzelman, with his wife and daughter, spends the evening at the White House and learns from MTL that his son has been appointed to West Point.

April 19, Sunday

❖ AL and others leave before dawn for an unpublicized trip to Falmouth, Virginia, to confer with Gen. Hooker, returning late. (There is no record of what transpired.)

April 20, Monday

❖ AL signs a proclamation admitting West Virginia to the Union.

❖ Delphy Carlin of St. Louis sees AL and asks that her son not be forced to face his brother in the Confederate army in battle. (The outcome of her request is not known.)

April 21, Tuesday

❖ AL attends a Cabinet meeting that deals with "light matters."

❖ AL asks Welles and Seward for their positions, in writing, on how to handle mail from a neutral power that is found aboard captured blockade runners. (Welles wanted to read it. Seward disagreed. A court later ordered that it be handed over to the neutral power.)

April 22, Wednesday

An eighteen-vessel river convoy runs past Vicksburg. Eleven get through.

❖ AL answers Gen. Rosecrans at Murfreesboro, Tennessee, who understands that people have been complaining about his military police: "I really cannot say that I have heard any complaints."

April 23, Thursday

❖ AL commutes one death sentence for a deserter but approves another.

❖ AL reportedly attends a spiritualist seance in the White House. Nothing happens while he is present.

April 24, Friday

❖ AL attends a Cabinet meeting.

April 25, Saturday

❖ AL meets with Francis L. Capen, "certified practical meteorologist" seeking a job as a weather consultant for the War Department.

April 26, Sunday

❖ AL visits Admiral Dahlgren in the morning at the Navy Bureau of Ordnance and reads telegrams.

April 27, Monday

Gen. Hooker launches his offensive, moving part of his force upstream along the Rappahannock River from Falmouth to outflank the Confederates. Another part remains at Falmouth to pin down the main Confederate force at Fredericksburg, Virginia.

❖ AL writes a telegram to Kansas Sen. James Lane in Leavenworth, Kansas, saying that Kansas Gov. Thomas Carney is with him in Washington, and Carney wants the commander of the 79th U.S. Colored Infantry removed, and is complaining that Gen. James Blunt interfered in recent municipal elections in Leavenworth. Then Carney asks AL not to send the telegram.

❖ At 3:30 p.m., AL telegraphs Gen. Hooker: "How does it look now?" (Hooker did not reply for two hours, and then said, "I am not sufficiently advanced to give an opinion.")

April 28, Tuesday

Gen. Hooker begins moving his army across the Rappahannock River into the Wilderness area.

❖ AL assures Pennsylvania Gov. Andrew Curtin that the people of Pennsylvania need not fear a Confederate invasion. (Curtin was alarmed by a Confederate cavalry raid.)

❖ AL visits the Navy Ordnance Bureau to settle a claim regarding an artillery contract.

❖ AL concludes that Francis L. Capen, "certified practical meteorologist," is an ignorant crank. "He told me three days ago that it would not rain again till the 30th of April or 1st of May. It is raining now and has been for ten hours. I cannot spare any more time to Mr. Capen."

April 29, Wednesday

Gen. Hooker's flanking force continues crossing the Rappahannock River.

❖ AL writes to the commanding officer of a frontier fort asking him to provide appropriate protection for John B. S. Todd, House delegate from the Dakota Territory and cousin of MTL, who is returning to his residence in the area after the Congressional session.

April 30, Thursday

Gen. Hooker masses his flanking force near Chancellorsville, Virginia.

Gen. Grant crosses the Mississippi River from west to east downstream from Vicksburg, using the vessels that previously ran past the city.

❖ AL tells Gen. David Hunter that he must restore a captain that Gen. Hunter dismissed if the only complaint against the captain was his refusal to endorse the Emancipation Proclamation.

MAY 1863

Summary: *Another Union offensive in Virginia collapses into bloody futility. In the west, Gen. Grant remains hard at work. But, war or no war, the work of governing never ends.*

May 1, Friday

In Virginia, Lee, although heavily outnumbered, divides his army, leaving a covering force at Fredericksburg while concentrating the rest against Gen. Hooker's position at Chancellorsville.

* AL assures Pennsylvania Gov. Andrew Curtin that the Confederates are not about to invade Pennsylvania.
* AL attends a Cabinet meeting.

May 2, Saturday

In Virginia, Lee further divides his outnumbered army, sending Stonewall Jackson's corps around to the far end of Gen. Hooker's line, where it smashes the Union flank. But amidst the resulting chaos, Jackson is mortally wounded by friendly fire.

In Mississippi. Gen. Grant moves his army rapidly away from the river, easily handling the confused Confederate forces that confront him.

* AL follows up with Pennsylvania Gov. Andrew Curtin: "…I really do not yet see the justification for incurring the trouble and expense of calling out the militia." (Curtin agreed.)

❖ AL supposedly tells an individual who applies for a pass to go to Richmond: "Well, I would be very happy to oblige you, if my passes were respected; but the fact is, sir, I have, within the past two years given passes to 250,000 men to go to Richmond, and not one has got there yet."

May 3, Sunday

In Virginia, Gen. Hooker stabilizes his position around Chancellorsville. He is then stunned by an artillery near-miss yet remains in command. The small Union covering force at Falmouth, Virginia, drives the Confederates out of Fredericksburg, and moves in Hooker's direction. Lee concentrates against the covering force, stripping the lines facing Hooker's main force.

In Mississippi, Gen. Grant's moves toward the state capital at Jackson, forcing the army defending Vicksburg to come out and fight.

❖ AL hears from Gen. Hooker's chief of staff in the morning that a battle has begun. Hearing nothing more by afternoon he replies: "Where is Gen. Hooker? Where is Sedgwick? Where is Stoneman?" (The chief of staff later replied with basic information, not mentioning Hooker's condition.)
❖ In the afternoon AL meets with Stanton, Gen. Halleck, and others. He stays at the telegraph office until 11 p.m.

May 4, Monday

In Virginia, the Union covering force that took Fredericksburg yesterday is forced back by converging Confederates. Gen. Hooker does not to take advantage of Lee's face-about.

In Mississippi, Gen. Grant's army continues eastward.

❖ AL waits for news at the War Department.

❖ After 3 p.m., AL telegraphs Gen. Hooker: "We have news here that the enemy has reoccupied heights above Fredericksburg. Is that so?" (Hooker replied: "I am informed that it is so, but attach no importance to it.")

May 5, Tuesday

In Virginia, Gen. Hooker's main force begins retreating across the river.

❖ AL attends a Cabinet meeting and reads the telegram from Gen. Hooker admitting that the rebels again hold the heights above Fredericksburg. (The Union lost 12,000 men trying to take those heights in December.)
❖ In the afternoon, AL discusses the military situation with Massachusetts Sen. Charles Sumner and with Welles.

May 6, Wednesday

On the Red River, Union river forces take Alexandria, Louisiana.

❖ AL sends a telegram to Gen. Hooker noting that the Richmond newspapers report that Lee has beaten him.
❖ AL gets a reply in the afternoon from Gen. Hooker admitting he has retreated: "I saw no way of giving the enemy a general battle with the prospect of success which I desire."
❖ AL leaves at about 4 p.m. to visit the army, taking Gen. Halleck with him.

May 7, Thursday

❖ AL, in the Falmouth, Virginia, area, spends the day visiting with Gen. Hooker. He returns to Washington that night.
❖ AL later writes to Hooker: "What next?" (Hooker's answer was vague.)

❖ AL tells Gen. Meigs: "The troops are none the worse for the campaign."

May 8, Friday

❖ AL issues a proclamation stating that being an alien does not exempt a person from military service if that person has declared an intention to become a U.S. citizen.

❖ AL orders the seizure of the New Almaden Quicksilver Mine near San Jose, California, on the understanding that the land's title had been proven fraudulent. (Actually, the title was still in litigation. The order triggered a political crisis in California, which was not firmly Unionist.)

❖ AL attends a Cabinet meeting where Welles reports on progress on the Mississippi River campaign.

May 9, Saturday

❖ AL asks for information on damages inflicted on the Confederate railroads north of Richmond during the recent Union cavalry raids. (Damage was limited—bridges proved hard for horsemen to destroy.)

❖ AL, with Stanton, watches a demonstration of liquid fire.

May 10, Sunday

Stonewall Jackson dies of his wounds. Last words: "Let us cross over the river, and rest under the shade of the trees."

May 11, Monday

❖ AL tells Stanton that he had decided to relieve Gen. Samuel Curtis in Missouri for failing to maintain order and for taking sides among feuding Republicans.

❖ Chase resigns after AL fires a Chase appointee for cause, without consulting Chase. AL manages to talk him out of it.

❖ AL asks the commander of Fortress Monroe if the Richmond papers have any news from Vicksburg. (They did not. AL was receiving no reports from Gen. Grant.)

May 13, Wednesday

❖ AL consults with Stanton about former congressman Clement Vallandigham, a prominent Copperhead recently arrested for treason by Gen. Burnside, producing an uproar. (Stanton later exiled Vallandigham to the Confederacy. The Confederates sent him to Canada.)
❖ AL appoints to West Point the son of a general who was killed at Chancellorsville, Virginia.

May 14, Thursday

Gen. Grant takes Jackson, Mississippi.

❖ Apparently following up on the conversation they had yesterday, AL writes to Gen. Hooker saying that he does not have to attack again immediately, and that his subordinates are unhappy about him and complaining—just as Hooker used to complain about Gen. McClellan.

May 15, Friday

Gen. Grant begins moving his forces west toward Vicksburg.

❖ AL appeals to Republicans in Missouri to stop feuding: "Neither side pays the least respect to my appeals to your reason."
❖ AL announces the resumption of Saturday concerts by the Marine band on the White House grounds. (MTL had called them off after Willie's death as they reminded her of him.)

May 16, Saturday

The rebel force that Gen. Grant had lured out of Vicksburg is defeated and forced back into the city.

❖ AL endorses an appeal by the father of a Confederate officer who was captured in Kentucky, who asks that his son be released on condition that he go to some other country besides the Confederacy for the duration of the war. (But the War Department wants all the POWs it can get for prisoner exchanges, and the son is exchanged back to the Confederacy.)

❖ AL, Seward, and Stanton go on a trip down the Potomac to inspect troop transports.

May 17, Sunday

❖ AL consults a map with Massachusetts Rep. George Boutwell to locate where Gen. Grant's troops crossed the Mississippi.

May 18, Monday

Gen. Grant lays siege to Vicksburg.

May 19, Tuesday

Gen. Grant launches a direct assault on Vicksburg. It fails.

May 20, Wednesday

❖ AL pardons Albert Horn, who was convicted of fitting out a vessel to engage in the slave trade.

May 21, Thursday

❖ AL refers complaints to Welles that American vessels are annoying neutral ships in Cuban waters.

May 22, Friday

Gen. Grant launches a second, larger direct assault on Vicksburg. It too fails.

❖ AL asks Gen. Stephen Hurlbut in Nashville, Tennessee, about recent reports in the Richmond newspapers of repeated Confederate defeats at the hands of Gen. Grant around Vicksburg. (Hurlbut forwarded a belated situation report, confirming the news reports.)
❖ AL meets with a delegation of one-legged convalescents from a local military hospital.

May 23, Saturday

❖ AL confers with Stanton, Welles, Fox, and Gen. Halleck concerning the failed attack on Charleston, South Carolina.

May 24, Sunday

❖ AL, accompanied by Wisconsin Sen. James Doolittle, visits three military hospitals and shakes hands with about a thousand men.

May 25, Monday

Union forces advancing from the south besiege the other rebel Mississippi River fortress at Port Hudson, Louisiana.

❖ AL continues visiting area hospitals.

May 26, Tuesday

❖ AL attends a Cabinet meeting where they discuss pardoning a condemned spy.

May 27, Wednesday

A Union direct assault on Port Hudson fails.

❖ AL writes to Gen. John Schofield in Missouri, who has been sent to replace Gen. Samuel Curtis, explaining that Curtis had to be replaced because he kept feuding with Missouri Gov. Hamilton Gamble. "Let your military measures be strong enough to repel the invader and keep the peace, and not so strong as to unnecessarily harass and persecute the people. It is a difficult role, and so much greater will be the honor if you perform it well."

❖ AL telegraphs various headquarters to see if they have heard any news about Gen. Grant.

May 29, Friday

❖ AL does not accept the resignation of Gen. Burnside, who thought that the Cabinet did not support his arrest of Clement Vallandigham: "When I shall wish to supersede you I will let you know."

❖ AL and Stanton observe the firing of a new kind of gun at the Navy Yard.

May 30, Saturday

❖ AL meets with a delegation from New York who urges him to put Gen. Frémont in command of a force of 10,000 black troops. (Frémont later turned it down, the proposed force being too small.)

JUNE 1863

Summary: Positive news elsewhere is overshadowed by an invasion of Pennsylvania. To confront it, AL must yet again replace the commander of the Army of the Potomac.

June 1, Monday

- ❖ AL tells a California land-claim litigant that courts rather than the president must decide land titles: "Vague assertions that the decisions of the courts are fraudulent, with appeals to me to reverse them, cannot be entertained."
- ❖ AL asks the Union prisoner exchange agent to arrange the release of two New York newspaper correspondents held by the Confederates. (He tried but could not.)
- ❖ AL confers with Stanton about Gen. Burnside's recent suppression of disloyal newspapers in Indiana. (Stanton had the order rescinded.)

June 2, Tuesday

- ❖ AL interviews Gen. John Reynolds to see if he would be interested in commanding the Army of the Potomac. (He turned it down, and died at Gettysburg.)
- ❖ AL attends a Cabinet meeting where they discuss events at Vicksburg.

June 3, Wednesday

Lee begins moving his army west, out of Fredericksburg, Virginia.

❖ AL forwards to Gen. Halleck a plan proposed by the
president of the Metropolitan Railroad, under which the
government would raise units of immigrants and blacks who
would work on railroad construction for part of the day and
receive military training and drills for the rest of the day,
and thus build a planned railroad between Washington and
Pittsburgh. (Gen. Halleck replied that the army could not
find enough laborers to finish local fortifications. "Moreover,
working on fortifications is much better military training
than working on railroads.")

June 4, Thursday

❖ AL suspends the execution of three soldiers condemned for
desertion. They thought they had enlisted for six months.
❖ AL and MTL attend a Shakespeare recitation at a private
residence.

June 5, Friday

❖ AL advises Gen. Hooker that, if Lee moves his force north of
the Rappahannock River, Gen. Hooker should not respond
by moving south of the river. "I would not take any risk of
being entangled upon the river, like an ox jumped half over
a fence, and liable to be torn by dogs, front and rear, without
a fair chance to gore one way or kick the other."

June 7, Sunday

French troops enter Mexico City.

June 8, Monday

❖ AL tries to reassure Gen. Samuel Curtis after firing him for
feuding with Missouri Gov. Hamilton Gamble: "With me

the presumption is still in your favor that you are honest, capable, faithful, and patriotic."

❖ AL discusses Pennsylvania politics with Chase.

❖ MTL and Tad take a train to Philadelphia.

June 9, Tuesday

A powerful Union cavalry probe collides with Lee's cavalry at Brandy Station, Virginia, triggering the largest cavalry battle in American history.

❖ AL telegraphs MTL in Philadelphia: "Think you better put Tad's pistol away. I had an ugly dream about him." (Tad had acquired an old pistol as a toy.)

June 10, Wednesday

The Lee's army heads northwest from Culpepper Court House, Virginia. Invasion fears begin spreading in the North.

❖ AL replies to a suggestion from Gen. Hooker that the Union army move against Richmond while Lee's army is moving north: "I think Lee's Army, and not Richmond, is your true objective point."

❖ Accompanied by Stanton and others, AL visits a fort outside Alexandria, Virginia, where a magazine explosion yesterday killed twenty-two men.

❖ AL completely forgets a noon appointment (apparently with the Nicaraguan minister).

June 11, Thursday

❖ AL telegraphs MTL in Philadelphia: "Your three dispatches received. I am very well; and am glad to know that you and Tad are so."

June 12, Friday

The vanguard of Lee's army reaches the Shenandoah Valley.

❖ AL responds to resolutions passed at a public meeting in Albany, New York, complaining that certain arrests made by the administration during the war have been unconstitutional. AL argues that they were not.

June 13, Saturday

Gen. Hooker begins moving his army northward to shadow Lee's movements.

❖ AL and Gen. Meigs board a tug at 1 p.m. to visit the army at Falmouth, Virginia. But then Hooker asks them to postpone the visit, so they return to Washington at about 3:30 p.m.

June 14, Sunday

Lee's forces attack Winchester, Virginia.

❖ AL tells Gen. Hooker that Winchester, Virginia, is apparently surrounded by the enemy.
❖ AL meets with Stanton, Welles, and Gen. Halleck in the evening at the War Department to try to establish what Lee is doing.
❖ AL tells Gen. Hooker: "If the head of Lee's army is at Martinsburg and the tail of it on the Plank Road between Fredericksburg and Chancellorsville, the animal must be very slim somewhere. Could you not break him?"

June 15, Monday

❖ AL calls up 100,000 state militia to combat the Confederate invasion: 50,000 in Pennsylvania, 30,000 in Ohio, and 10,000 each in Maryland and West Virginia.

❖ AL tells Gen. Hooker that Martinsburg, West Virginia, and Winchester, Virginia, have both fallen and the surviving defenders have retreated to Harpers Ferry, West Virginia.

❖ AL asks the commander of Harpers Ferry, West Virginia, about Confederate strength in the area.

❖ AL tells MTL in Philadelphia that he is doing "tolerably well," that he has not gotten out much, but has gotten new tires on the carriage.

June 16, Tuesday

Lee's vanguard crosses the Potomac. Evacuations begin at Harrisburg, Pennsylvania.

❖ AL sends a private letter to Gen. Hooker saying that he and Gen. Halleck do trust him, although Halleck is a little worried about Hooker's habit of writing directly to AL rather than through Halleck.

❖ In a separate message, AL tells Gen. Hooker that he is disappointed that he is using his cavalry defensively rather than attempting to attack Lee's strung-out army.

❖ AL attends a Cabinet meeting where Chase suggests that the army move directly to Richmond, but AL rejects the idea.

❖ AL sends a general to Philadelphia to organize troops there.

❖ AL tells MTL in Philadelphia that there is no reason she should come home. "I do not think the raid in Pennsylvania amounts to anything at all."

June 17, Wednesday

❖ Gen. Hooker asks AL for all available information on Confederate activity north of the Potomac, and AL tells him that he will get a copy of everything that comes through the telegraph office.

June 18, Thursday

Gen. Grant relieves Gen. John McClernand after he issues a congratulatory order to his troops denigrating other commands.

❖ AL turns down the offer of a battalion of Canadian militia to defend Washington, saying that Washington is not in danger.

❖ AL reduces the sentence of an army surgeon, convicted of discussing troop movements in front of a Virginian, from dismissal to a severe reprimand.

June 19, Friday

❖ AL hears from a delegation of Louisiana planters asking that local elections be held under the existing state constitution.

❖ AL consults with the mayor of Boston about the city's defenses.

June 20, Saturday

❖ AL hears from the Missouri state convention that it might adopt gradual emancipation if in the interim they would be "protected in their slave property" by the Federal Government.

June 21, Sunday

❖ AL tells Gen. Hooker that the telegraph operator in Leesburg, Virginia, reports battle noises to the south.

June 22, Monday

❖ AL answers Saturday's question about supporting gradual emancipation: "My impulse is to say that such protection would be given."

❖ AL begins summer residence at the Soldiers' Home.

❖ AL passes on more reports of battle noises from Leesburg.

June 23, Tuesday

Gen. Rosecrans launches an offensive that maneuvers the Confederates out of central Tennessee without major fighting.

❖ AL asks the Army quartermaster in New York if he has received any news from the front.
❖ AL attends a Cabinet meeting and is described as looking sad and careworn.

June 24, Wednesday

❖ AL forwards to Gen. Hooker reports of Confederate troops in southeast Pennsylvania.

June 25, Thursday

❖ AL receives a delegation from the Ohio State Democratic Convention protesting the Administration's perceived civil rights abuses.

June 26, Friday

After taking twenty-one prizes in nineteen days, a Confederate commerce raider is defeated near Portland, Maine.

❖ AL commutes six military death sentences.
❖ AL receives a message from New York Gov. Horatio Seymour saying that the (typically quite partisan) Democrat will stand behind the Administration during the current emergency.

June 27, Saturday

Confederate forces take York, Pennsylvania.

❖ AL relieves Gen. Hooker as commander of the Army of the Potomac and replaces him with Gen. Meade, one of the corps commanders. (When a dispute arose about defending Harpers Ferry, which Hooker did not want to do, he offered to resign, and the offer was accepted.)

June 28, Sunday

❖ AL attends a Cabinet meeting and announces the replacement of Gen. Hooker.
❖ AL inquires about battle noises reported near Harrisburg, Pennsylvania.

June 29, Monday

Newly installed Gen. Meade has his forces overtake Lee's forces, which are concentrating near Gettysburg.

❖ AL writes a personal letter to Gen. Robert Millroy saying he does not accept Millroy's excuse for losing half his men and all his artillery and wagons at Winchester. (Millroy's excuse was that his superiors were out to get him because he was not a West Point graduate.)
❖ Fox presents a plan to capture Richmond from Fortress Monroe, but Gen. Halleck vetoes the idea

June 30, Tuesday

❖ AL confers with Stanton and Gen. Halleck and misses a Cabinet meeting.
❖ AL sends an inquiry to Harrisburg, asking if the Confederates are crossing the Susquehanna River.

❖ In response to various parties demanding that Gen. McClellan be restored to command, AL replies: "Do we gain anything by opening one leak to stop another?"

❖ AL tells Gen. David Hunter that his removal as commander of the Department of the South (as of June 3) was not a reflection on him personally.

JULY, 1863

Summary: *Lee is defeated in Pennsylvania, the rebels lose an entire army at Vicksburg, they continue retreating in Tennessee, and Charleston, South Carolina, remains besieged. AL momentarily believes his armies are about to win the war—and is bitterly disappointed.*

July 1, Wednesday

At Gettysburg Union forces are driven to a low ridge south of town, where they are joined by reinforcements.

On the Mississippi, the siege of Vicksburg continues.

In Missouri, the state convention abolishes slavery as of July 4, 1870.

❖ AL spends time in the War Department telegraph office reading dispatches, now that a major battle is taking place.

July 2, Thursday

At Gettysburg, Lee's attacks on the flanks of the Union position are repelled, most unexpectedly on the extreme southern flank by an insignificant force at Little Round Top.

❖ AL spends hours in the telegraph room of the War Department, reading dispatches.
❖ AL asks Stanton to allow government advertising in the Washington-based pro-AL *National Republican* newspaper, presumably to keep it out of financial trouble. (It would receive about $500 in government advertising that year.)

❖ MTL is thrown from her carriage when the horses bolt between the Soldiers' Home to the White House. She is initially thought to be slightly injured, but infections, migraines, and behavior changes ensue, possibly making the accident a turning point in her life.

July 3, Friday

At Gettysburg, a morning of minor actions is followed by a massive artillery duel, and then Lee launches a major attack against the Union center. Called Picket's Charge, it's a debacle.

At Vicksburg, the Confederates ask for terms. Grant offers parole, so he won't have to feed them.

❖ AL reads dispatches at the War Department during the morning and confers there with Welles and Seward about the situation.
❖ AL sends a telegram to RTL, away at Harvard, saying his mother is not in danger from her injuries.
❖ AL intervenes with Gen. Burnside, now commanding the largely quiet Department of the Ohio, to prevent a soldier from being shot for desertion without a case review. (AL pardoned the man a month later.)

July 4, Saturday, Independence Day

At Gettysburg, both sides initially stand in place. The Union artillery fires a noon salute at the enemy to mark Independence Day. Torrential rain commences. The Confederates begin withdrawing, largely unmolested. The wagon train carrying the wounded is twenty miles long.

At Vicksburg, 29,000 Confederates surrender.

Incidents of the War.

The war's mounting casualties, on both sides, greatly distressed Lincoln.

❖ AL at 10 a.m. telegraphs a press release: "The President announces to the country that news from the Army of the Potomac, up to 10 p.m. of the 3rd, is such as to cover that Army with the highest honor."

❖ A friend of AL from Springfield, Archimedes "Dick" Dickson, acting as an industrial salesman, tries to interest AL in a new pattern artillery projectile called the Absterdam shell, whose flanges expand when fired, fitting the shell snug in the barrel.

❖ AL learns that Alexander Stephens has arrived under a flag of truce at Fortress Monroe, asking to come to Washington to talk to AL, ostensibly about a prisoner exchange. (AL knew the Confederate vice president when they were both congressmen. Presumably, Stephens' real motivation was to be on hand should the Administration become favorable to peace negotiations following a Confederate triumph in Pennsylvania.)

❖ AL helps set up fireworks on the White House grounds.

July 5, Sunday

Lee's retreating army heads toward Hagerstown, Maryland.

❖ AL attends an 11 a.m. Cabinet meeting which discusses Alexander Stephens' request.

❖ AL, bringing Tad, visits Gen. Dan Sickles, who has been brought to Washington after being wounded at Gettysburg. (He had impetuously positioned his troops, the III Corps, in a salient where they suffered heavy casualties. Sickles himself lost his right leg to a cannon ball. In Washington, he wanted to tell AL about the victory—and presumably control the narrative about III Corps. He had been the only corps commander there who was not a West Point graduate.)

❖ Having seen his report about a Union cavalry raid Saturday destroying a Confederate pontoon bridge across the now-swollen Potomac at Falling Waters, West Virginia (near Hagerstown), AL telegraphs directly to Gen. William French asking if the Potomac could be forded. (It could not.)

July 6, Monday

Lee's army, harassed by Union cavalry, continues concentrating near Hagerstown, waiting for the Potomac to fall.

❖ AL attends a 9 a.m. Cabinet meeting, again discussing Alexander Stephens' request. They finally agree that Stephens should use existing channels if he really wants to talk about prisoner exchanges.

❖ Gen. Herman Haupt, the chief railroad engineer of the Union army, arrives from Gettysburg, on one of his trains and consults with AL and others to express his fear that Gen. Meade is going to let Lee get away. (Haupt had spoken with Meade Saturday and heard him say that the Union army had almost been defeated and needed to rest, and since Lee did not have a pontoon train the Confederates would be stuck on the north side of the rain-swollen Potomac. Haupt told him that the

Confederates could extemporize a bridge by tearing down local buildings for lumber, but Meade remained convinced that the Union force needed rest. Haupt feels that the end of the war is within reach if Meade will move aggressively and catch Lee.)

❖ RTL comes upon AL after Gen. Haupt leaves and sees that his father is greatly troubled by what Haupt told him. (RTL is so struck with his father's reaction that he asks Haupt about it when they happen to meet again twenty-one years later.)

❖ After spending hours in the telegraph room of the War Department, AL returns home at about 7 p.m.

❖ Once there, he sends Gen. Halleck a complaint that the dispatches he saw in the telegraph room indicate a general policy of herding enemy forces across the river rather than preventing their crossing and destroying them.

July 7, Tuesday

Gen. Meade finally sends his infantry after Lee.

In Tennessee, the Confederates begin concentrating at Chattanooga.

The Union Conscription Act takes effect, triggering discontent in many locations, but especially in New York City, a Democratic hotbed.

❖ AL is at the War Department telegraph office in the morning and sees the dispatch from Gen. Grant announcing the July 4 surrender of Vicksburg. Welles almost knocks AL over, rushing to show him the dispatch.

❖ Maine's two senators and Hamlin confer with AL, urging better coastal defenses to deter Confederate commerce raiders. They seem reassured when told that maritime patrols would be maintained during the fishing season.

❖ In the evening, a celebratory crowd serenades AL, who responds with his longest known off-the-cuff speech. He uses several ideas that show up in the speech he gives in

November: "On the 4th the cohorts of those who opposed the declaration that all men are created equal turned tail and run."

July 8, Wednesday

The Potomac remains swollen. Union infantry catches up with Lee's outside Hagerstown.

On the Mississippi, Port Hudson, Louisiana, surrenders, opening the entire river to the Union.

- ❖ AL separately assures the customs collector in San Francisco, and the U.S. attorney in New York, that the recent victories are not rumors.
- ❖ AL complains to Adjutant Gen. Lorenzo Thomas about Gen. Meade's lack of aggressiveness, saying he is "as likely to capture the Man-in-the Moon, as any part of Lee's army."

July 9, Thursday

Gen. Meade's army concentrates south of Boonsboro, Maryland, facing the Confederate concentration on the banks of the flooded Potomac at Williamsport, Maryland, where a small ferry operates.

- ❖ AL issues two pardons, one for counterfeiting and one for inciting soldiers to desert.
- ❖ AL advises local officials to use discretion and "not have a riot" in the case of the New Almaden Quicksilver Mine in California. (They met armed resistance when they tried to take possession of the mine.)

July 10, Friday

Lee's and Meade's armies probe each other near Williamsport.

Near Charleston, Union forces lay siege to Battery Wagner near the harbor entrance.

❖ AL has another meeting about the Absterdam shell.
❖ AL writes to Gen. Dan Sickles saying his old unit (III Corps) has not suffered any disasters since Sickles left, regardless of rumors. (Sickles later sends the bones of his amputated leg to a museum, visiting them occasionally.)
❖ AL telegraphs assurances to his former Springfield, Illinois, neighbor, Jesse Dubois, currently the Illinois Auditor of Public Accounts, that Lee has been defeated.

July 11, Saturday

Gen. Meade meets with his six corps commanders. Only one favors attacking Lee's army.

Near Charleston, a Union attack on Battery Wagner fails.

❖ AL orders the Naval Ordnance Department to conduct trials of the Absterdam shell.
❖ AL telegraphs RTL (in New York City at the time) to return to Washington.
❖ AL is seen to be in a good mood due to reports that Gen. Meade has decided to attack.

July 12, Sunday

Gen. Meade decides to attack Lee's trapped army— eventually, after reconnaissance is complete. The Potomac recedes.

❖ AL is at the War Department telegraph room and sees that Gen. Meade plans to attack the next day. He displays considerable anxiety, muttering, "Too late!"

July 13, Monday

The bulk of Lee's army escapes across the falling Potomac.

Draft riots break out in New York City.

❖ AL sends a thank-you letter to Gen. Grant for his recent victory. AL said he was worried about Grant's plans to operate inland away from the river and take the city from the land side, but "you were right and I was wrong." (The taciturn Grant took more than a month to reply.)

❖ AL sends a letter to Gen John Schofield in St. Louis asking him to stop investigating how a letter from AL to him ended up, without authorization, in an opposition newspaper, as the issue is not worth the political blowback. (That letter also ended up in print.)

July 14, Tuesday

Union forces probe Lee's rear guard.

Draft riots continue in New York City.

❖ AL is dejected to learn that Lee's army has escaped.

❖ AL writes a thank-you letter to Gen. Meade for his victory at Gettysburg. AL then adds that he feels "deep distress" concerning the failure to pursue Lee, complaining that Meade should have crushed the retreating Confederates. He files the letter and never sends it.

❖ AL watches the test firing of twenty Absterdam shells.

July 15, Wednesday

Draft riots continue in New York City.

❖ AL issues a proclamation of thanksgiving for the recent Union victories, setting aside August 6 as a day of praise and prayer.

- ❖ Responding to reports that only one of the six corps commanders had favored attacking the trapped Confederates on Saturday, AL asks who that one general was. (No answer is recorded.)
- ❖ Responding to numerous protests, and concerned about California's loyalty to the Union, AL reverses his decision to seize the New Almaden Quicksilver Mine.
- ❖ AL endorses a letter to Zebulon Vance, governor of Confederate North Carolina, hailing his reported statements calling for an end to the war, and offering to facilitate negotiations on the basis of the abolition of slavery.

July 16, Thursday

New York City draft riots end.

The USS Wyoming wins a naval battle against anti-foreign elements in the Straits of Shimonoseki, Japan.

- ❖ AL confers with Kansas Gov. Thomas Carney regarding the right of a governor to appoint military officers.

July 17, Friday

Black troops win a Union victory at Honey Springs, Indian Territory.

- ❖ AL affirms his faith in Gen. Meade at a Cabinet meeting.
- ❖ AL directs Stanton to give the governor of Kansas the same authority as other loyal governors to confer military commissions.

July 18, Saturday

A second, heavier Union assault against Battery Wagner, spearheaded by black troops, is a bloody failure. Among the dead is Col. Robert Gould Shaw, who met AL in April 1861.

- ❖ AL spends six hours reviewing court-martial sentences, and proves averse to hanging anyone for cowardice. He jokes that a captain charged with furtively watching a woman undress should be elevated to the peerage as Count Peeper. With his Kentucky accent he pronounces the name like that of Count Piper, the Swedish minister.
- ❖ AL misses an appointment with Gov. Thomas Carney of Kansas, who wanted to see AL again before leaving town. Carney wants the state to be put under a military commander other than Gen. James Blunt.

July 19, Sunday

Gen. Meade's army finally moves south of the Potomac, following Lee.

- ❖ AL is feeling upbeat enough to write doggerel and show it to his secretary, Hay.
- ❖ AL has an evening meeting with Lord Lyons, the British minister.

July 20, Monday

Gen. Meade's army probes the Blue Ridge, seeking Lee's army.

- ❖ AL writes to New Jersey Gov. Joel Parker saying he can't delay the draft in his state since then every governor will want a delay.
- ❖ Two Illinois congressmen confer with AL about slavery and the Border States.

July 21, Tuesday

- ❖ AL writes to Gen. O. O. Howard expressing confidence in Gen. Meade.

- ❖ AL directs Stanton to renew efforts to raise black troops along the Mississippi River.
- ❖ AL tells Gov. Thomas Carney of Kansas that getting rid of Gen. James Blunt (who nearly twenty years later died in a mental institution) cannot be done offhandedly, but Blunt will be told to stop turning prisoners over to lynch mobs.

July 22, Wednesday

- ❖ AL feels sick, skips meals, and misses an appointment with Gen. Robert Schenck, VIII Corps commander.
- ❖ AL sets $2,500 as the annual salary for the chief chemist at the new Department of Agriculture.

July 23, Thursday

Union forces make contact with Lee's army at Manassas Gap but do not press their advantage.

- ❖ AL confers with Nehemiah Ordway, chairman of Republican Central Committee of New Hampshire, regarding draft quotas.
- ❖ AL writes to a Missouri Gov. Hamilton Gamble about factional feuding among Missouri Republicans, hoping to defuse him.
- ❖ AL writes Gen. Robert Schenck to assure him that he was not trying to snub him yesterday.

July 24, Friday

Lee's army crosses the Rappahannock and breaks contact with Union forces.

- ❖ AL attends a Cabinet meeting.
- ❖ AL suspends the death sentences of six deserters.
- ❖ AL writes to Blair urging the advisability of giving postal jobs to military widows and disabled soldiers.

July 25, Saturday

❖ AL tells the governor of New Jersey that he can't make special deals with the governors of each state concerning draft quotas, but new volunteers from his state will be deducted from the state's draft quota.

❖ AL tells Welles to stop seizing suspected blockade runners as they leave neutral ports and detaining their neutral crews as prisoners of war.

July 26, Sunday

❖ AL confers with Welles about reinforcements for the siege of Charleston.

July 27, Monday

❖ AL asks Gen. Meade if he is still willing to employ Gen. Hooker as a corps commander.

July 28, Tuesday

❖ AL permits a wounded Confederate captain, taken at Gettysburg, to be transferred to the care of relatives in Washington.

July 29, Wednesday

❖ AL tells Halleck that he opposes "pressing" Gen. Meade into offensive operations.

❖ AL tells Stanton to start preparing an expedition against Texas.

July 30, Thursday

❖ AL authorizes retaliation if black soldiers are enslaved or sold after being captured by the Confederates.

❖ AL tells Francis Blair Sr. that he has begun preparing an expedition to Texas.

July 31, Friday

❖ AL interviews the lawyer of Dr. David Wright. (Wright was convicted of murdering 2nd Lt. Alanson Sanborn because Lt. Sanborn was leading black troops down a street.)
❖ The Cabinet hears a two-hour report on the capture of Vicksburg.
❖ AL successfully asks Gen. Stephen Hurlbut, an old political ally, to reconsider his decision to resign from the army.

AUGUST 1863

Summary: *After a series of unaccustomed victories in July, August sees a comparative lull on the battlefronts. The draft proceeds without disturbances, except among certain politicians.*

August 1, Saturday

Another cavalry battle at Brandy Station, Virginia, marks the end of the Gettysburg Campaign.

- ❖ AL receives a petition from citizens in the Shenandoah Valley asking that Gen. Robert Milroy be restored to command. (He wasn't.)
- ❖ AL and Hay attend the dedication of a new printing office for the *Washington Chronicle*.

August 3, Monday

- ❖ AL orders a stay of execution for Dr. David Wright of Norfolk, Virginia, until AL can review the case file.

August 4, Tuesday

- ❖ AL attends a Cabinet meeting where they discuss prizes and prize courts (i.e., for the disposition of captured enemy vessels, typically blockade runners).

August 5, Wednesday

- ❖ AL writes to Gen. Nathaniel Banks regarding Louisiana's possible readmission into the Union: "I would be glad for her to make a new constitution recognizing the Emancipation Proclamation.... Education for young blacks should be included in the plan."

❖ AL telegraphs the *Cincinnati Gazette* asking if they have any Kentucky election results.

❖ AL asks the Department of the Agriculture to pay the salary of the chemist who has been formulating experimental gunpowder invented by Capt. Isaac R. Diller.

August 6, Thursday

As proclaimed by AL, the Union observes a day of thanksgiving for recent victories.

❖ AL attends church thanksgiving services and a large pro-Union rally.

August 7, Friday

❖ AL answers a letter from New York Gov. Horatio Seymour demanding that the draft be canceled in New York, citing the draft riots, unequal draft quotas between districts, and his presumption that the law is unconstitutional. (AL responded that he was willing to adjust quotas, but the draft must go on.)

❖ RTL, MTL, and Tad are in the White Mountains of New Hampshire.

August 8, Saturday

❖ AL writes to MTL and breaks the news that Tad's pet goat has disappeared. He also discusses recent Kentucky election results.

❖ AL sends Francis Pierpont, governor of Union-controlled Virginia, to Norfolk, to settle a dispute about how relief funds for destitute families should be raised.

August 9, Sunday

❖ AL acknowledges receipt of a petition from eastern Tennessee Unionists asking for effective government protection against Confederate repression, saying he is doing all he can, and it would be pointless to meet with them.

❖ AL writes to Gen. Grant urging him to recruit and use black soldiers. "It works doubly, weakening the enemy and strengthening us."

❖ Accompanied by Hay, AL poses for several photographs at the new Alexander Gardner studio.

August 10, Monday

❖ AL provides a letter of introduction for abolitionist and former slave Frederick Douglass, who intends to help recruit black units.

❖ AL tells Gen. Meade that Gen. Joe Hooker has agreed to a subordinate assignment in the Army of the Potomac, which he used to command. (Meade replied that he wasn't interested.)

❖ AL attends a Cabinet meeting and reviews his communication with New York Gov. Horatio Seymour.

August 11, Tuesday

❖ AL, after consulting with the Cabinet, replies to another letter of complaint from New York Gov. Horatio Seymour, and agrees to further adjustments to district draft quotas, but insists that the draft proceed.

❖ The Cabinet also discusses the problem of drafting skilled workers.

❖ AL writes a check for $5.00: "Pay to Colored man with one leg or bearer."

August 12, Wednesday

Union forces besieging Charleston, South Carolina, begin bombarding Fort Sumter, demolishing it.

❖ Responding to urgings that he restore Gen. John McClernand to the position from which he was dismissed by Gen. Grant, AL writes directly to McClernand: "For me to force you back upon Gen. Grant would be forcing him to resign. I cannot give you a new command, because we have no forces except such as already have commanders."

August 13, Thursday

❖ AL agrees to a personal appeal from Major Alexander Montgomery that the major deserves a court-martial, as opposed to a dismissal from the army, as his actions were "merely personally offensive to me," as opposed to treasonous. (He had been quoted as saying that AL ought to have his "damned black heart cut out" for issuing the Emancipation Proclamation. He was reinstated in June 1864.)

❖ AL tours the Capitol with Hay to see the progress of the rebuilding program.

August 14, Friday

❖ AL attends a Cabinet meeting where Gen. Meade describes the Battle of Gettysburg.

❖ AL assures Elizabeth Todd Grimsley (cousin of MTL) that he still intends to appoint her son John Todd Grimsley to the Naval Academy.

August 15, Saturday

❖ AL offers Gen. Robert Anderson (former commander of Fort Sumter) command of Fort Adams in Rhode Island as a sinecure, as he is in poor health. (He took it but then went on disability retirement.)

❖ AL issues a proclamation calling up the New York state militia to help enforce the draft laws. (New York Gov. Horatio Seymour had said he did not want U.S. troops involved.)

August 16, Sunday

Gen. Rosecrans begins operations against Chattanooga.

❖ AL begins writing a letter to be read aloud ("very slowly") at a pro-Union rally September 3 at his home town of Springfield, Illinois: "I do not believe any compromise, embracing the maintenance of the Union, is now possible.... You say you will not fight to free negroes. Some of them seem willing to fight for you.... Peace does not appear so distant as it did. I hope it will come soon, and come to stay; and so come as to be worth the keeping in all future time. It will then have been proved that, among free men, there can be no successful appeal from the ballot to the bullet."

August 17, Monday

❖ AL writes to Shakespearean actor James Hackett, in response to a gift of a book of Shakespearean criticism from Hackett: "I think the soliloquy in *Hamlet* commencing 'O, my offence is rank' surpasses that commencing 'To be, or not to be.' But pardon this small attempt at criticism. I should like to hear you pronounce the opening speech of *Richard the Third*. Will you not soon visit Washington again?" (The letter got published, political opponents used it to make fun of AL, Hackett apologized to AL, AL accepted, and their correspondence continued.)

❖ Christopher Spencer, inventor of the Spencer seven-round lever-operated repeating rifle, presents an example to AL and shows him how to assemble it.

August 18, Tuesday

❖ AL writes to Gen. James Blunt, who's been the object of complaints by Kansas Gov. Thomas Carney: "I regret to find you denouncing so many persons as liars, scoundrels, fools, thieves, and persecutors of yourself. To take men charged with no offence against the military, out of the hands of the courts, to be turned over to a mob to be hanged, can find no precedent or principle to justify it." (Blunt replied that the hangings stopped too soon.)

August 19, Wednesday

❖ AL endorses a request by Judge James Colt of Missouri that his POW teenage stepson be released to him. (Stanton blocked the release, as the boy had been voluntarily in the Confederate army for two years.)

❖ The minister of Austria presents his credentials without any formalities. Austria had recently ejected a U.S. envoy for favoring Hungarian independence.

August 20, Thursday

❖ AL visits the telegraph office at the War Department and then takes a boat trip down the Potomac to see new fort construction, returning after dark.

August 21, Friday

Confederate guerrillas sack and burn Lawrence, Kansas, killing all the men and boys (nearly 200) they can find.

❖ AL confers about naval matters and the appointment of a governor for Arizona Territory.

❖ AL writes a pass for a delegation of black Baptist ministers so they may cross military lines to "minister to their brethren there."

❖ AL, Stanton, and others take a boat trip to Alexandria, Virginia, to visit defense fortifications.

August 22, Saturday

❖ AL tells Gen. Dan Sickles (still recuperating from his wounds) that AL can't help him with a California real estate lawsuit, as no law "assigns any duty to the President in the case."

❖ In the evening, Hay falls asleep listening to AL read Shakespeare.

August 23, Sunday

❖ AL continues writing his letter to be read aloud at the September 3 Union rally in Springfield.

August 25, Tuesday

Union authorities order the evacuation of most of four western Missouri counties where the guerillas who sacked Lawrence, were based. About 20,000 people are forced from their homes.

August 26, Wednesday

❖ AL continues writing his letter to be read aloud at the September 3 Union rally in Springfield.

August 27, Thursday

❖ AL receives a complaint about the "unfairness" of the draft from municipal officials in Chicago. He tells them that the matter must be addressed at the state level.

❖ AL declines to grant a stay of execution for five bounty jumpers (men who enlisted, pocketed local enlistment bounties, and then deserted, probably multiple times). (They were executed two days later.)

❖ AL mails the letter for the Union rally in Springfield.

August 28, Friday

❖ AL confers with Pennsylvania Gov. Andrew Curtin regarding draft quotas.

August 29, Saturday

❖ AL writes to MTL in New Hampshire reporting that the siege of Charleston, is going well.

August 31, Monday

❖ AL responds to a letter from Gen. Rosecrans, basically telling Rosecrans that he is not mad at him for not having advanced farther.

❖ AL confers with two Virginia politicians about a tax imposed on the people of Northampton County, Virginia, to rebuild a lighthouse that pro-Confederates damaged.

SEPTEMBER 1863

Summary: *A rebel counterattack shatters a major Union army in Tennessee. There, AL's favorite brother-in-law is killed in action — in the Confederate army.*

September 1, Tuesday

❖ AL tells Stanton to suspend orders expelling paroled POWs from Northampton County, Virginia, and assessing the residents for the cost of a vandalized lighthouse, "till I can at least be better satisfied of their propriety than I now am."

September 2, Wednesday

Union forces under Gen. Burnside take Knoxville, Tennessee, cutting a major Confederate rail link.

❖ AL is startled to see that the letter he wrote for tomorrow's Union rally in Springfield, Illinois, is being printed in east coast newspapers.

❖ AL explains to Chase that the parts of Virginia and Louisiana that were exempted from the Emancipation Proclamation last January cannot now be covered by it.

September 3, Thursday

❖ AL writes to MTL in New Hampshire that things are going fine in Washington and that her friend Gen. Abner Doubleday can expect a new assignment soon.

September 4, Friday

❖ AL declares that livestock may be exported from the Pacific Coast.

September 5, Saturday

❖ AL is told that the people of Northampton County are jubilant over his suspension of collections to cover damages to a lighthouse, seeing it as a victory over the government. He answers: "No dollar shall be refunded by my order, until it shall appear that my act in the case has been accepted in the right spirit."

September 6, Sunday

The Confederates evacuate Battery Wagner outside Charleston, South Carolina.

❖ AL writes to MTL in New Hampshire: "All well, and no news, except that Gen. Burnside has Knoxville, Tennessee."
❖ AL directs that the $4,000 collected for lighthouse repairs in Northampton County be held until further notice.

September 7, Monday

Advancing Union forces swing south around Chattanooga.

September 8, Tuesday

The Union invasion of Texas is defeated at Sabine Pass, Texas.

September 9, Wednesday

In Tennessee, Union forces take Chattanooga, as Confederate authorities decide to send a corps from Lee's army to spearhead a counterattack.

September 10, Thursday

Union forces take Little Rock, Arkansas.

❖ AL replies to a letter from a local restaurant owner who was fined for selling liquor to soldiers but insists he is innocent: "I cannot listen to a man's own story, unsupported by any evidence, who has been convicted of violating the law; because that would put an end to all law."

September 11, Friday

❖ AL directs Johnson to begin organizing a loyal civilian government in Tennessee.
❖ AL discusses the situation in Charleston, with Stanton, Fox, and Gen. Halleck.
❖ AL receives a report from Hamlin's son, commander of a black regiment in Louisiana, of the "difficulties and embarrassments" his unit deals with.

September 13, Sunday

❖ AL forwards to the examining physician the names of people who have supplied affidavits concerning the sanity of Dr. David Wright of Norfolk, Virginia, condemned for killing a commander of black troops. (AL let the sentence stand and Wright was executed October 23.)

September 14, Monday

❖ AL calls a Cabinet meeting to discuss the fact that certain judges are releasing drafted men on writs of habeas corpus.

September 15, Tuesday

❖ AL attends a Cabinet meeting where they decide that the only way to prevent courts from interfering with the draft is a presidential proclamation suspending habeas corpus in military cases. Seward prepares one and it is issued that afternoon.

❖ AL responds to a request by Gen. Meade that AL indicate the government's wishes: "My opinion is that he should move upon Lee at once in the manner of a general attack, leaving to developments whether he will make it a real attack. I think this would develop Lee's real condition and purposes better than the cavalry alone can do."

September 16, Wednesday

South of Chattanooga, the Union and Confederate armies make contact and begin concentrating.

September 17, Thursday

❖ AL asks for more information on the "misconduct of the people on the Eastern Shore of Virginia" (i.e., the lighthouse case in Northampton County).

September 18, Friday

❖ AL orders the discharge from the army, for ill health, of William "Duff" Armstrong, whom AL successfully defended (pro bono) against a murder charge in the so-called Almanac Case in 1858. (A witness testified that he saw the crime plainly under a full moon. AL showed that there was only a quarter moon that night.)
❖ AL pardons a soldier who deserted one unit to serve in another as a paid substitute. However, the soldier must return to his original unit and serve his original enlistment.
❖ AL urges Johnson to press ahead with recruiting, "allowing all the better trained soldiers to go forward to Rosecrans."

September 19, Saturday

Heavy fighting breaks out southeast of Chattanooga, along Chickamauga Creek.

- ❖ AL names Gen. Andrew Hamilton (an exiled Texas Unionist) military governor of Texas, although no part of Texas was occupied by the Union.
- ❖ AL tells Gen. Halleck to avoid attacking Richmond: "If our army cannot fall upon the enemy and hurt him where he is, it is plain to me it can gain nothing by attempting to follow him over a succession of entrenched lines into a fortified city."

September 20, Sunday

A botched Union maneuver at Chickamauga allows a Confederate breakthrough and half the Union army flees back to Chattanooga, with Gen. Rosecrans and two corps commanders. The other half mounts an epic defense and retires in good order that evening.

- ❖ AL express anxiety about yesterday's fighting.
- ❖ AL tells MTL, in New York, that he knows of no sickness in Washington and she can return home.

September 21, Monday

The defeated Union army under Gen. Rosecrans is besieged in Chattanooga.

- ❖ AL sends two separate messages to Gen. Burnside in Knoxville, Tennessee, urging him to try to send help to Gen. Rosecrans in Chattanooga, sixty miles away.
- ❖ AL tells Gen. Halleck that Gen. Rosecrans' army must remain in the Chattanooga, area, to keep the enemy out of most of Tennessee and break an important Confederate rail link.
- ❖ AL telegraphs Gen. Rosecrans: "Be of good cheer. We have unabated confidence in you, and in your soldiers and officers. In the main you must be the judge as to what is to be done."

September 22, Tuesday

❖ AL learns that his favorite brother-in-law (husband of a younger half-sister of MTL) Ben Hardin Helm was killed at Chickamauga. He had been a general in the Confederate army.

❖ AL attends a Cabinet meeting where they review the Battle of Chickamauga.

September 23, Wednesday

❖ AL forwards to Gen. Rosecrans at Chattanooga, a copy of the report sent by the Confederate commander at the Battle of Chickamauga to Richmond, noting that he claims to have captured fewer Union prisoners and guns than Rosecrans admits to losing.

❖ Stanton calls AL out of bed for a late-night Cabinet meeting at the War Department. They agree to send two corps from the Washington area to reinforce Chattanooga. The troops can get there by rail in seven days.

September 24, Thursday

❖ AL sends a summation of the Battle of Chickamauga to MTL, including confirmation of the death of her brother-in-law.

September 25, Friday

❖ AL writes a telegram to Gen. Burnside: "Yours of the 23rd is just received, and it makes me doubt whether I am awake or dreaming. I have been struggling for ten days, first through Gen. Halleck, and then directly, to get you to go to assist Gen. Rosecrans in an extremity, and you have repeatedly declared you would do it, and yet you steadily move the contrary way." He then does not send the telegram.

September 26, Saturday

❖ AL is angered, along with Stanton, by press reports of troop movements.

❖ AL confers with Bates about events in Missouri.

September 27, Sunday

❖ AL sends a telegram to Gen. Burnside in Knoxville: "Hold your present positions, and send Rosecrans what you can spare, in the quickest and safest way."

September 28, Monday

❖ AL confers with Seward and Welles about military events.

❖ MTL arrives at home with Tad.

September 29, Tuesday

❖ AL addresses a delegation of the Sons of Temperance in the White House, and praises their aims. (AL does not drink.)

❖ Chase notes that Seward and Stanton rarely attend Cabinet meetings and is considering following their example.

❖ A delegation from Missouri, unhappy about the success of Confederate guerrillas there, unsuccessfully asks AL to remove Gen. John Schofield, the department commander.

September 30, Wednesday

❖ AL sees his podiatrist.

OCTOBER 1863

Summary: The Union situation around Chattanooga improves after Gen. Grant is put in charge. In politics, everyone who comes to AL has a pet complaint—especially if they are from Missouri.

October 1, Thursday

- ❖ AL sends specific instructions to Gen. John Schofield, commander in Missouri: Promote military efficiency; suppress individuals and newspapers that injure the military; conduct mass expulsions at his discretion (as he was doing); neither return fugitive slaves nor entice them to escape; allow property confiscation only under orders; allow only those qualified under Missouri law to vote; expel the guerrillas.
- ❖ AL learns that his nephew, John Todd Grimsley, has failed to meet the Naval Academy entrance requirements. (He became a dry-goods merchant instead.)

October 3, Saturday

- ❖ AL proclaims that the last Thursday of November will be a day of thanksgiving.

October 4, Sunday

- ❖ AL tells Gen. Rosecrans, besieged in Chattanooga: "If we can hold Chattanooga, and East Tennessee, I think the rebellion must dwindle and die. I think you and Burnside can do this; and hence doing so is your main object."

October 5, Monday

❖ AL sends a formal answer to the Missouri delegation he saw last week, again refusing to dismiss Gen. John Schofield.

October 6, Tuesday

❖ AL watches Shakespeare's *Othello* at Grover's Theater, with his family and others.

October 7, Wednesday

❖ AL asks Johnson if he has any news from the Union army at Chattanooga. (He didn't. Confederate raiders had cut the telegraph connection.)

October 8, Thursday

❖ AL suspends the executions of two underage deserters.

October 10, Saturday

❖ AL receives British Minister Lord Lyons and three British naval officers.
❖ Gen. Meade reports that the Confederates appear to be moving in force toward the Shenandoah Valley and he is falling back as a precaution.

October 11, Sunday

❖ AL is introduced by Seward at the White House to Miss Charlotte Cushman, an actress who performed frequently for U.S. Sanitary Commission benefits.

October 12, Monday

❖ AL sends further encouragement to Gen. Rosecrans, besieged with dwindling supplies at Chattanooga: "You and

Burnside now have him by the throat, and he must break
your hold, or perish."

October 13, Tuesday

*Unionists win critical governor elections in Ohio and
Pennsylvania.*

❖ AL attends a Cabinet meeting and reads a dispatch from Gen.
Meade stating that if Lee does not attack, he will attack Lee.

October 14, Wednesday

❖ AL sends an apology to Thurlow Weed: "I have been
brought to fear recently that somehow, by commission or
omission, I have caused you some degree of pain." (Weed
explained that he had been misunderstood.)

October 15, Thursday

❖ AL telegraphs a pass to Mrs. Robert Todd (step-mother of
MTL) to bring her daughter, widow of Confederate Gen. Ben
Hardin Helm, north to Kentucky.
❖ AL writes to Stanton: "This lady, Abigail C. Berea, had a
husband and three sons in the war, and has been a nurse
herself, without pay, during nearly the whole war. Her
husband was killed at Gettysburg, and one of her sons also
has died in the service. One other son she is willing to leave
in the service where he still is, but the youngest...she asks to
have discharged. Let it be done."
❖ AL tabulates the political situation and decides that the next
presidential election will be close.

October 16, Friday

Gen. Grant is put in charge of most troops in the west.

❖ AL writes to Gen. Halleck expressing the hope that Gen. Meade will attack Lee: "The honor will be his if he succeeds, and the blame may be mine if he fails."

❖ AL receives a favorable report on the experimental gunpowder invented by Capt. Isaac R. Diller. (There is no further record of the project.)

October 17, Saturday

❖ AL issues a proclamation calling for another 300,000 volunteers, to serve three years or for the duration of the war.

❖ AL watches Shakespeare's *Macbeth* at Grover's Theater, with MTL, Tad, and others.

October 18, Sunday

❖ AL receives a report from Hay concerning public opinion in the West.

October 19, Monday

In Chattanooga, Gen. Rosecrans is replaced with Gen. George Thomas.

❖ AL responds to a letter from Missouri Gov. Hamilton Gamble demanding that AL have Gen. John Schofield "maintain the integrity of the state government" against incipient violence, asking what violence Gamble is talking about.

October 20, Tuesday

❖ AL confers with Thomas Durant, promoter for the Union Pacific Railroad, about construction plans.

❖ Gen. Dan Sickles meets with AL about his real estate dispute in California.

October 21, Wednesday

❖ AL hears from a delegation from St. Mary's County, Maryland, complaining that black troops on the Patuxent River are causing "disturbances." (AL is later informed that the troops are under discipline, but the locals are "rabid secessionists" who have killed a white officer, and he should pay no attention to them.)

October 22, Thursday

❖ AL tells the military authorities it might be better to withdraw black troops from the Patuxent River, and send white men in to do recruiting, rather than risk homicides.

October 23, Friday

Gen. Grant arrives in Chattanooga.

❖ AL consults with Gen. Robert Schenck about the situation in Maryland, especially along the Patuxent River.

October 24, Saturday

❖ Responding to a (false) report that another of Lee's corps has been sent to Tennessee, AL writes to the Gen. Halleck urging that the Army of the Potomac attack Lee (now presumably weakened) "with all possible expedition."
❖ AL consults with Chase about patronage in Maine.
❖ AL notes to Hay that reports from Gen. George Thomas display a different (presumably more positive) outlook than those of the Gen. Rosecrans.

October 25, Sunday

❖ In the afternoon, AL discusses possible plans for attacking Charleston, South Carolina.

October 26, Monday

❖ AL replies to a query from Illinois Rep. Elihu Washburne about AL running for reelection: "A second term would be a great honor and a great labor, which together, perhaps I would not decline, if tendered."

❖ AL approves court-martial findings against Capt. James Cutts Jr., brother of the second wife of the late senator Stephen A. Douglas, and reduces the sentence from dismissal to a reprimand, which AL apparently delivers in person: "No man resolved to make the most of himself can spare time for personal contention." (Cutts had been convicted with conduct unbecoming an officer, for quarreling and for eavesdropping. He returned to duty and received the Medal of Honor for gallantry during the Wilderness Campaign. In 1868 he was dismissed after another "conduct unbecoming" charge.)

❖ AL and Tad attend two comedies at the Grover Theater.

October 27, Tuesday

Through various maneuvers, the Union supply line is restored to Chattanooga.

❖ Upon reviewing the case file, AL agrees that court-martial proceedings are not warranted in the case of Gen. Robert Milroy, whose command was destroyed in June at Winchester, Virginia. (He had not been positively ordered to withdraw before he was cut off.)

October 28, Wednesday

❖ AL informs Gen. John Schofield in Missouri that he has received multiple complaints that the authorities in Missouri are "arming the disloyal, and disarming the loyal." (Schofield replied that reorganizing the militia would handle the problem.)

October 29, Thursday

❖ AL reminds certain individuals that they need to use specific forms to certify the election of congressmen.

October 30, Friday

❖ AL and MTL attends *Fanchon, the Cricket* at Ford's Theater.

October 31, Saturday

❖ AL continues warning congressmen-elect of the new credentialing requirements.

NOVEMBER 1863

Summary: *AL uses the dedication of the battlefield cemetery at Gettysburg to tie the outcome of the war to the fate of humanity. Soon thereafter, the resurgent Confederate position in Tennessee abruptly collapses.*

November 1, Sunday

- ❖ AL issues an order clarifying the intent of the draft law: Those who pay the $300 commutation fee or pay for a substitute have satisfied their military requirement and are credited to their states (against the draft quota) as if they had volunteered. Towns may also pay commutation fees, also earning credit against the quota.
- ❖ AL forwards news about Chattanooga to Seward, who is an Auburn, New York, due to the illness of his son.
- ❖ AL consults with various parties about upcoming elections in Maryland.

November 2, Monday

- ❖ AL receives a pro-forma invitation to attend the dedication of a new national cemetery in Gettysburg, and make "a few appropriate remarks." He accepts.
- ❖ AL confers with more officials about possible violence doing Maryland's election day, on Wednesday.

November 3, Tuesday

- ❖ AL inquires to Gen. Meade about a soldier who was supposed to be shot for desertion in three days.

❖ AL meets with William Evans, in English liberal studying American democracy.

November 4, Wednesday

A third of the Confederate force besieging Chattanooga is sent sixty miles up the Tennessee River in an unsuccessful attempt to retake Knoxville, Tennessee.

❖ AL oversees movers hauling nineteen loads of furniture from the Soldiers' Home to the White House as the Lincoln family moves back for the winter.

November 5, Thursday

❖ AL writes to Gen. Nathaniel Banks complaining that little has been done in the previous three months to establish a Unionist state government in Louisiana.
❖ AL receives a delegation from the African Civilization Society (a black organization promoting emigration to Liberia) which asks for $5,000.

November 7, Saturday

Union forces take Brownsville, Texas.

❖ AL spends the morning reviewing court-martial cases.
❖ Thurlow Weed presents AL with a plan concerning amnesty and reconstruction.

November 8, Sunday

❖ AL poses for photographs with Nicolay and Hay.

Private secretaries John Nicolay and John Hay were immortalized in this photo, posing with their boss.

November 9, Monday

Heavy snow falls in Virginia.

* AL meets with a delegation from New York headed by John Jacob Astor Jr. and Robert Roosevelt (uncle of Theodore Roosevelt) urging that AL allow Gen. John Dix to run for mayor of New York. (AL had no objection, but Dix declined for personal reasons.)
* AL, MTL, Hay, and others attend *The Marble Heart* at Ford's Theater. (John Wilkes Booth played the villain and appeared to be delivering threatening lines directly at AL.)

November 10, Tuesday

* AL allows the export of tobacco belonging to friendly foreign governments that was purchased before March 4, 1861. (Tobacco was a government monopoly in many countries.)
* AL telegraphs Gen. John Schofield in Missouri asking about a report that he has refused leaves of absence to military officers, preventing them from attending sessions of the state legislature. (Gen. Schofield said that regulations allowed him to grant leaves of absence only for sickness.)

November 12, Thursday

* AL arrives late and without MTL for the wedding of Chase's daughter, the beautiful and accomplished Kate Chase, to Rhode Island Sen. William Sprague. (MTL despised Miss Chase as a social rival.)

November 13, Friday

* AL meets with Pennsylvania Gov. Andrew Curtin about various issues.

November 14, Saturday

❖ AL again meets with Pennsylvania Gov. Andrew Curtin.

❖ Tad receives a pony.

November 15, Sunday

❖ AL poses for more photographs.

❖ Ward Hill Lamon publishes the program for the upcoming event at Gettysburg.

November 16, Monday

❖ AL meets with Connecticut Sen. Lafayette Foster, with visitors from Montreal, and with two Italian naval officers.

❖ AL telegraphs Gen. Burnside at Knoxville, Tennessee: "What is the news?" (Burnside replied that his soldiers were retreating slowly into their fortifications.)

November 17, Tuesday

❖ AL tells Stanton did he does not like the idea of a one-day trip to Gettysburg, calling it a "breathless running of the gauntlet." (They organized an overnight trip instead.)

❖ AL attends a Cabinet with the intention of discussing the Pennsylvania trip with Chase, but Chase does not attend. (Chase did not go to Pennsylvania, either)

❖ AL reviews a parade of the Invalid Corps.

November 18, Wednesday

❖ Tad is too ill to eat breakfast. MTL is hysterical about it.

❖ AL announces that until Congress convenes in December he will be unable to receive visitors.

❖ AL and his party leaves Washington at noon on a train with four cars. The party includes his valet, Nicolay, Hay, Seward, Usher, Blair, several foreign diplomats and visitors, a military guard, several military officers, and the Marine band.

- ❖ They arrive at Gettysburg, at 5 p.m. AL stays in the home of David Wills, who instigated the organization of the cemetery.
- ❖ AL receives a telegram from Stanton saying that Tad is better.
- ❖ Various groups serenade AL and he addresses the crowd briefly.

November 19, Thursday

- ❖ AL, in Gettysburg, has breakfast and then retires to his room in the Wills residence with Nicolay and finishes his speech.
- ❖ AL leaves the house at about 10 a.m. The weather is fine, but the procession organizes slowly and AL spends the time shaking hands.
- ❖ Pennsylvania Gov. Andrew Curtin approaches AL and remarks on the serenade given last night to New York Gov. Horatio Seymour, a famously obstructionist Democrat. Lincoln replies (presumably tongue in cheek): "He deserves it. No man has shown greater interest and promptness in his cooperation with us."
- ❖ With AL riding a chestnut horse, the procession starts to move at about 11 a.m. They take their seats by noon.
- ❖ Ceremonies open with a dirge and then a prayer.
- ❖ Edward Everett delivers a polished, technically perfect but emotionally sterile two-hour oration from memory, covering the cause and course of war, and the battle itself.
- ❖ There is a musical interlude.
- ❖ After being introduced by Ward Hill Lamon, AL rises to speak.
- ❖ There is a disturbance as people in the back push forward to hear.
- ❖ After calm is restored AL puts on his glasses and pulls out a sheet of paper, but then does not appear to read from it.
- ❖ AL speaks for about three minutes. He says that the nation must press on to ultimate victory to keep faith with those who have died in the struggle so far, and to validate democracy for the sake of humanity's future. With that validation, "government of the people, by the people, for the people, shall not perish from the earth."

Lincoln's Address at the Dedication of the Gettysburg National Cemetery, November 19, 1863.

A fictionalized depiction of Lincoln in Gettysburg. Actual photographs captured a confused crowd scene, with Lincoln barely discernable.

- ❖ "Lamon, that speech won't scour!" AL tells Lamon as he sits down, referring to the need for a plow to cut cleanly through the earth.
- ❖ A reporter leans forward and asks AL if that is all. AL answers: "Yes, for the present."
- ❖ After the ceremony he returns to the Wills residence for dinner, and shakes hands for an hour.
- ❖ AL is introduced to John Burns, a local resident and veteran of the War of 1812 who traded fire with the Confederates during the Battle of Gettysburg.
- ❖ Then AL goes with Seward and Brown to the local Presbyterian Church to hear a speech by the incoming lieutenant governor of Ohio.

❖ AL's train leaves at about 7 p.m. and arrives in Washington after 1 a.m.

November 20, Friday

AL returns from Gettysburg, with a case of varioloid (mild smallpox) which limits access to him for three weeks.

❖ AL directs Gen. Meade to suspend the execution of a lieutenant condemned for desertion. (AL had been approached by the man's wife who was in such distress that he was not able to get many details. The man's sentence was later commuted to imprisonment.)
❖ Edward Everett writes to AL: "I should be glad, if I could flatter myself that I came as near to the central idea of the occasion, in two hours, as you did in two minutes." (AL replied: "I am pleased to know that, in your judgment, the little I did say was not entirely a failure.")
❖ AL tells Michigan Sen. Zachariah Chandler: "I hope to 'stand firm' enough to not go backward, and yet not go forward fast enough to wreck the country's cause." (Chandler had urged him to ignore the conservatives and the radicals and stick to his own philosophy.)

November 21, Saturday

❖ AL, acknowledging his illness, quips: "Now I have something I can give everybody."
❖ AL confers about the next presidential election with Blair and others.

November 22, Sunday

❖ AL talks to Norman Judd, the U.S. minister to Prussia, who says he wants to return to private life. (He agreed to stay on.)
❖ Seward reads to AL reports from Cassius Clay, minister to Russia, on European diplomacy and naval developments.

November 23, Monday

- ❖ AL forwards to Seward reports from Gen. Burnside stating that Knoxville, Tennessee, can be held.
- ❖ Tad is still sick.

November 24, Tuesday

Union troops take Lookout Mountain, overlooking Chattanooga.

- ❖ AL confers with Seward about a warning received from Spain not to interfere in Santo Domingo.
- ❖ AL is relieved to hear that Knoxville, Tennessee, is still holding out.

November 25, Wednesday

Union troops sent to take the foot of Missionary Ridge outside Chattanooga instead charge over the ridge, and the rebels retreat thirty miles before they can regroup.

- ❖ AL sends congratulations to Gen. Grant concerning the events of Monday and Tuesday: "Well done. Many thanks to all. Remember Burnside."
- ❖ Despite expecting war news, AL retires early due to illness.

November 26, Thursday

The nation celebrates the first instance of Thanksgiving as an official Federal holiday.

- ❖ AL is mostly confined to his bed.
- ❖ Gen. Thomas Meagher of the Irish Brigade introduces AL to Irish writer Charles G. Halpine, who uses the pen name "Private Miles O'Reilly."

November 27, Friday

- ❖ AL is prohibited by his physician from receiving visitors.

November 28, Saturday

- ❖ AL is reported to be better.
- ❖ Tad is also reported to be better.
- ❖ AL receives a report on conditions at Libby Prison, Richmond, prepared by surgeons who were recently released from it.

November 29, Sunday

- ❖ AL is reported to have improved.

November 30, Monday

- ❖ AL resumes work on his message to Congress.

DECEMBER 1863

Summary: AL recovers sufficiently to interact with Congress when it convenes, as the battle fronts slow down for winter. AL gives an old friend a special Christmas gift, one day late.

December 1, Tuesday

❖ AL is reported to be "recovering from his indisposition."

December 3, Thursday

❖ AL remains sick.
❖ MTL arrives in New York.

December 4, Friday

❖ Though confined to his room, AL works on his message to Congress.
❖ AL telegraphs MTL in the New York that "all is going well."
❖ Responding to a petition from the governor of Kentucky, AL orders the release of a POW whose mother is described as "one of the most active Union ladies" in Fayette County, Kentucky.

December 5, Saturday

❖ AL telegraphs MTL in New York: "All doing well."

December 6, Sunday

Union relief forces reach Knoxville, Tennessee.

❖ AL confers with Indiana Rep. Schuyler Colfax, newly elected Speaker of the House, concerning a plot by the rabidly anti-emancipation clerk of the House of Representatives (former Tennessee congressman Emerson Etheridge) to give control of the body to the Democrats by excluding newly elected congressmen who do not have the latest election certificates. (The "coup" was easily thwarted when Border State congressmen voted with the Republicans to admit the new members.)

❖ AL again telegraphs MTL in New York: "All doing well."

December 7, Monday

Congress convenes.

❖ AL issues a press release announcing the Union victory in Tennessee.

❖ AL complains that the Confederate force that was besieging Knoxville is being allowed to escape. (The corps eventually retreated through the mountains into Virginia and rejoined Lee's army.)

❖ Having sent Tad a book from New York, MTL announces she will return tomorrow.

December 8, Tuesday

❖ AL delivers his report to Congress, noting improvements in many national affairs over the last year. While he anticipates the resumption of national authority in the rebelling areas, war power is still the main reliance of the government and the military must be the priority.

❖ AL issues his "Proclamation of Amnesty and Reconstruction." Rebels who take an oath to support the Constitution will be granted a full pardon, except for those in certain high positions or guilty of mistreating POWs. Rebellious states can be readmitted by following certain procedures.

❖ AL sends his "profoundest gratitude" to Gen. Grant.

December 9, Wednesday

❖ AL receives many visitors at the White House congratulating him on his message to Congress. Chase is notably absent.

December 11, Friday

❖ AL is reported to be able to work several hours a day.
❖ AL pardons Edward Gantt of Arkansas for treason. He had been a brigadier general in the Confederate army.

December 13, Sunday

❖ AL confides to Browning (who is no longer a senator) that Emily Todd Helm, half-sister of MTL and widow of a Confederate general, is at the White House.
❖ Gen. Dan Sickles and Gen. James Wadsworth call on AL in the evening and find him with Shakespearean actor James Hackett.

December 14, Monday

❖ AL issues a pardon (under the terms of Tuesday's proclamation) to Emily Todd Helm, who took an oath of allegiance.
❖ AL declines to see New York Rep. Fernando Wood, who is seeking amnesty for Confederate sympathizers in the North.
❖ AL, his family, and Fox attend Shakespeare's *Henry IV* at Ford's Theater.

December 15, Tuesday

❖ AL is able to attend a Cabinet meeting.
❖ AL confers with Dr. Thomas Cottman about establishing a state government in Louisiana.

December 16, Wednesday

❖ AL pardons Alfred Rubery, a young British subject who had been sentenced to ten years for fitting out a Confederate privateer in San Francisco. (Pro-American British parliamentarian John Bright had sought the pardon.)

❖ Informed that Gen. John Buford is dying, AL promotes him to major general. (Gen. Buford died of typhoid fever that afternoon after hearing the news. He had led the initial Union defense of Gettysburg.)

❖ AL relents and confers with New York Rep. Fernando Wood concerning amnesty for Confederate sympathizers in the North. (Wood assured AL that letting Vallandigham return from exile would produce two Democrat candidates in the next presidential election, splitting the opposition.)

December 17, Thursday

❖ The Supreme Court justices make their annual visit to the president.

❖ AL attends Shakespeare's *The Merry Wives of Windsor* at Ford's Theater, starring James Hackett as Falstaff.

December 18, Friday

❖ AL tells Stanton that Gen. John Schofield must be removed from command in Missouri as he has interfered with state politics there.

❖ In response to a Congressional resolution calling for one, AL asks Illinois Rep. Elihu Washburne to oversee the creation of a medal to present to Gen. Grant. (Grant was a constituent of Washburne, who had advocated for his promotion.)

❖ AL confers with a representative of Pennsylvania Gov. Alexander Curtin.

❖ AL attends a public lecture on conditions in Russia by diplomat and writer Bayard Taylor.

December 19, Saturday

❖ To mollify the Indiana congressional delegation, AL asks Gen. Grant to find an assignment for Gen. Robert Milroy, who has been unemployed since his debacle at the beginning of the Gettysburg Campaign. (Grant found him a job behind the lines.)

❖ AL and MTL host a reception at the White House for officers of Russian naval vessels wintering in U.S. waters.

❖ Seward reads AL a dispatch from Cassius Clay in Russia, denouncing French Emperor Napoleon III.

December 20, Sunday

❖ AL replies to Henry Wright of the Massachusetts Anti-Slavery Society, who asks him to write the sentence "I shall not attempt to retract or modify the Emancipation Proclamation; nor shall I return to slavery any person who is free by the terms of the proclamation or by any of the acts of Congress," on a piece of paper, sign it, and send it back. AL does.

December 21, Monday

❖ At the War Department, AL watches cryptanalysts read intercepted messages intended for the Confederate secretary of state.

❖ AL nominates Gen. John Schofield for promotion, to make his removal from Missouri less painful.

December 22, Tuesday

❖ AL attends a cabinet meeting attended by only Seward and Welles.

❖ At the request of fellow Illinois attorney, circuit court rider, and raconteur Usher Linder, AL directs that Usher's son, POW Daniel Linder, be sent to him at the White House. (In 1856 the younger Linder, then about 18, shot someone in a quarrel. His father was sick, so AL defended the youth pro bono, getting the charges dismissed. Daniel Linder thereafter moved to Kentucky and ended up in the Confederate army.)

❖ AL tells Welles to suppress further publication of a batch of intercepted correspondence between the Confederacy and its agents in Europe. (A nephew of Seward's was mentioned in the intercepts as being involved in blockade running, greatly upsetting Seward.)

December 23, Wednesday

❖ AL tells Hay about a dream he had: He is among plain people. One of them remarks: "He is a very common-looking man." AL replies in the dream: "Common-looking people are the best in the world. That is the reason the Lord makes so many of them."

❖ Approached in person by a deserter fearing arrest, AL gives him a pardon on condition he return to his unit and serve out his enlistment. (He is also given a rail pass to get there.)

❖ AL confers with various people about conditions in Missouri.

December 24, Thursday

❖ AL assures Gen. Nathaniel Banks that he is in charge of reconstruction in Louisiana and need not defer to anyone else. (Local officials held an unauthorized election while Banks was away taking Brownsville, Texas.)

December 25, Friday

❖ AL sends a suggestion to diplomat and writer Bayard Taylor that he prepare a lecture on "Serfs, Serfdom, and Emancipation in Russia." (Taylor replied, diplomatically, that he would try to get around to it but there was little resemblance between Russian serfdom and American slavery.)

December 26, Saturday

❖ Confederate POW Daniel Linder is brought before AL, who has him administered the oath of allegiance, freed, and sent to his father in Chicago.

❖ AL approves a court-martial for Army Surgeon General William Hammond. (He was later convicted of contract irregularities and dismissed. More than 10 years later the finding was reversed.)

December 27, Sunday

❖ AL, with Stanton, takes an overnight boat trip to the POW camp at Point Lookout, Maryland. (Apparently, they were interested in how many of the prisoners would be willing to join the Union. Of the 10,000 prisoners, maybe a 10th were willing.)

December 28, Monday

❖ AL, with Stanton, returns to Washington from their trip to Point Lookout.

December 29, Tuesday

❖ AL attends a Cabinet meeting without Seward, Chase, or Blair.

❧1864 ❧

JANUARY 1
THROUGH DECEMBER 31

JANUARY 1864

Summary: *Winter chills both military operations and the flow of office-seekers. AL hopes that his December 8 amnesty proclamation will trigger an outpouring of closet Unionists.*

January 1, Friday

❖ AL and MTL host the annual New Year's Day reception at the White House. Four black people attend, and AL greets them like the others.

January 2, Saturday

❖ AL sends Hay to the POW camp at Point Lookout, Maryland, with blank forms for those prisoners who want to take the oath of allegiance. Those who do, and want to join the Union army or have family within the Union lines, will be released.

❖ AL discusses events in Arkansas with Browning.

January 3, Sunday

❖ AL discusses possible replacements for Chief Justice Roger Taney with New York politician John Hall. (Taney, however, survived until October.)

January 5, Tuesday

❖ AL asks Congress to reconsider its ban on the payment of $300 bounties to veterans who reenlist, as it is more efficient to retain veterans than to train new recruits.

❖ AL attends a Cabinet meeting that is sparsely attended.

❖ MTL is in Philadelphia. AL telegraphs her: "All very well."

January 6, Wednesday

French troops take Guadalajara, Mexico.

❖ AL responds to a complaint from Kentucky Gov. Thomas Bramlette that troops raised specifically to protect Kentucky had been moved to Knoxville, Tennessee, presumably on the orders of Gen. Grant: "True, these troops are, in strict law, only to be removed by my order; but Gen. Grant's judgment would be the highest incentive to me to make such order."

January 7, Thursday

❖ AL commutes the death sentence of a deserter to imprisonment for the war, "not on any merit in the case, but because I am trying to evade the butchering business lately."

❖ AL telegraphs MTL in Philadelphia: "We are all well, and have not been otherwise."

January 8, Friday

❖ AL attends a Cabinet meeting attended by only Welles and Usher.

❖ Seward presents members of the National Academy of Sciences to AL.

January 9, Saturday

❖ AL declares two weeks of mourning for Caleb Smith, former Secretary of the Interior, who died Thursday.

❖ MTL resumes her Saturday receptions.

January 10, Sunday

❖ AL confers with Welles, Frances Blair Sr., and others concerning the upcoming presidential election, especially the possibility of a third-party run by Chase or by Gen. Frémont.

January 11, Monday

The 13th Amendment (abolishing slavery) is introduced in the Senate.

January 12, Tuesday

❖ AL, responding to a Senate resolution asking information concerning an accusation by Kansas Sen. James Lane that Kansas troops are invariably put to death when captured by the rebels, reports that there is no evidence that such is the case.

❖ The Cabinet meets with only three members.

❖ AL attends an evening reception at the White House.

January 13, Wednesday

❖ AL sends Hay to Florida to help form a Unionist state government there. (He found that the population of the Union-held areas had largely fled.)

❖ AL orders further trials of the Absterdam artillery projectile.

❖ AL writes to Gen. Nathaniel Banks urging him to expedite the creation of the Unionist state government in Louisiana.

January 14, Thursday

❖ AL frees two POWs. "Today Hon. [Kentucky Rep.] Brutus J. Clay calls with Mrs. Haggard, and asks that her son, Edward Haggard, now in his 19th year, and a prisoner of war at Camp Douglas [in Chicago] may be discharged. Let him take the oath [of allegiance] of December 8. and be discharged. Do the same for William H. Moore."

❖ The payment of veteran reenlistment bounties is extended to March 1.

January 15, Friday

❖ AL sends a judge to Tennessee to help administer loyalty oaths.

January 16, Saturday

- ❖ AL attends a lecture by twenty-one-year-old Anna Dickinson in the House chamber. (The abolitionist and women's rights advocate, who had campaigned for the Republicans, was described as a spellbinding orator.)
- ❖ MTL hosts an afternoon reception.
- ❖ AL writes to the editors of *The North American Review* saying an article in the January edition is wrong about one of his policies: "I have never had a theory that secession could absolve states or people from their obligations." (They print his response in the April edition.)

January 17, Sunday

- ❖ AL writes to Kentucky Gov. Thomas Bramlette, who is still upset that certain troops were moved from Kentucky to Tennessee, suggesting he confer with Gen. Grant.

January 18, Monday

- ❖ AL orders Gen. Butler to suspend certain financial regulations he has imposed in Union-occupied Norfolk, Virginia, and Portsmouth, Virginia, which disregard the authority of the Unionist Virginia state government. (Butler replied with a forty-page justification.)
- ❖ AL pardons another deserter who personally appealed to him for help, on condition he return to his unit and serve his enlistment.

January 19, Tuesday

- ❖ AL telegraphs RTL in Cambridge, Massachusetts: "There is a good deal of smallpox here. Your friends must judge for themselves whether they ought to come or not."
- ❖ Former Ohio congressman Joshua Giddings lobbies AL to get his son, a major, promoted to brigadier general in a black unit. (He got bumped up to lieutenant colonel instead.)

January 20, Wednesday

❖ AL forwards to Congress a report from former Indiana governor Joseph Wright concerning what he saw last year at the international agricultural exhibition in Hamburg, with a suggestion that Wright be reimbursed for his expenses. (Apparently, he never was.)

❖ AL orders Gen. Frederick Steele to organize an election for the Arkansas governor's office under the state's pre-war constitution.

January 21, Thursday

❖ AL forwards a report to the Senate by the minister to Chile describing the part Americans played in fighting the fire and rescuing victims when the Iglesia de la Compañía de Jesús in Santiago, Chile, burned on December 8, 1863. (The church doors only opened inward, trapping the fleeing congregants, and about 2,500 people died.)

❖ AL and MTL host a dinner for members of the Cabinet and the Supreme Court.

January 22, Friday

❖ AL announces that Gen. Frederick Steele will be both the military governor and the military commander of Arkansas, to avoid the conflict between the two offices that he has seen elsewhere.

❖ AL attends a Cabinet meeting.

January 23, Saturday

❖ AL signs a permit for two relatives of Kentucky Rep. Brutus Clay to put their pre-war plantations in Mississippi and Arkansas back under cultivation, as long as they use only non-slave labor.

❖ MTL hosts a reception that is well attended.

January 24, Sunday

❖ AL and MTL host a dinner party at the White House for a number of congressmen and military officers.

January 25, Monday

❖ AL works with Chase on new trade regulations.
❖ RTL is home for college vacation.
❖ AL, MTL, RTL, and guests hear opera singer Felicita Vestvali at Grover's Theater.

January 26, Tuesday

❖ AL suspends nine executions pending case reviews.
❖ About 8,000 people attend the evening reception at the White House.

January 27, Wednesday

❖ AL asks Gen. John Foster in Knoxville if newspaper stories about him trading messages with Pete Longstreet, a rebel general, are true. (They were. Longstreet had sent Foster a complaint about the circulation of handbills touting AL's amnesty proclamation, stressing "the propriety of communicating any views that your Government may have upon this subject through me, rather than by handbills." So Foster sent him a batch of the handbills.)
❖ AL confers with Browning and others about the Absterdam artillery projectile.

January 28, Thursday

❖ AL also asks Chase to appoint a friend of Gen. Nathaniel Banks' as a treasury agent.

January 29, Friday

- ❖ AL reports to the Senate that the Administration has asked Great Britain for permission to pursue hostile Sioux into Canada.
- ❖ AL attends a Cabinet meeting.

January 30, Saturday

- ❖ AL again writes to Gen. Frederick Steele with advice about setting up a Unionist state government in Arkansas.
- ❖ MTL hosts a Saturday reception.

January 31, Sunday

- ❖ AL answers a question from Gen. Nathaniel Banks in Louisiana regarding loyal people who wish to avoid taking the oath of allegiance: "You are at liberty to adopt any rule which shall admit to vote any unquestionably loyal free-state men and none others."

FEBRUARY 1864

Summary: *With the battle fronts quiet during winter, AL can pay more attention to politics—and discover that Chase is running against him. MTL begins to display unsettling behavior in public.*

February 1, Monday

- ❖ AL orders the draft of an additional 500,000 men to take place on March 10. They will serve for three years or for the duration of the war.
- ❖ AL orders a ship sent to the Ile à Vache (Cow Island) off the southern coast of Haiti to rescue members of the failed freedmen's colony there.
- ❖ Having waited five hours to see AL, Col. Ulric Dahlgren (son of AL's friend Admiral Dahlgren) talks to AL about personal and military matters while AL is being shaved.

February 2, Tuesday

- ❖ AL attends a Cabinet meeting, with no recorded outcome.
- ❖ AL and MTL attend the second anniversary meeting of the U.S. Christian Commission, held in the House chamber.

February 3, Wednesday

- ❖ AL authorizes the use of government property in Springfield, IL, for a soldiers' home. (The locals erect a lounge and sleeping rooms for furloughed soldiers.)
- ❖ AL observes trials of the Absterdam artillery projectile at the Washington arsenal.

February 4, Thursday

- ❖ AL sends Edward Everett a copy of the "remarks" he made at Gettysburg, to be sold for charity. (This is now known as the Everett Copy of the Gettysburg Address.)
- ❖ AL sends the Senate copies of correspondence between the Union and rebel authorities concerning the exchange of prisoners of war. (The exchange cartel had broken down over the issue of black POWs.)
- ❖ AL hosts a state dinner for foreign diplomats.

February 5, Friday

- ❖ AL and Tad attend another performance by opera singer Felicita Vestvali at Grover's Theater.

February 6, Saturday

French troops take Zacatecas, Mexico.

- ❖ AL visits the sickbed of Illinois Rep. Owen Lovejoy. AL tells him: "This war is eating my life out. I have a strong impression that I shall not live to see the end." (Lovejoy died six weeks later.)
- ❖ MTL hosts a Saturday reception.
- ❖ During the reception, AL discusses with artist Francis Carpenter ideas for portraying the first reading of the Emancipation Proclamation. (AL allowed him to live in the White House while working on the painting, which now hangs in the U.S. Capitol.)

February 7, Sunday

- ❖ AL endorses the release from prison of a "Union man" who had been drafted by the Confederates.

February 8, Monday

❖ AL assures Arkansas Gov. Isaac Murphy that the army will support his state election plans.

❖ AL, MTL, and others attend *The Sea of Ice* starring British actress Laura Keene at the Washington Theater.

February 9, Tuesday

❖ AL poses for photographs. (One of them was later used as the basis for the five-dollar bill.)

❖ RTL is among the attendees at the Tuesday evening reception.

February 10, Wednesday

❖ AL spends the morning on court-martial cases.

❖ AL discusses a possible anti-slavery constitutional amendment with a delegation from Pennsylvania.

❖ The White House stables catch fire after 8 p.m. Six animals die, two belonging to AL, two belonging to Nicolay, and two belonging to Tad. AL is seen to weep over the loss.

February 11, Thursday

❖ AL asks Congress to appropriate $800,000 to cover the expenses that the Pennsylvania militia incurred during the Gettysburg Campaign. (Congress took more than two years to do it.)

❖ AL confers with the local building commissioner concerning the replacement of the White House stables.

❖ AL tells Stanton that he cannot take over churches in loyal states, or churches with loyal congregations in rebel areas.

February 12, Friday

❖ AL expresses concern to Chase about the management of the New York customs house, as the designated collector (Hiram

Barney) does not seem to be running the place. AL suggests making Barney minister to Portugal.

❖ AL attends a Cabinet meeting with no recorded outcome.

February 13, Saturday

❖ AL consults with Bates about the upcoming presidential election.
❖ Congress appropriates $12,000 to replace the White House stables.
❖ MTL hosts a Saturday afternoon reception. AL attends but is not well.

February 15, Monday

❖ AL sends Gen. Dan Sickles (now able to walk again) on a tour of inspection down the Mississippi and along the coast to inquire about progress toward reconstruction, reactions to the amnesty offer, conditions of the black population, etc.
❖ AL confers about court-martial cases.
❖ MTL, RTL, and his friends attend an amateur performance of "tableaux" at Willard's Hotel benefiting the U.S. Sanitary Commission.

February 16, Tuesday

❖ AL forwards to the House documents concerning the arrest of the U.S. consul to Montreal on bogus charges brought by a Southern sympathizer.
❖ AL attends a Cabinet meeting with no recorded outcome.

February 17, Wednesday

Off Charleston, South Carolina, a Union warship is sunk by a hand-cranked Confederate submarine (which also sinks).

❖ AL instructs Gen. Fredericks Steele to set an election day for Arkansas.

February 18, Thursday

❖ AL assures the governor of Massachusetts that the Federal Government is not trying to prevent him from recruiting blacks in Virginia for Massachusetts regiments, although the governor of (Union-controlled) Virginia doesn't like it.

February 19, Friday

❖ AL attends a Cabinet meeting that is interrupted by "a fair, plump lady" from Dubuque, Iowa, who merely wants to see AL.

❖ AL and his family host a reception for a delegation of show business midgets.

❖ AL and family attend performances by Edwin Booth at Grover's Theater.

February 20, Saturday

❖ MTL hosts her afternoon reception, which AL attends.

February 22, Monday

❖ AL signs legislation reviving the rank of three-star lieutenant general, and nominating Gen. Grant to fill the slot.

❖ AL confers with Bates about Missouri politics.

❖ AL gives an impromptu speech at a charity benefit at the Patent Office building. MTL complains bitterly to him when he is done, saying it was the worst speech she had ever heard in her life.

February 23, Tuesday

❖ AL responds to a letter from Chase claiming he knows nothing about a circular produced by Kansas Sen. Samuel Pomeroy calling for the Republican Party to drop AL and replace him with Chase in the upcoming presidential election. (He admits that Pomeroy's people did contact him and he did let them use his name.): "I will answer a little more fully when I can find the leisure to do so."

❖ AL confers with Hugh McCulloch, comptroller of currency, on financial matters.

❖ The Tuesday evening reception is well attended. AL chats with two black army surgeons who attend.

February 24, Wednesday

❖ AL issues a pass to Simon Cameron to visit Fortress Monroe.

❖ AL meets with a political delegation from New York.

February 25, Thursday

❖ AL interviews J. F. Bailey about the organization of the New York customs house.

❖ AL telegraphs Gen. Frederick Steele in Arkansas: "General Sickles is not going to Arkansas.... He will not meddle in your affairs."

❖ AL and MTL attend Grover's Theater to see Edwin Booth in John Howard Payne's *Brutus*.

February 26, Friday

❖ AL orders that the sentences of all condemned deserters are to be commuted to imprisonment for the course of the war. Commanders are authorized to restore sentenced deserters to duty if it would benefit the service.

❖ AL attends a Cabinet meeting where they discuss politics.

❖ AL again sees Edwin Booth perform at Grover's Theater.

February 27, Saturday

❖ MTL's Saturday afternoon reception is well attended.

February 28, Sunday

❖ AL tells Gen. Lorenzo Thomas to take over the leasing of abandoned plantations along the Mississippi. (Gen. Thomas had complained that the Treasury Department would not be able to hire labor under the terms it was offering.)

February 29, Monday

❖ Responding to Chase's claim that he had nothing to do with the "Pomeroy Circular," AL says that neither he nor Chase should be "held responsible for what our respective friends may do."

MARCH 1864

Summary: *As the weather warms up so do the battle fronts — leading to a tragedy in AL's circle. On the political front, Chase is caught intriguing.*

March 1, Tuesday

> *A large Federal cavalry raid reaches the defenses of Richmond, stalls, and retreats.*

❖ AL nominates Gen. Grant for the newly created rank of lieutenant general.
❖ AL orders Stanton to allow a soldier (who had been previously punished by having his pay withheld) to reenlist for a new term so that his widowed mother can have some income. (Stanton complied.)
❖ AL attends a Cabinet meeting.
❖ AL and MTL host an evening reception at the White House for congressmen and their wives.

March 2, Wednesday

> *Col. Ulric Dahlgren (son of AL's friend Admiral John Dahlgren) is killed during the retreat of the cavalry raid from Richmond. Papers (possibly bogus) surface indicating he planned to assassinate Confederate leaders.*

❖ AL confers with a delegation from Toledo, Ohio, about the appointment of a postmaster there.
❖ AL confers about affairs in Kansas.
❖ While sitting for painter Francis Carpenter, AL recites passages from Shakespeare.

❖ AL and family members see Shakespeare's *Hamlet* starring Edwin Booth at Grover's Theater.

March 3, Thursday

❖ AL confers with the Joint Committee on the Conduct of the War, which is pushing for a new commander for the Army of the Potomac.
❖ AL approves an address by Gen. Frederick Steele to the people of Arkansas calling for the restoration of civil government through the election process.

March 4, Friday

❖ AL meets with his friend, Admiral John Dahlgren, about what is known so far about the fate of his son, Col. Ulric Dahlgren. (At that point he was only known to be missing.)
❖ AL attends a Cabinet meeting without Chase or Blair. Seward and Stanton think Chase's situation is amusing.
❖ AL and family attend Grover's Theater to see Edwin Booth in Edward Bulwer-Lytton's *Richelieu*.

March 5, Saturday

❖ MTL hosts her usual Saturday-afternoon reception.

March 6, Sunday

❖ AL attends church.
❖ AL and Stanton call on Admiral John Dahlgren with (false) news that his son, Col. Ulric Dahlgren, is alive.

March 7, Monday

❖ AL allows a specific amount of tobacco owned by the French government to be exported from rebel territory.

❖ AL confers with Missouri Gov. Willard Hall on conditions in Missouri.

❖ Richmond papers have announced the death of Col. Ulric Dahlgren. AL asks Gen. Butler at Fortress Monroe to get more information.

❖ AL see Edwin Booth in *The Fool's Revenge* at Grover's Theater.

March 8, Tuesday

❖ AL meets Gen. Grant for the first time when he shows up during the Tuesday evening public reception.

❖ AL learns that the recent New Hampshire election greatly favored the Union ticket.

March 9, Wednesday

❖ AL presents a lieutenant general's commission to Gen. Grant at a cabinet meeting. AL and Grant read short statements and then discuss military affairs.

❖ AL receives a copy of a letter by Chase withdrawing from the presidential race.

❖ AL proclaims a new eastern terminus for the Union Pacific transcontinental railroad in accordance with the latest surveys.

March 10, Thursday

❖ AL officially puts Gen. Grant in charge of the armies of the United States.

❖ George Ramsay reports to AL that the parties supplying the experimental Absterdam artillery projectiles want to charge excessive prices and there appears to be a patent dispute. AL tells him to proceed if he can get a good price. (AL was not thereafter involved in the project. The vendor did get a contract, but then got embroiled in quality assurance issues.)

March 11, Friday

* AL attends a Cabinet meeting that is interrupted by Gen. Grant informing AL that he is leaving for Nashville, Tennessee.

March 12, Saturday

Gen. Nathanial Banks launches an offensive up the Red River into the heart of Louisiana.

* AL forwards to the Senate Usher's report on freedman colonization efforts. (No copy of this report has survived.)
* MTL hosts the regular Saturday-afternoon reception. AL attends.
* AL holds a party for about fifteen military officers. Gen. Grant was invited but has left town.

March 13, Sunday

* AL writes to Gov. Michael Hahn and congratulates him on his recent election to head the reconstructed state government in Union-occupied Louisiana. He advocates that the upcoming state constitutional convention consider giving the vote to "some of the colored people," especially veterans and the "very intelligent."
* AL meets again with a Shakespearean actor James Hackett.
* AL informs Gen. Carl Schurz that he needs to resign from the army if he is going to participate in politics, but getting back into the army thereafter as a general could be difficult.

March 14, Monday

* AL orders an additional draft of 200,000 men, to meet the needs of the navy and to form a reserve over and above the 500,000 drafts ordered February 1.
* AL meets with Pennsylvania Gov. Alexander Curtin.

March 15, Tuesday

- ❖ AL assigns Louisiana reconstruction Gov. Michael Hahn with all powers previously vested in the state's military governor.
- ❖ AL attends a Cabinet meeting where they talk about yesterday's draft proclamation.
- ❖ AL calls Stanton's attention to the "gallant drummer boy" Robert Hendershot, who was cited for meritorious service in the Fredericksburg Campaign when he was only twelve years old, and asks Stanton to find a "situation suitable to him." (Hendershot, who had been given a disability discharge for epilepsy, had become an attraction of Barnum's Museum in New York. AL probably meant for Stanton to get the boy a job as a government messenger. He later enlisted in the navy.)
- ❖ AL endorses the army's takeover of St. Paul's Church in New Orleans: "If the building is needed for military purposes, take it; if it is not so needed, let its church people have it."

March 16, Wednesday

Union forces reach Alexandria, Louisiana, on the Red River.

- ❖ AL asks Arkansas reconstruction government Gov. Isaac Murphy, "What of your election on the 14th?" (It was actually held that day, resulting in a pro-Union state constitution with abolition.)

March 17, Thursday

- ❖ AL tells Gen. Butler, commander of Fortress Monroe, to inform him immediately if he's able to obtain the remains of Col. Ulric Dahlgren. (Gen. Butler did later retrieve the remains, albeit at the risk of exposing the Union spy network in Richmond.)

❖ AL writes to Maryland Rep James Criswell: "It needs not be a secret, that I wish success to emancipation in Maryland." (A convention was then rewriting the Maryland constitution and the resulting document did end slavery in the state.)

March 18, Friday

❖ AL attends a Cabinet meeting where they discuss emigration law.
❖ AL and MTL attend the closing of the Christian Commission benefit fair at the capacious Patent Office Building.
❖ AL tells Stanton that he would be happy to see the release of POWs who were willing to take the oath of allegiance and whose families are within Union lines.
❖ AL endorses the application of an old acquaintance, Benjamin Watson, to be a camp sutler.

March 19, Saturday

❖ AL lists sixteen Indian prisoners who are to be released.
❖ MTL hosts her Saturday-afternoon reception. AL attends.

March 21, Monday

Washington suffers a snow storm.

❖ AL proclaims the admission of Nevada into the union.
❖ AL refers to Blair two young ladies who "want employment."

March 22, Tuesday

❖ AL attends a Cabinet meeting.
❖ Attendance at the Tuesday evening reception is good despite the weather.

- ❖ AL writes in an autograph album: "I never knew a man who wished to be himself a slave. Consider if you know any good thing, that no man desires for himself."

March 23, Wednesday

- ❖ AL again tells Gen. Carl Schurz that he cannot be a politician and a general: "Speaking in the North, and fighting in the South, at the same time, are not possible."
- ❖ AL sends Ohio Rep. Robert Schenck an apology concerning some (unspecified) slight at last night's reception. (Schenck replied that he had not noticed it until he got the apology.)
- ❖ Ohio Sen. Benjamin Wade and Michigan Sen. Zechariah Chandler call on AL demanding the removal of Gen. Meade.

March 24, Thursday

- ❖ AL confers with Hay about the political situation in Florida.
- ❖ In response to a Senate resolution, AL forwards a report from Seward concerning the establishment of monarchical governments in Central and South America. (Seward reported that, rumors aside, no one was trying to do it. Events in Mexico, where it was really happening, were a separate concern.)
- ❖ Gen. Grant returns to the White House and has a meeting with AL.

March 25, Friday

- ❖ AL attends a Cabinet meeting where Welles complains about the scarcity of seamen and suggests transferring 12,000 men from the army.
- ❖ AL is in his study all evening and sits for painter Francis Carpenter while discussing and reciting Shakespeare.
- ❖ AL writes to Benjamin French, commissioner of public works, about a bill before Congress that would enlarge French's office and remove it from the Department of the

Interior. AL tells French that if the bill does pass, "I do not think I can allow you to retain the office; because that would be encouraging officers to be constantly intriguing, to the detriment of the public interest, in order to profit themselves." (French replied that he had not been intriguing and AL did not know the full story.)

❖ AL writes to Thurlow Weed asking if it is true that Weed is hurt because one of his suggestions. (Thurlow responded, through a third party, that he was more concerned about the quarrelsomeness of the Cabinet.)

March 26, Saturday

❖ AL issues a proclamation highlighting cases entitled to the benefit of the December 8 Amnesty Proclamation. (It applies to those "at large" who come forward voluntarily.)

❖ AL discusses black enlistment in Kentucky with Kentucky Gov. Thomas Bramlette and others.

❖ AL confers with Welles about transferring men from the army to the navy.

❖ Nicolay, representing AL, goes to New York to confer with Thurlow Weed concerning political questions.

March 27, Sunday

❖ AL has an evening conference with Gen. Grant, Gen. Halleck, and Stanton.

March 28, Monday

Rioting Copperheads attack Federal troops on leave in Charleston, Illinois, leaving nine dead and twelve wounded.

❖ AL is disturbed in his office by an intruder who calls himself Francis Xavier and who tries to convince AL that he (Xavier) was elected president in 1856.

March 29, Tuesday

❖ AL is introduced by Welles to a group of navy admirals and construction officials.

❖ AL writes to Gen. Grant suggesting he assign a certain captain (a friend of a senator's wife) to his staff. Grant demurs.

❖ AL tells Gen. Meade that there is no point of having a court of inquiry about the source of recent negative press concerning his performance at Gettysburg. (Meade was convinced that Gen. Dan Sickles was behind it.)

March 30, Wednesday

❖ AL receives Nicolay's political reports from New York.

March 31, Thursday

❖ AL, after meeting with a colonel who had been dismissed from the service more than a year earlier but wants back in, writes: "Today I verbally told Colonel [Thomas] Worthington that I did not think him fit for a colonel; and now, upon his urgent request, I put it in writing." (After the Battle of Shiloh Worthington, who had commanded a regiment there, started feuding with Gen. Sherman, and his intemperate statements got him thrown out of the army.)

APRIL 1864

Summary: AL has time to spend on politics as the military fronts largely remain quiet—for the moment.

April 1, Friday

- ❖ AL attends a Cabinet meeting.
- ❖ Iowa Sen. James Harlan lobbies AL to get Col. Edward Hatch nominated for promotion to brigadier general. (He does get the promotion.)

April 2, Saturday

- ❖ AL forbids the exportation of salted provisions except through ports bordering the Pacific Ocean. (Salted meat was a military resource.)
- ❖ AL, MTL, and Mrs. Grant see Charles Gounod's *Faust* at Grover's Theater.

April 3, Sunday

- ❖ Browning calls on AL, seeking the release of a POW.

April 4, Monday

- ❖ AL discusses the situation in Mexico with Seward as Congress passes a resolution opposing the establishment of a monarchy there. Officially, the Administration has supported neither side in Mexico.
- ❖ AL is introduced to Gen. Philip Sheridan, who is the new cavalry commander of the Army of the Potomac.
- ❖ In an open letter, AL repeats some comments he made to a delegation from Kentucky on March 26: "If slavery is not

wrong, nothing is wrong…. And yet I have never understood that the presidency conferred upon me an unrestricted right to act officially upon this judgment…. [After the Border States rejected compensated emancipation] I was, in my best judgment, driven to the alternative of either surrendering the Union, and with it, the Constitution, or of laying strong hand upon the colored element. I chose the latter…. [The result is] a gain of quite 130,000 soldiers, seamen, and laborers…. I claim not to have controlled events, but confess plainly that events have controlled me."

❖ AL writes to Gen. Rosecrans in Missouri: "It is said, I know not whether truly, that in some parts of Missouri, assassinations are systematically committed upon returned rebels….Again, it is complained that the enlistment of negroes is not conducted in as orderly a manner, and with as little collateral provocation, as it might be."

❖ AL and MTL attend Grover's Theater to see Carl von Weber's *The Marksman*, an opera with spoken dialogue.

April 5, Tuesday

❖ AL calls off the regular Tuesday evening reception due to bad weather.

❖ AL writes to the widow of education pioneer Horace Mann, who forwarded a petition signed by 195 young people asking AL to "free all slave children." He replies: "…I have not the power to grant all they ask, I trust they will remember that God has, and that, as it seems, He wills to do it."

❖ AL and MTL see the comic opera *Martha* by Friedrich von Flotow at Grover's Theater.

April 6, Wednesday

❖ AL attends a night meeting of the House of Representatives to hear a speech by English parliamentarian and antislavery orator George Thompson.

April 7, Thursday

Gen. Nathaniel Banks is defeated while advancing toward Shreveport, Louisiana.

❖ AL has a personal meeting with British antislavery orator George Thompson.

April 8, Friday

The Confederate force that defeated Gen. Nathaniel Banks' force yesterday is itself defeated. But the Union force continues retreating downriver, aborting of the only Union offensive then underway.

❖ AL approves legislation authorizing the Columbia Institution for the Deaf and Dumb and Blind (modern Gallaudet University) to confer degrees.
❖ AL attends a Cabinet meeting, with no recorded outcome.
❖ AL, MTL, Seward, and others see Shakespeare's *King Lear* at Ford's Theater.

April 9, Saturday

❖ AL confers with Massachusetts Sen. Charles Sumner.
❖ MTL hosts the last Saturday reception of the season.

April 11, Monday

❖ AL endorses the renewal of a military pass for ten-year-old John Ehler, who was not able to use his original pass to visit a relative in the Army of the Potomac due to problems with a bridge.

April 12, Tuesday

Confederate raiders overrun Fort Pillow, Tennessee. About half the garrison was black, and many do not survive. Whether they died during or after the fighting is disputed.

- ❖ AL attends a Cabinet meeting where they discuss the national debt and the exportation of French-owned tobacco.
- ❖ A Washington city council delegation complains to AL about excessive draft quotas for the District of Columbia.

April 14, Thursday

- ❖ AL reviews sixty-seven court-martial cases.
- ❖ AL confers with Henry Lea, a Philadelphia Unionist pamphleteer.

April 15, Friday

- ❖ AL attends a Cabinet meeting where Chase, Stanton, and Blair are absent.

April 16, Saturday

- ❖ AL is described as "indisposed."
- ❖ AL agrees to certain adjustments for Philadelphia's draft quota.
- ❖ Indian Territory is added to the Military Department of Arkansas.

April 17, Sunday

Gen. Grant officially ends the prisoner exchange program.

April 18, Monday

- ❖ AL meets with a delegation of Chippewa chiefs and gives them a tour of the White House.
- ❖ AL commutes the death sentences of twenty prisoners to imprisonment at Dry Tortugas.
- ❖ AL goes to Baltimore for the opening of the Maryland Sanitary Commission Fair and makes a short speech calling

for restraint concerning Fort Pillow, as the matter must be fully investigated.

April 19, Tuesday

- ❖ AL returns in the morning from Baltimore.
- ❖ The Cabinet meets, but AL does not attend.
- ❖ AL rests before the Tuesday-evening reception, the last of the season. It is heavily attended.

April 20, Wednesday

Supported by an ironclad, the rebels retake Plymouth, North Carolina.

- ❖ AL confers with Gen. Grant.
- ❖ AL poses in his office for photographs requested by painter Francis Carpenter.
- ❖ AL confers with Pennsylvania Rep. Joseph Bailey, Ohio Lt. Gov. Thomas Ford, and others.

April 21, Thursday

- ❖ AL reviews seventy-two court-martial cases.
- ❖ AL authorizes Gen. Meade to commute court-martial sentences according to his own judgment.
- ❖ AL confers about enlistments with the governors of Ohio, Indiana, Illinois, and Iowa, and they meet again in the evening with Stanton and Gen. Halleck.

April 22, Friday

- ❖ AL signs legislation placing the inscription, "In God We Trust" on coins.
- ❖ AL attends a Cabinet meeting where Seward, Chase, and Stanton are absent.

April 23, Saturday

- ❖ AL allows Missouri Rep. Francis Blair Jr. to return to the army as a general.
- ❖ AL accepts an offer from the governors of Ohio, Indiana, Illinois, Iowa, and Wisconsin to raise a total of 85,000 militiamen to serve one hundred days during the upcoming spring campaign. (Gen. Grant accepted the idea only if they did not count against three-year draftees.)
- ❖ AL asks Gen. Rosecrans can allow "Mrs. Ward," who has been banned from St. Louis, to return to her home. (Rosecrans declined, saying she should not even have been allowed into Washington where she made her appeal to AL.)

April 24, Sunday

- ❖ AL loafs with Hay while reading a Richmond newspaper.
- ❖ AL consults with Gen. Butler concerning the upcoming spring offensive.

April 25, Monday

- ❖ AL directs that mental health specialist Dr. John Gray go to Elmira, New York, to examine a private who has been condemned for murder and "make [his] own conclusions" regarding his sanity.
- ❖ AL reviews Gen. Burnside's troops as they leave for Annapolis, Maryland.
- ❖ Pennsylvania Gov. Alexander Curtin visits AL in the evening and discusses Francis Carpenter's painting with him.

April 26, Tuesday

Retreating Union forces on the Red River begin concentrating at Alexandria, Louisiana, where the gunboats are blocked by low water.

- ❖ AL reviews another fifty-one court-martial cases.

- ❖ AL attends a Cabinet meeting where Chase, Stanton, and Blair are absent.
- ❖ Photographers from Mathew Brady's studio take stereoscopic views of AL in his office.

In this first-ever White House photo-op, Lincoln is captured in his study. (Credit: Public Domain)

April 27, Wednesday

- ❖ AL reviews another thirty-six court-martial cases.
- ❖ AL endorses a request to promote Herman Huidekoper, whose brother, an acquaintance of AL, lost an arm at Gettysburg. (He was made commander of a black regiment.)
- ❖ AL confers with former Ohio congressman Albert Riddle, who is being sent as U.S. consul to Mantazas, Cuba.
- ❖ AL congratulates Arkansas Gov. Isaac Murphy on the successful formation of a new pro-Union state government.

April 28, Thursday

- ❖ AL tells the House that both Robert Schenck and Francis Blair Jr. had special permission to resign from the army to serve in Congress.
- ❖ On the personal appeal of a deserter, AL pardons him on condition that he return to his unit and serve his enlistment. (This was the third such recorded case.)
- ❖ AL sends an appeal the Congress to do something for the loyal people of eastern Tennessee, especially building a direct rail link between Knoxville and Cincinnati by way of central Kentucky. (Congress never acts on the suggestion.)
- ❖ MTL arrives in New York with Tad. AL sends her fifty dollars and sends assurances to Tad that his goats are fine.

April 29, Friday

- ❖ AL spends part of the evening at the War Department.

April 30, Saturday

- ❖ AL pardons twenty-five Sioux Indians who have been imprisoned since November 1862.
- ❖ AL meets women's-rights advocate Elizabeth Cady Stanton.
- ❖ AL writes to Gen. Grant to express his "entire satisfaction with what you have done up to this time."

MAY 1864

Summary: Finally using their numerical advantage, Union forces launch sustained offensives of unprecedented violence in Virginia and Georgia. But the rebels match every move.

May 1, Sunday

- ❖ AL goes for an afternoon drive with Michigan Rep. Francis Kellogg and Michigan Gov. Austin Blair.

May 2, Monday

- ❖ AL advises Gen. Stephen Hurlbut to not demand a court of inquiry at this time into why he was replaced, as it would "divert" his superiors. (Gen. Sherman had replaced Hurlbut for "timidity.")
- ❖ AL forwards to the House documents concerning the military status of Gen. Francis Blair Jr. (He was allowed to resign and then later was reinstated.)

May 3, Tuesday

- ❖ AL asks each Cabinet for a written opinion on what course to take regarding Fort Pillow.
- ❖ AL sends Lucius Chittenden to Annapolis, Maryland, to investigate the condition of exchanged POWs arriving there.

May 4, Wednesday

In Virginia, the Army of the Potomac sorties south across the Rapidan River, beginning the long-awaited Union spring offensive.

❖ AL asks Gen. Sherman at Chattanooga, to do anything he can consistent with military operations to relieve the suffering of the Nashville, Tennessee, population. (Sherman replied that limited railroad freight capacity forced him to stop feeding civilians south of Nashville. "All who won't fight or work should go away and we offer them free transportation.")

❖ Lucius Chittenden reports that the exchanged prisoners he examined were in terrible condition.

May 5, Thursday

The Battle of the Wilderness begins north of Richmond. South of Richmond, Gen. Butler's army lands on the James River.

❖ AL authorizes the exportation of horses for the personal use of the Emperor of France and the Captain General of Cuba. (Exporting livestock had been banned as a war measure.)

May 6, Friday

Fighting rages in the Wilderness.

❖ AL attends a Cabinet meeting where each member presents his position on the Fort Pillow incident.

❖ AL confers with Cornelius Agnew, surgeon general of New York, and diarist George Templeton Strong of the U.S. Sanitary Commission.

May 7, Saturday

In the Wilderness, forest fires force both armies to retreat. In Georgia, Gen. Sherman begins an offensive toward Atlanta.

❖ AL hears a report of the Battle of the Wilderness from *New York Tribune* reporter Henry Wing, who arrives from the front at 2 a.m. Wing repeats a message from Gen. Grant: "Whatever happens, there is to be no turning back." AL, delighted, kisses Wing on the forehead.
❖ The Marine band resumes playing Saturday concerts on the White House grounds.

May 8, Sunday

In Virginia, fighting resumes at Spotsylvania Court House, continuing for the next thirteen days.

❖ Indiana Rep. Schuyler Colfax visits AL and has the impression AL is telling stories to hide his anxiety and sadness about what is happening at the front.

May 9, Monday

In Virginia, a Union corps commander is killed by a rebel sniper. Last words: "They couldn't hit an elephant at this distance."

❖ AL learns of the failure of the Red River campaign.
❖ AL issues a press release: "Enough is known of Army operations within the last five days to claim our especial gratitude to God."
❖ Interpreting the news of the Union movement to Spotsylvania Court House as a victory, a boisterous crowd serenades AL at the White House.

May 10, Tuesday

❖ AL asks Gen. Lew Wallace in Baltimore why he told the rector of a church to take the oath of allegiance or leave town. (Gen. Wallace replied that the man was a closet secessionist and chose to leave town.)

❖ AL attends a Cabinet meeting and reads reports from the front.

May 11, Wednesday

On the Red River, trapped gunboats are freed by building a dam to raise the river level, breaking the dam, and letting the vessels wash downstream.

❖ AL spends time at the War Department waiting for reports from the front.

May 12, Thursday

In Virginia the fighting is so intense that large trees are cut down by rifle fire.

❖ AL meets with sixteen-year-old temperance lecturer Susannah Evans.

❖ AL urges the two Kansas senators (Samuel Pomeroy and James Lane) to stop feuding over a patronage issues. "It gives you the means of tormenting my life out of me, and nothing else."

May 13, Friday

On the Red River, the Federals complete their retreat, effectively taking a Union field army out of play.

❖ AL responds to yet another scandal involving control of a church building: "If the military have military need of the church building, let them keep it; otherwise let them get out of it."

❖ AL and Seward are seen reading telegrams early in the morning.

May 14, Saturday

❖ AL learns of the death of Gen. James Wadsworth, a leading Republican, who was mortally wounded in the Wilderness and fell into enemy hands, dying in a Confederate field hospital.

❖ AL tells Kansas Gov. Thomas Carney that the raising of troops should be free from patronage disputes. (Carney and Kansas Sen. James Lane had been feuding about it.)

❖ AL responds to a Senate resolution demanding to know why refugee Indians in Kansas have not been returned to their homes: "The presence of Confederates and hostile Indians in the territory made it inadvisable."

May 15, Sunday

A rebel counterattack in the Shenandoah Valley ends the Union advance on that front, (and the military career of Gen. Franz Sigel).

❖ Nicolay thinks AL looks more relaxed and confident.

May 16, Monday

Gen. Butler makes an inept move against Richmond from the south and is driven back.

❖ AL confers about the idea of the government offering 6 percent bonds instead of 5 percent bonds. (Nothing comes of it.)

May 17, Tuesday

Chess-like maneuvering continues in Georgia. In the Spotsylvania, Virginia area, the Union army continually shifts its flanks to the left (east and south). Lee's forces invariably match those moves.

❖ AL attends a Cabinet meeting.

❖ AL writes an order for the draft of an additional 300,000 men, but it is never issued.

❖ AL sends to Stanton a draft of instructions for handling the Fort Pillow incident: Some Confederate POWs will be set aside as hostages. If the Confederate government does not respond with assurances that no such thing will happen again, the government will "take such action as may then appear expedient and just" against the hostages. (It was never enacted.)

May 18, Wednesday

In the Spotsylvania area, a major Union probe fails.

❖ AL orders the suppression of two newspapers in New York for printing a fake presidential proclamation ordering a new draft of an additional 400,000 men. (This was probably the reason why the previous day's real draft proclamation was never issued. After the hoaxer was identified the newspapers were allowed to resume operation.)

❖ AL attends a lecture on the Battle of Gettysburg held in the House chamber.

May 19, Thursday

In Georgia, the rebels try to catch the advancing Union army on the march but fall into confusion.

❖ After talking to the widow of a black officer killed at Fort Pillow, Alabama sends her to Massachusetts Sen. Charles

Sumner with the suggestion that Sumner find a way to make the law recognize the marriages of black soldiers so that their widows and orphans can get the same benefits as white soldiers.

May 20, Friday

❖ AL issues an order stating that no persons engaged in trade who are following the published regulations of the Treasury Department shall be hindered by the military.

May 21, Saturday

❖ AL sends identical letters the governors of Indiana, Illinois, Iowa, and Wisconsin, urging them to hurry their hundred-day troops forward so they can be used to guard the lengthening supply lines of Gen. Sherman.

❖ Legislation having passed creating a temporary government for Montana Territory, AL tells Seward and Bates to assemble applicants for the territorial offices relating to their departments.

❖ AL sends a telegram to Christina Sack in Baltimore, who had telegraphed AL saying she can prove that her condemned brother is not a spy: "I cannot postpone the execution of a convicted spy on a mere telegraphic dispatch signed with a name I never heard before. Gen. [Lew] Wallace may give you a pass to see him, if he chooses." (Apparently, Gen. Wallace did see her, as her brother's sentence was commuted on Tuesday to imprisonment for the duration of the war.)

May 23, Monday

❖ AL spends the day on miscellaneous appointments and trial matters. (This includes releasing an imprisoned Confederate who had ministered to Union wounded during the Fredericksburg Campaign. The five-year sentence of another man who had enslaved freedmen was confirmed.)

May 24, Tuesday

* ❖ AL attends a Cabinet meeting with no recorded outcome.
* ❖ In response to a telegram from the governor of Ohio asking for news, AL cites yesterday's dispatch from the Gen. Grant, which ends with the words, "Everything looks exceedingly favorable for us."
* ❖ Seward reports that the French government has been informed that the Congressional resolution of April 4, 1864, expressing opposition to a monarchy in Mexico, was not an executive action, and that the French government would be duly notified of any change in U.S. policy.
* ❖ AL nominates for promotion two naval officers who rammed a rebel ironclad with a wooden sidewheeler.
* ❖ AL spends the evening with Seward and with Simon Cameron.

May 25, Wednesday

In Georgia, Union forces are within twenty-five miles of Atlanta.

* ❖ AL endorses a request from a rag-picker to follow the Army of the Potomac to pick up discarded clothing. (He was willing to pay $200 a month for exclusive permission. Apparently, nothing came of it.)

May 26, Thursday

* ❖ AL discusses pay for black chaplains with Bates and with Massachusetts Sen. Charles Sumner.

May 27, Friday

* ❖ AL shakes hands with the son of Michigan Rep. John Driggs, Driggs having brought him (and several other people) to AL for that purpose.

❖ Augustus Dickens of Chicago, the brother of novelist Charles Dickens, asks AL for his autograph.

May 28, Saturday

French "puppet" Maximillian of Hapsburg lands in Veracruz to become emperor of Mexico.

❖ AL sends more documents to the Senate concerning Mexican affairs.
❖ MTL visits the Armory Square Hospital.

May 30, Monday

❖ AL shakes hands with the small son of Maryland Sen. Thomas Hicks after he climbs the stairs of the White House accompanied by a servant. AL gives "the little gentleman" a note to take back to his father. (The child had wanted to meet AL before returning home to Baltimore. His father had lost a foot to illness the previous year and was unable to climb the stairs.)

May 31, Tuesday

After nearly a month of fighting and maneuvering, the Army of the Potomac now confronts Lee outside Cold Harbor, Virginia.

❖ AL transmits to the Senate documents relating to the case of José Arguëlles, who was extradited to Cuba even though there is no extradition treaty between Spain and the U.S. (Arguëlles, a Cuban government officer, had seized a cargo of slaves that had landed in Cuba, declared that 141 of them had died, fraudulently sold those 141, and fled to the U.S.
❖ In the morning, AL reviews groups of children participating in a "Sunday School Celebration" parade past the White House.

- ❖ AL attends a Cabinet meeting.
- ❖ AL consults with various people about the Radical Republican splinter group convention underway in Cleveland. (They nominate John Frémont.)

JUNE 1864

Summary: *The offensives started last month drag on. Meanwhile, AL is nominated for another presidential term.*

June 1, Wednesday

In Virginia, heavy back and forth fighting breaks out in the Cold Harbor area, within eight miles of Richmond. In Georgia, Union forces capture strategic Allatoona Pass.

❖ AL confers with Welles on the appointment of navy midshipmen, and with Ohio Rep. Robert Schenck on the selection of retired officers' board members.
❖ Visiting the telegraph office for news, AL reads aloud the *New York Herald* report on the Radical Republican splinter convention in Cleveland, Ohio. That done, he reads aloud from the Bible.

June 2, Thursday

In Virginia, Union forces mass at Cold Harbor for a climatic assault. But the men write their names on slips of paper and pin them to their uniforms.

❖ AL paroles a POW for three weeks so he can visit his dying father, who is the postmaster of Quincy, Illinois.
❖ AL receives information from Gen. Rosecrans of a conspiracy led by former Ohio congressman Clement Vallandigham to overthrow government.
❖ Alexander McClure, delegate-at-large from Pennsylvania to the National Union Party Convention, calls on AL.
❖ MTL attends an opera with Blair and Blair's daughter.

June 3, Friday

In Virginia, the attempted Cold Harbor breakthrough is a fiasco, costing 7,000 men.

French troops take Acapulco, Mexico.

❖ AL signs legislation providing for a national currency secured by a pledge of U.S. bonds.
❖ AL confers with groups of delegates headed to the National Union Convention in Baltimore.
❖ AL declines an invitation to attend a mass meeting honoring Gen. Grant.

June 4, Saturday

Amidst torrential rain, the rebels outside Atlanta again shift position to block a Union move.

❖ AL welcomes more delegates on their way to the national convention in Baltimore.
❖ The Marine band plays another concert on the White House grounds.

June 5, Sunday

Rebel forces in the Shenandoah Valley are routed at Piedmont, Virginia, by Gen. Franz Sigel's replacement, AL's friend Gen. David Hunter.

❖ AL declines to select a vice president for his second term, leaving it up to the convention.

June 6, Monday

❖ AL listens while Hay reads a letter from Nicolay describing pre-convention activities in Baltimore. AL dictates a reply: He has no selection for vice president, and he has no suggestions for a platform or for the convention's organization.

❖ After an appeal by two university professors, AL moves to pardon a soldier for "attempting to desert," but only if his commanders will take him back.

❖ AL consults at length with Kansas Sen. James Lane about national politics.

❖ AL consults with Chase about the New York collector of customs.

June 7, Tuesday

❖ AL is officially notified that the Baltimore convention of the National Union Party (which combines mainstream Republicans with War Democrats) has been called into session.

❖ Ward Hill Lamon telegraphs AL from the Baltimore convention: "Enthusiastic unanimity beyond even my expectations."

❖ MTL sees the *Barber of Seville* at Grover's Theater.

June 8, Wednesday

❖ AL spends much of the day at the War Department telegraph office receiving reports from the front and from the convention. He learns of his reelection nomination in the afternoon and then later of the nomination of Johnson for vice president.

❖ AL refuses to permit a man to return to Beaufort, South Carolina, who had been expelled for providing whiskey to soldiers.

❖ Congratulations begin arriving in the evening.

❖ AL hears Beethoven's *Fidelio* at Grover's Theater.

June 9, Thursday

- ❖ AL replies to the delegation from the Baltimore convention that officially notifies him of his nomination: "I have not permitted myself, gentlemen, to conclude that I am the best man in the country; but I am reminded, in this connection, of a story of an old Dutch farmer, who remarked to a companion once that 'it was not best to swap horses when crossing streams.'"
- ❖ Congratulations continue to arrive, including a serenade by an Ohio delegation.

June 10, Friday

- ❖ AL hears back about the private he was willing to pardon on June 6: his commanders don't want him back. He was a draftee who deserted almost immediately and was caught trying to bribe his way through the outpost line to get to the enemy.
- ❖ Browning lobbies AL to appoint the widow of the Quincy, IL, postmaster to be the new postmaster there.

June 11, Saturday

- ❖ AL signs legislation providing for the execution of treaties regarding consular jurisdiction over crews of foreign vessels in U.S. waters.
- ❖ AL addresses some of the Ohio hundred-day troops who recently arrived in Washington.
- ❖ AL confers with Bates about confiscation orders issued by Gen. Lew Wallace in Baltimore.

June 12, Sunday, First-Quarter

In Virginia, the Union army slips away from the stalemated Cold Harbor position to cross to the south side of the James River.

June 13, Monday

Lee sends reinforcements from Richmond to the Shenandoah Valley.

❖ AL tells Bates to give Gen. Lew Wallace's objectionable confiscation orders to Stanton, who will revoke them.

❖ AL asks for an investigation into a complaint that "our military are seizing negroes and carrying them off without their own consent" in the vicinity of Henderson, Kentucky. (The complaint was confirmed. Orders were issued against kidnapping.)

❖ AL sends to the Senate Stanton's report on the case of William Yocum, convicted in January of kidnapping, while suspending his own pardon action. (Yocum had returned a slave to a loyal slave-owner. AL thought Yocum had suffered enough. Stanton disagreed.)

June 14, Tuesday

In Virginia, Union forces begin crossing the James River on the longest pontoon bridge ever built, to converge on the rail junction of Petersburg, Virginia.

❖ AL remarks to a reporter that he will be satisfied if the war in Virginia is over within a year.

June 15, Wednesday

The Union attack on Petersburg fails when Lee gets reinforcements there just in time.

❖ After seeing reports of his movement toward Petersburg, AL telegraphs Gen. Grant: "I begin to see it. You will succeed. God bless you all."

June 16, Thursday

The Union assault against Petersburg continues to fail.

❖ AL and entourage leave Washington on a special train at 7 a.m. for Philadelphia, to attend the Great Central Fair, a benefit for the U.S. Sanitary Commission. He arrives in the city for lunch and is at the fairgrounds at about 4 p.m.

❖ AL, at the fair's banquet, makes a speech-length response to a toast: "General Grant is reported to have said, 'I am going through on this line if it takes all summer.' This war has taken three years…. I say we are going through on this line if it takes three years more."

❖ Responding to a midnight serenade, AL explains that he has nothing to say and just wants to see them.

June 17, Friday

Union assaults against Petersburg remain unsuccessful, but they have cut two of its five railroad lines. In the Shenandoah Valley, Union forces begin retreating in the face of the reinforced Confederates.

❖ AL, in Philadelphia, departs for Washington at about 8 a.m.

❖ AL supplies information to Illinois Sen. Lyman Trumbull, chairman of the Senate Committee on the Judiciary, about the formation of the Arkansas reconstruction state government, as the Senate is examining the credentials of the two senators sent by Arkansas.

June 18, Saturday

Gen. Grant begins siege warfare against Petersburg. In Georgia, the rebels dig in along Kennesaw Mountain, outside Marietta.

❖ AL consults with Browning about patronage in the new Montana Territory.

❖ AL asks Welles to do what he can for "[his] old friend C. B. Denio," who is stuck in Chicago after trying to get to Washington to complain about rampant thievery at the Mare Island Navy Yard in California, where he was a master mason.

❖ AL sends to the Senate further information concerning the case of Cuban official José Arguëlles, with additional proof that he had been involved in fraudulent slave sales.

June 19, Sunday

Off Cherbourg, France, the USS Kearsarge *sinks the CSS* Alabama, *while throngs ashore watch.*

❖ AL attends the funeral of eighteen women killed in an explosion at a local munitions plant.

❖ With Hay, AL attends a concert at Ford's Theater.

June 20, Monday

❖ AL reprimands the postmaster of Philadelphia for trying to influence a congressional race.

❖ AL leaves Washington at about 5 p.m. with Tad and Fox on the USS *Baltimore* to visit Gen. Grant's headquarters.

June 21, Tuesday

❖ AL and his party, aboard the USS *Baltimore*, arrives at City Point, Virginia, at about noon.

❖ AL and Gen. Grant, on horseback, tour the Union lines outside Petersburg.

❖ AL reviews black troops.

❖ AL tells stories with Gen. Grant and his staff in front of Grant's tent in the evening.

❖ That night AL sleeps aboard ship.

June 22, Wednesday

Outside Petersburg, a Union attempt to cut another rail line into the city is defeated.

❖ AL goes upstream with Gen. Grant to tour other parts of the line, including the area of Bermuda Hundred, Virginia.
❖ They return in the early afternoon and AL and his party leaves for Washington on the USS *Baltimore*.

June 23, Thursday

In Georgia, the rain stops.

❖ AL and party, traveling aboard the USS *Baltimore*, arrive in Washington at about 5 p.m.
❖ AL is described as sunburned and tired, but refreshed and cheered.

June 24, Friday

❖ AL tells Gen. Rosecrans to look into complaints that Gen. Egbert Brown is not doing his best to suppress bushwhackers in central Missouri. (Rosecrans replied that Brown is reliable enough, but would be better at a desk job.)
❖ AL attends a Cabinet meeting and appears to be in good humor.
❖ AL asks Bates for an opinion as to what "pay, bounty, and clothing are allowed by law to persons of color who were free on the 19th day of April 1861 and who have been enlisted and mustered into the military service of the United States between the month of December 1862 and the 16th of June 1864." (Bates initially expressed mystification at the question, which was derived from the circular wording of an enabling act. He eventually decides that black soldiers are owed the same pay, bounty, and clothing as any others.)

❖ AL telegraphs MTL in Boston: "All well, and very warm. Tad and I have been to Gen. Grant's army. Returned yesterday safe and sound."

By all accounts, Lincoln cherished his time with youngest son Tad.

June 25, Saturday

- ❖ AL assures Bates that Gen. Lew Wallace's objectionable confiscation orders have been revoked.
- ❖ AL, Fox, and Browning go to the Navy Yard after dark to see a demonstration of artillery firing signal shells.

June 27, Monday

In Georgia, Gen. Sherman attacks Kennesaw Mountain, losing 3,000 men.

- ❖ AL approves legislation intended to prevent smuggling.
- ❖ AL confers with Welles concerning the removal of a navy agent at New York who has been arrested for fraud, although his backers say the charges are trumped up.

June 28, Tuesday

- ❖ AL signs legislation repealing the Fugitive Slave Act of 1850 and all acts and parts of acts that required the return of fugitive slaves.
- ❖ AL attends a Cabinet meeting.
- ❖ In response to a Senate resolution seeking information about alleged Union army recruitment taking place in Canada or Ireland, AL reports that no such enlistment has been authorized.
- ❖ AL approves a joint resolution incorporating the Young Men's Christian Association in Washington.
- ❖ AL assures Chase that Maunsell Field cannot be appointed assistant U.S. treasurer at New York as powerful New Yorkers oppose him—something to do with public intoxication.

June 29, Wednesday

- ❖ In response to AL's refusal yesterday to back one of Chase's appointments, Chase offers to resign.

❖ AL accepts.

❖ AL confers with various people about Chase's resignation and the interim operation of the Treasury Department.

❖ Congress having declined to seat the congressmen sent by the new reconstruction state government of Arkansas, AL directs Gen. Frederick Steele in Arkansas to continue giving the state government the same protection as previously.

❖ AL telegraphs MTL, who is now in New York: "All well. Tom is moving things out."

❖ AL, Tad, Hay, and Nicolay attend a performance at Grover's Theater.

June 30, Thursday

❖ AL nominates a replacement for Chase: former Ohio governor David Tod (no relation to MTL). Tod later begs off.

❖ AL abandons the idea of colonizing the Chiriqui region of Panama with freed blacks, as the idea was opposed by Honduras, Nicaragua, and Costa Rica, plus Seward.

❖ AL consents to the use of the grounds between the White House and the War Department by the St. Matthew's Colored Sunday School for a Fourth of July celebration.

❖ AL signs internal revenue legislation.

JULY 1864

Summary: A sudden Confederate attempt to sack Washington is narrowly defeated. AL, meanwhile, defeats a sudden Congressional attempt to seize control of reconstruction.

July 1, Friday

In Virginia, the reinforced Confederates continue pressing north through the Shenandoah Valley.

❖ AL decides to nominate Maine Sen. William Fessenden, chairman of the Senate Finance Committee, to replace Chase, and calls him to the White House for an interview. While Fessenden is waiting in the reception room, AL sends Hay to the Senate with the nomination, where it is immediately ratified. Confronted with this development, the amazed Fessenden declines, but AL ignores him, and other Republicans pressure him to accept.

July 2, Saturday

In Georgia, the rebels fall back to yet another new trench line, this time behind Marietta.

❖ AL signs legislation allowing land grants to aid railroad and telegraph construction from Lake Superior to the Pacific.
❖ AL has a long interview with Fessenden.
❖ AL confers with Indiana Rep. George Julian on the power of Congress to confiscate the landed estates of Confederates.
❖ AL confers with Gen. Meigs on the status of Fort Leavenworth, Kansas.

- ❖ AL seeks information on the deadly March 28 Copperhead riot in Charleston, Illinois, and is told the case has been turned over to the civil authorities.
- ❖ MTL and RTL are back in Washington, and the family moves to the Soldiers' Home for the summer.

July 3, Sunday

French troops take Durango, Mexico.

- ❖ Fessenden again tries to decline his Cabinet appointment, but AL convinces him to accept.

July 4, Monday

- ❖ AL provides Fessenden with a memo assuring him that he (Fessenden) is in complete control of the Treasury Department.
- ❖ AL spends much of the morning in the President's Room at the Capitol, signing legislation and conferring with congressmen prior to Congress adjourning.
- ❖ There, amidst angry words from Michigan Sen. Zachariah Chandler, AL pocket vetoes the Wade—Davis Bill, which would have put reconstruction under Congressional control. (AL, whose position was that the states never left the Union despite the rebellion of certain inhabitants, required that 10 percent of the 1860 voter headcount swear allegiance, facilitating reconstruction. Wade—Davis' position was that the seceded states needed to rejoin the Union and were meanwhile conquered territory. A majority had to swear allegiance and only those who could swear they had never supported the rebellion in any way could initially vote. It would have facilitated social reengineering.)
- ❖ Congress adjourns.

July 5, Tuesday

The Confederates in the Shenandoah Valley erupt into Maryland, constituting a corps-size raiding force heading toward Washington, spreading out to extort cash from small towns.

* AL suspends the writ of habeas corpus in Kentucky in response to insurgent activity there.
* AL attends a Cabinet meeting where Fessenden appears for the first time.

July 6, Wednesday

* AL confers with Gen. Allan Hitchcock concerning the defense of Washington as a powerful Confederate force approaches.
* AL allows James Gilmore to go south again on another errand to broker peace.

July 7, Thursday

* In response to a Congressional resolution, AL proclaims the first Thursday of the coming August as a "day of national humiliation and prayer."
* AL pardons yet another deserter who has appealed directly to him, on condition that he return to his unit and serve his enlistment.

July 8, Friday

In Georgia, Union forces cross the Chattahoochee River, forcing another rebel retreat.

* AL, having killed the Wade–Davis Bill, issues a statement on reconstruction: There can be no single plan for restoration; he was not going to set aside the reconstruction governments already installed in Louisiana and Arkansas; Congress does

not have the power to abolish slavery in states as implied in Wade–Davis; he favors a constitutional amendment abolishing slavery nationwide; the Wade–Davis template would be fine for any state that chose to adopt it.

❖ AL reviews thirty-five court-martial cases.

❖ In the evening, AL discusses the Baltimore convention with painter Francis Carpenter and with Hay.

July 9, Saturday

Amidst rising panic Gen. Lew Wallace tries to stop the invaders on the Monocacy River. His scratch force is defeated, opening the road to Washington, forty miles away.

❖ AL reviews thirty-one court-martial cases.

❖ AL telegraphs John Garrett, head of the Baltimore and Ohio Railroad: "What have you heard about a battle at Monocacy today? We have nothing about it here except what you say." (Garrett forwarded reports from his telegraphers of heavy fighting, retreats, and defeat.)

❖ AL releases Copperhead leader Dr. James Barrett. (Gen. Grant had asked for his release as he knew the man and did not think he was worth arresting.)

❖ AL replies to *New York Tribune* editor Horace Greeley, who has heard from people claiming to have peace feelers from Jefferson Davis. AL says he would be glad to hear from any- one who has a proposition from Davis, in writing, agreeing to reunion and emancipation, "whatever else it embraces."

July 10, Sunday

❖ AL visits some of the city's fortifications in the morning.

❖ AL responds to a Baltimore committee begging for military reinforcements: "I have not a single soldier but whom is being disposed by the military…. Let us be vigilant but keep cool. I hope neither Baltimore or Washington will be sacked."

❖ AL moves his family from the Soldiers' Home back to the White House, as the suburbs may no longer be safe.

❖ AL urges Gen. Grant to transfer reinforcements from the front line at Petersburg, Virginia, and "make a vigorous effort to destroy the enemy's force in this vicinity."

July 11, Monday

In Maryland, after burning the Blair home in Silver Spring the rebels reach the Washington suburbs and begin probing the city's ring of forts, which are rapidly filling with soldiers hurriedly shipped from the Union lines outside Petersburg.

❖ AL gets notice that the equivalent of a corps is on the way to reinforce Washington.

❖ AL orders local militia and volunteers into Federal service for sixty days.

❖ AL and MTL, with a mounted escort, ride out to Fort Stevens on the city's northern periphery. He watches skirmishing with probing Confederate infantry until the defenders insist that he get off the parapet.

❖ Later AL goes to the wharf to greet arriving reinforcements.

July 12, Tuesday

Satisfied that the city is fully defended, the rebels withdraw from Washington after dark.

❖ AL attends a cabinet meeting where they discuss the situation.

❖ In the afternoon, AL, MTL, Seward, and others drive out to Fort Stevens again and watch operations. AL gets on the parapet again. A man is shot by his side. A general politely asks AL to move. AL ignores him. A young officer (reputedly future Supreme Court Justice Oliver Wendell Holmes Jr.) screams at him to get down, reverting to the vernacular. AL moves.

❖ At night, AL and MTL drive along the city's forts and are greeted by soldiers.

July 13, Wednesday

❖ Bates confers with AL concerning various aspects of the Baltimore convention.

July 14, Thursday

In Maryland, the pursuing Federals fail to catch the retreating rebels.

❖ AL moves his family back into the Soldiers' Home.
❖ AL prepares a memorandum urging Cabinet members not to feud, nor to intrigue for each other's removal.
❖ AL responds to Stanton regarding a letter he forwarded from Gen. Halleck suggesting AL remove Blair for disparaging remarks he made about local military officers (calling them "poltroons") after Confederate raiders burned Blair's home: AL does not approve of the remarks but says, "I propose continuing to be myself the judge as to when a member of the Cabinet shall be dismissed."

July 15, Friday

❖ AL attends a Cabinet meeting where they mostly discuss the Confederate raid.
❖ AL meets with Virginia Unionist Gov. Francis Pierpont and with the Peruvian minister.
❖ AL confers with Bates, who remains contemptuous of Gen. Halleck.
❖ Browning finds AL is upset that the raiders appear to be escaping.

July 16, Saturday

- ❖ AL authorizes Hay (currently in New York) to write safe-conduct passes for the four Confederate representatives in Canada that Horace Greeley has contacted.
- ❖ AL talks to Browning about the feud between Blair and Gen. Halleck.
- ❖ AL, alone, attends the Marine band concert at the White House.

July 17, Sunday

Tired of retreats, Jefferson Davis replaces the rebel commander at Atlanta with Hood, who believes vigorous attacks will make up for inferior numbers.

- ❖ AL writes to Gen. David Hunter to assure him that he is not being used as a scapegoat for the recent fiasco in Maryland, and will remain commander of his department.

July 18, Monday

- ❖ AL issues a call for another 500,000 volunteers, who may elect to enlist for one, two, or three years.
- ❖ James Gilmore reports to AL that he interviewed Jefferson Davis, who said that the South is fighting for independence rather than slavery, and peace must be based on independence.
- ❖ AL discusses patronage issues with Pennsylvania Rep. E. J. Moore.
- ❖ AL writes a position paper for the Confederate representatives in Canada who contacted Horace Greeley: "Any proposition which embraces the restoration of peace, the integrity of the whole Union, and the abandonment of slavery, and which comes by and with an authority that can control the armies now at war against the United States will be received and considered by the executive government of

the United States, and will be met by liberal terms on other substantial and collateral points."

❖ AL telegraphs Gen. Sherman to assure him that the state recruiting officers hanging around his camps and enlisting black men have legal authority to do so.

July 19, Tuesday

❖ AL attends a Cabinet meeting whose agenda includes the March 28 Copperhead riot in Illinois, and the dispute between Gen. Butler and Virginia Unionist Gov. Francis Pierpont.

July 20, Wednesday

Outside Atlanta, Hood launches his first boss-pleasing attack against the Union trenches. It is a confused, bloody failure. He blames subordinates for not being vigorous enough.

❖ AL telegraphs Gen. Grant: "Yours of yesterday about a call for 300,000 is received. I suppose you had not seen the call for 500,000 made the day before, and which I suppose covers the case." (Grant had written to AL urging heavy reinforcements.)

❖ Harvard College confers on RTL a Bachelor of Arts degree.

Robert Todd Lincoln, the family's oldest son, who outlived his parents and siblings but left no heirs.

July 21, Thursday

❖ AL recommends Mrs. Ann Sprigg to Fessenden: "The bearer of this is a most estimable widow lady, at whose house I boarded many years ago when a member of Congress. She now is very needy; and any employment suitable to a lady could not be bestowed on a more worthy person." (She was made a clerk in the loan branch of the Treasury Department.)

July 22, Friday

Outside Atlanta, Hood launches an even bigger attack, with worse results and more blame-shifting. In Virginia, the reinforcements that had pursued the raiders' return to Petersburg, leaving the Shenandoah Valley as it was before the raid—dominated by the rebels.

❖ AL attends a Cabinet meeting where he discussed the correspondence between himself and Horace Greeley concerning the so-called Niagara Falls negotiations.

❖ AL and the Cabinet view Francis Carpenter's unfinished painting of AL reading the Emancipation Proclamation.

July 23, Saturday

❖ AL telegraphs Gen. David Hunter at Harpers Ferry, West Virginia: "Are you able to take care of the enemy when he turns back upon you, as he probably will on finding that Wright has left?" (Gen. Horatio Wright had commanded the Union reinforcements that had pursued the raiders. Hunter responded that he was not strong enough, but he did not think the enemy would return. He was wrong.)

July 24, Sunday

In the Shenandoah Valley, a Union force is routed at Kernstown, Virginia, but rain intervenes with the pursuit.

July 25, Monday

❖ AL writes a public letter noting that since the Confederate representatives at Niagara Falls are not empowered to negotiate, they must be there to influence the upcoming Democratic convention in Chicago.

❖ AL confers with Gen. Meigs about a proposal to destroy the fords across Potomac between Washington and Harper's Ferry by building dams. (The raiders used the fords.)

July 26, Tuesday

❖ AL attends a Cabinet meeting with only Welles, Usher, and Bates present.

❖ AL sends a long telegram to Gen. Sherman, who had complained that the promotion of two particular generals was the result of lobbying rather than front-line service. AL contends the promotions were made in good faith. "I beg you to believe we do not act in a spirit of disregarding merit."

❖ Welles and Mrs. Welles visit the Soldiers' Home in the evening.

July 27, Wednesday

Outside Petersburg, the Federals extend their trenches to the north side of the James River.

❖ AL responds to an inquiry from Johnson about whatever happened to the promotion that Col. A. C. Gillett was supposed to get. (They discovered that his name was really Gillem, and so the paperwork had gone astray.)

❖ AL tells Stanton to look into what can be done for women employed at the Philadelphia arsenal, who protested that their pay has not kept up with inflation since the start of the war.

❖ AL asks Gen. David Hunter at Harpers Ferry, "Please send any recent news you have—particularly as to movements of the enemy." (Hunter replied that the rebels had not moved. He was wrong.)

July 28, Thursday

Outside Atlanta, Hood launches a third bloody, futile attack. In the Shenandoah Valley, rebel cavalry again emerges into Maryland and Pennsylvania.

July 30, Saturday

Union besiegers detonate a tunnel under a rebel trench outside Petersburg, but the botched assault costs 4,000 men. In Pennsylvania, rebel raiders burn Chambersburg when the cash they demand is not forthcoming.

❖ AL approves the latest regulations governing commercial intercourse and directs military personnel to assist the Treasury Department in executing them.

❖ The Marine band performs a Saturday evening concert on the White House grounds.

❖ AL (plus MTL and Fox) leaves for Fortress Monroe in the evening aboard the USS *Baltimore* for a scheduled meeting with Gen. Grant.

July 31, Sunday

Confederate raiders in Pennsylvania fall back ahead of Union cavalry.

❖ AL arrives at Fortress Monroe in the morning. AL confers with Gen. Grant and they both visit the Navy Yard at Norfolk, Virginia. AL leaves for Washington in the afternoon.

AUGUST 1864

Summary: With the battle fronts locked in bloody stale-mates, AL begins to lose hope for his chances of reelection, and with that any hope of achieving his war aims.

August 1, Monday

Gen. Philip Sheridan is given three corps to rid the Shenandoah Valley of Confederates.

❖ AL arrives in Washington in the morning, accompanied by MTL, Fox, and others.
❖ Welles confers with AL about the Smith brothers' fraud case in Boston.

August 2, Tuesday

Union forces begin operating against Mobile, Alabama, one of two remaining Confederate seaports.

❖ AL attends a Cabinet meeting where military affairs are discussed.
❖ AL declines to meet with the wife of Surgeon General William A. Hammond, who wants to present evidence that had not been introduced at the latter's trial. (Hammond's conviction was later overturned.)
❖ AL confers with New York Sen. Edwin Morgan about the circumstances of Chase's resignation (which had involved New York patronage issues).

August 3, Wednesday

❖ AL shares his frustrations in a telegraph to Gen. Grant: "I have seen your dispatch in which you say 'I want Sheridan put in command of all the troops in the field, with instructions to put himself south of the enemy, and follow him to the death. Wherever the enemy goes, let our troops go also.' This, I think, is exactly right, as to how our forces should move. But please look over the dispatches you may have received from here, even since you made that order, and discover, if you can, that there is any idea in the head of any one here, of 'putting our army south of the enemy' or of 'following him to the death' in any direction. I repeat to you it will neither be done nor attempted unless you watch it every day, and hour, and force it."

❖ AL tells Stanton to suspend Gen. David Hunter's order to exile to the South secessionist residents of Frederick, Maryland, until he forwards the details of each case. (In response, Hunter resigned his post. He stayed in the army but had no further field commands.)

August 4, Thursday

"Damn the torpedoes, full speed ahead," says the commander of the Union fleet as it storms past the forts guarding the entrance of Mobile Bay, right after his lead ship hits a "torpedo" (i.e., a moored mine) and sinks. But the fleet gets through, defeats a rebel ironclad, and gains control of the bay (although not the city).

❖ Marking the Day of National Humiliation and Prayer, AL attends church with Blair.

August 5, Friday

❖ AL listens while Seward reads the so-called Wade–Davis Manifesto in which the authors of the Wade–David Bill accuse AL of killing the bill so he can create a bloc of reconstructed Southern voters under his control.

- ❖ Gen. Grant is in town, and AL meets with him at the War Department. He also meets with Gen. Philip Sheridan.
- ❖ AL confers with Bates about conditions in Missouri.
- ❖ AL attends a Cabinet meeting.

August 6, Saturday

- ❖ AL endorses the promotion of Col. Griffin Stedman, who is dying of wounds received at Petersburg, Virginia.
- ❖ AL approves the publication of redacted correspondence between himself and Horace Greeley concerning the Niagara Falls peace effort.

August 7, Sunday

- ❖ AL meets with Stanton, Welles, Gen. Grant, and Gen. Halleck. They learn that Col. Stedman, promoted yesterday, has died.

August 8, Monday

- ❖ AL tells an official in Kentucky that the pass he gave MTL's half-sister Emily Todd Helm was to protect her against the fact of her being the widow of a Confederate general and not against the consequences of any subsequent disloyal act. (AL must have been responding to a rumor, as she was never arrested.)

August 9, Tuesday

- ❖ AL sends Horace Greeley, so he can reprint it, a copy of their correspondence concerning the Niagara Falls negotiations, printed as a six-page pamphlet.

❖ AL tells Gen. Butler in Norfolk, Virginia, if military necessity demands that he clean up the city, then he should do so and not have the citizens vote on the subject.

❖ AL tells Gen. Nathaniel Banks in Louisiana that he is anxious for the new state constitution, adopted by a convention, to be ratified by the electorate.

August 10, Wednesday

Gen. Philip Sheridan's forces begin moving south into the Shenandoah Valley.

❖ AL confers with Col. John Eaton Jr., superintendent of freedman for the Department of the Tennessee, on the condition of blacks there.

August 12, Friday

❖ AL attends a Cabinet meeting.
❖ Thurlow Weed warns AL that his reelection is impossible.
❖ AL sends an emissary to Gen. Grant to probe his attitude about being a presidential candidate. (Grant hated the idea.)
❖ Poet Walt Whitman reports routinely exchanging courteous bows when encountering AL between the Soldiers' Home and the White House. AL's brown face has deep cut lines, with an expression of "latent sadness."

August 13, Saturday

At Petersburg, Union forces continue probing the east flank of the Confederate trench line.

❖ AL dines with Gen. Robert Anderson.

August 14, Sunday

- ❖ AL suggests that Gen. Grant confer with Lee and mutually ban "house-burning and other destruction of private property." (Grant disagreed: "Experience has taught us that agreements made with rebels are binding upon us but are not observed by them longer than suits their convenience." He offered instead a general order against wanton destruction.)

August 15, Monday

Gen. Sherman's forces probe Atlanta's fortifications.

- ❖ AL sends copies of his correspondence with Horace Greeley regarding the Niagara Falls peace effort to the *New York Times* for publication there.
- ❖ AL asks Usher about the case of Patrice DeJanon. (DeJanon had been dismissed as a professor of Spanish at West Point and his wife was angry at AL for perceived rudeness to her when she tried to get an interview. DeJanon was later reinstated.)

August 16, Tuesday

- ❖ AL attends a Cabinet meeting where Seward and Bates argue over procedures for handling captured cotton.
- ❖ AL replies to a Democrat newspaper editor in Wisconsin who complains that AL's recent statements that peace required reunion and emancipation left out pro-slavery War Democrats like himself: "If Jefferson Davis wishes…to know what I would do if he were to offer peace and reunion, saying nothing about slavery, let him try me." But AL does not send the letter.

August 17, Wednesday

- ❖ AL reviews fifteen court-martial cases.

❖ AL telegraphs Gen. Grant: "I have seen your dispatch expressing your unwillingness to break your hold where you are. Neither am I willing."

August 18, Thursday

Outside Petersburg, the Federals push their trench line west, block another railroad, and hold it against counterattacks.

❖ Leonard Swett, one of his 1860 campaign organizers, tells AL that he cannot be reelected and asks if AL will withdraw.
❖ AL addresses a regiment of discharged hundred-day men returning to Ohio: "Every form of human right is endangered if our enemies succeed."

August 19, Friday

❖ AL attends a Cabinet meeting.
❖ AL confers with followers about reelection.
❖ AL has his second meeting with Frederick Douglass, who sees Tuesday's letter to the *Democrat Wisconsin* editor and warns him that it might be seen as backsliding on the Emancipation Proclamation. So AL does not send it, although it gets leaked. (Douglass later marveled at how AL treated him as an equal.)

August 20, Saturday

❖ AL suspends the death sentence of a teenage private who was drunk when he committed murder.
❖ AL addresses another discharged regiment of hundred-day men.

August 21, Sunday

❖ AL establishes an ordnance board to test a new wrought-iron cannon offered to the government by Horatio Ames.

August 22, Monday

- ❖ AL addresses another discharged hundred-day regiment: "I am a living witness that any one of your children may look to come here as my father's child has."
- ❖ AL confers with Stanton concerning the release of Joseph Howard Jr., who perpetrated the May 18 presidential proclamation hoax. (He is released Tuesday.)

August 23, Tuesday

- ❖ AL attends a Cabinet meeting and has each member sign a memorandum without knowing the contents: "This morning, as for some days past, it seems exceedingly probable that this Administration will not be reelected. Then it will be my duty to so co-operate with the president-elect, as to save the Union between the election and the inauguration; as he will have secured his election on such ground that he cannot possibly save it afterwards."
- ❖ At about this time, MTL admits to her dress designer (freedwoman Elizabeth Keckley) that she is $27,000 in debt. She hopes to get Republican politicians to bail her out.

August 24, Wednesday

- ❖ Responding to a letter from *New York Times* editor Harry Raymond suggesting that AL appoint a peace commissioner to meet with the Confederates, AL drafts a letter appointing Raymond as that commissioner.
- ❖ In the evening, AL watches a demonstration of Morse code signaling from a tower at the Soldiers' Home to the roof of the Smithsonian Institution.

August 25, Thursday

- ❖ AL confers with Seward, Stanton, and Fessenden, and reject yesterday's idea of sending Harry Raymond to the South as a peace commissioner, as defeatist.

❖ AL meets with British minister Lord Lyons.

August 26, Friday

❖ AL attends a Cabinet meeting.

August 27, Saturday

❖ AL tells Stanton that Gen. Franz Sigel can have a court of inquiry into the reasons for his dismissal. (Stanton never acted. Gen. Grant relieved Siegel July 7, commenting: "All of Gen. Sigel's operations from the beginning of the war have been so unsuccessful that I think it advisable to relieve him from all duty.")

August 28, Sunday

❖ AL commutes the death sentence of four men convicted of espionage in Baltimore after a direct appeal from their lawyer. (They got imprisonment for the duration of the war.)
❖ AL asks Welles to "find some way to relieve [him] from the embarrassment of this case" concerning the Smith brothers in Boston who are charged with making fraudulent deliveries to the navy. (Most of the Massachusetts congressional delegation was watching the case.)

August 29, Monday

The Democratic Convention convenes in Chicago, nominating Gen. McClellan as their anti-war presidential candidate.

❖ AL confers with Welles about the Smith brothers' case and agrees to transfer jurisdiction to the Boston civil courts.
❖ AL interviews Paul Brinck of New Jersey, who thinks the draft quota for his township is too large.

❖ Thomas Worthington, the cashiered colonel and gadfly whom AL told in March that he was not fit to be a colonel, asks AL for permission to visit Gen. Grant, apparently to pursue his feud. (Grant declined: "I should be very sorry to see the colonel. He has nearly worried the life out of me at times when I could not prevent an interview.")

August 30, Tuesday

❖ AL attends a Cabinet meeting. They get confirmation of the capture of Confederate Fort Morgan, at the entrance of Mobile Bay, Alabama.

August 31, Wednesday

Gen. Sherman cuts Atlanta's last rail connection. Hood's vigorous counterattack is another bloody failure.

❖ Concerning the case of man caught in possession of a contract to provide supplies for the Confederacy with the absurd excuse that he hoped to let the Union government profit from the deal, AL says he will pardon the man if New York Sen. Edwin Morgan, New York Republican activist Thurlow Weed, and *New York Times* editor Harry Raymond will endorse the request. (Raymond and Weed did endorse the request. Morgan agreed with AL that the man should go to jail.)

❖ AL addresses another discharged regiment of hundred-day men returning to Ohio.

❖ MTL is in Manchester, Vermont.

SEPTEMBER 1864

Summary: Things become less gloomy with the collapse of the enemy in Georgia and in the Shenandoah Valley. But the election remains in doubt.

September 1, Thursday

The Confederates evacuate Atlanta.

❖ AL confers with Louisiana Gov. Michael Hahn about the new Louisiana state constitution and the electoral campaign there.
❖ AL sends an officer to the POW camp at Rock Island, Illinois, to get the names of prisoners who wish to take the oath of allegiance and join the Union army.

September 2, Friday

❖ AL confers about politics in New York.

September 3, Saturday

❖ AL proclaims Sunday, September 11, as a Day of Thanksgiving and Prayer in response to the recent Union victories at Atlanta and Mobile Bay.
❖ AL confers with Michigan Sen. Zachariah Chandler about the latter's plans for winning the November election. This includes the removal of Blair from the Cabinet.

September 4, Sunday

❖ AL writes to Quaker minister Eliza P. Gurney, of New Jersey, to thank her for her wartime support despite her pacifism.

September 5, Monday

❖ AL orders the firing of a noon salute to honor recent victories.

September 6, Tuesday

❖ AL attends a Cabinet meeting.
❖ AL meets with Mary Wise, who served in an Indiana regiment until she was wounded and found to be a woman. AL orders that her withheld pay be restored.
❖ A Congregationalist minister meets with AL and finds him with a stack of documents and a basket of peaches.

September 7, Wednesday

Gen. Sherman expels Atlanta's remaining civilians (about 1,600).

❖ AL meets with a delegation of "loyal colored men of Baltimore" who present AL with an elaborately bound Bible. AL responds: "I can only say…it has always been a sentiment with me that all mankind should be free."

September 8, Thursday

❖ AL sends a congratulatory telegram to the governor of Washington Territory on the opening of the telegraph line to that area.
❖ AL telegraphs MTL in Manchester, Vermont, that the wife of the governor of the Soldiers' Home has died.

September 9, Friday

❖ AL attends a Cabinet meeting where they discuss trading with the enemy for cotton and decide they might as well allow it.

❖ AL meets with Indiana Judge David McDonald, who later confides in his diary that AL "is very far from being a fool."

❖ AL confers with a woman whose husband served a full enlistment but was then imprisoned for desertion during a previous enlistment. (AL later pardoned him.)

September 10, Saturday

❖ AL meets with Fessenden and Simeon Draper.

❖ AL confers about politics in Connecticut.

❖ A battalion of Treasury Department clerks parade in front of the White House.

September 11, Sunday

❖ AL meets with New York Rep. Fernando Wood.

❖ MTL remains in Manchester.

September 12, Monday

❖ AL confers with cannon manufacturer Norman Wiard about conditions in the armaments industry.

❖ AL sends a suggestion to Gen. Grant that he send reinforcements to Gen. Philip Sheridan in the Shenandoah Valley.

September 13, Tuesday

❖ AL delivers a short speech to a large political rally on Pennsylvania Avenue.

❖ Gen. Butler asks for some of new Ames wrought-iron cannons to use their reputedly high penetrating power against rebel ironclads. AL responds that they are untested and possibly overpriced.

September 14, Wednesday

A Confederate division is withdrawn from the Shenandoah Valley to reinforce the thinning rebel lines at Petersburg, Virginia.

❖ Responding to the appeal of a local magistrate for the release of an imprisoned private whose wife and child are destitute, AL orders his pardon on the condition that his commander will take him back. (It took his wife nearly a month to get the commander to respond, but then the pardon did go through.)

September 15, Thursday

❖ AL allows the widow of a Confederate officer to return to Knoxville, Tennessee. (There she took the oath of allegiance.)
❖ AL confers with Francis Blair Sr. on political conditions in Tennessee.
❖ MTL and Tad return to Washington.

September 16, Friday

❖ AL attends a Cabinet meeting.
❖ AL confers with two officials about draft quotas in Illinois.

September 17, Saturday

John Frémont, the Radical Republican presidential nominee, withdraws from the race, avoiding Republican fragmentation.

❖ AL telegraphs Gen. Sherman: "I feel great interest in the subjects of your dispatch mentioning corn and sorghum, and a contemplated visit to you." (Sherman had reported that Georgia Gov. Joe Brown had, despite the Union invasion, demobilized the state militia to harvest corn and sorghum.

Sherman hoped to meet with Brown about Georgia leaving the Confederacy. The meeting did not take place.)

❖ AL attends a Cabinet meeting where they discuss returning plantations in Louisiana.

❖ AL meets with a District of Columbia delegation asking for a two-week postponement of the draft. AL says he cannot promise to make exceptions.

September 19, Monday

The remaining Confederates in the Shenandoah Valley are badly defeated at Winchester, Virginia.

❖ AL asks Gen. Sherman to release Indiana soldiers to return home to participate in the October 11 state election (i.e., not the November national election) as Indiana is the only major state whose soldiers cannot vote in the field. (Indiana's Republican governor told AL he feared a major defeat otherwise.)

September 20, Tuesday

❖ AL attends a Cabinet meeting where Stanton announces that the Confederates have captured two steamers on Lake Erie. (It was part of a scheme to free Confederate POWs that immediately fell apart.)

❖ AL confers about the sale of public lands in Kansas.

❖ AL authorizes the release of Francis Mallison, who was involved in the bogus presidential proclamation in May.

September 21, Wednesday

❖ AL asks Gen. Edward Canby if he can get aid to destitute Union people reportedly living beyond Union lines near Alexandria, Louisiana. (Canby replied that, unfortunately, he could not.)

❖ AL confers with Seward about the political situation in New York and sends Nicolay to discuss political strategy with Thurlow Weed.

❖ AL endorses an effort by a New York merchant to go to Richmond to supply clothes and blankets to Union prisoners held by the Confederacy.

September 22, Thursday

Gen. Philip Sheridan, pursuing the retreating rebels in the Shenandoah Valley, catches and defeats them again.

❖ AL attends a Cabinet meeting where they discuss Frémont's withdrawal from the presidential race.

❖ AL assures Gen. Grant that no further recruiting of Confederate POWs will occur without Grant's clearance. (A Pennsylvania draft district was organizing a unit at a POW camp, presumably to count against the district's draft quota. Grant insisted the unit be sent to New Mexico or to fight Indians.)

❖ AL discusses politics with Michigan Sen. Zachariah Chandler and Michigan State Sen. David Jerome.

September 23, Friday

❖ AL accepts Blair's standing offer to resign. (Blair's removal satisfied the Radical Republicans, who backed John Frémont and disliked Blair.)

❖ AL attends a Cabinet meeting where Blair's resignation is announced.

September 24, Saturday

❖ AL issues new orders by which trade with the South can be conducted at set locations.

❖ AL telegraphs former Ohio governor William Dennison: "Mr. Blair has resigned, and I appoint you Post-Master General. Come on immediately."

❖ AL asks the judge advocate general to look into the court-martial case of man whose wife has been lobbying AL. (They found no such case.)

September 25, Sunday

Union forces commence destroying the agricultural resources of the Shenandoah Valley.

September 26, Monday

❖ AL confers about selecting a treasury agent at Memphis, Tennessee.

❖ AL reminds Gen. Rosecrans in Missouri that he must permit soldiers to vote. (Rosecrans said he had no plan to do otherwise.)

September 27, Tuesday

❖ AL asks Gen. Butler about the complaints of "assistant surgeon" William Crouse who says Butler dismissed him and threw him out of his department. (Butler quickly replied that Crouse never actually accepted his appointment as assistant surgeon and was thrown out after he started drinking and acting crazy.)

❖ AL interviews John W. Wilson, who has arrived from England with a letter of introduction from British Liberal member of parliament John Bright.

❖ Dennison reports that he missed a train connection and is stuck in Steubenville, Ohio.

September 28, Wednesday

- ❖ AL confers with Pennsylvania Gov. Andrew Curtin to clear the air between them on various (unstated) issues.

September 29, Thursday

Outside Petersburg, Union forces launch offensives around both flanks of the trench line.

- ❖ AL tells Gen. Grant that he fears Lee might send reinforcements to the Shenandoah Valley.

September 30, Friday

Outside Petersburg, the Union forces hold most of the gains they made yesterday. In Georgia, Hood moves against the railroad between Chattanooga and Atlanta.

- ❖ AL hires John Summerfield Staples to serve in the army as his draftee substitute. (Staples mostly served behind the lines. His hometown later put up a monument to him.)
- ❖ AL attends a Cabinet meeting where they discuss the admission of Nevada into the Union.

OCTOBER 1864

Summary: *The battle fronts and state elections shift decidedly in AL's favor.*

October 1, Saturday

- ❖ AL endorses a plan to buy clothes and food on credit for refugee Indians in Kansas.
- ❖ Welles confers with AL about naval operations in the Gulf of Mexico.

October 2, Sunday

- ❖ AL looks into vacant judge positions to which he could appoint Bates.
- ❖ AL interviews a Missouri newspaper editor concerning politics in St. Louis.

October 3, Monday

Hood interrupts Gen. Sherman's rail link.

- ❖ AL meets his official draft substitute, John Summerfield Staples, plus Staples' father and others. AL expresses hope that Staples will be "one of the fortunate ones." (The arrangement costs AL $750.)
- ❖ Browning visits AL in the evening.

October 4, Tuesday

- ❖ AL attends a Cabinet meeting were Dennison is sworn in as the new postmaster general.
- ❖ AL sends Nicolay to gauge political feelings in St. Louis.

❖ AL meets with an organization interested in distributing literature to soldiers.

❖ AL confers with Welles about possible arrangements for exchanging naval prisoners.

October 5, Wednesday

The dramatic Union defense of the railroad fort at Allatoona, Georgia, popularizes the phrase, "Hold the fort."

❖ AL is worried about the proposed exchange of naval prisoners, as other prisoner exchanges have been called off. After consulting with Seward, Stanton, Gen. Halleck and others, he decides to go ahead.

October 6, Thursday

❖ AL meets with Richard Graves MacDonnell, governor general of Nova Scotia.

❖ AL interviews a Kentucky delegation about political conditions there.

❖ Tad sends a carriage bill to Gus Gumpert for payment, saying: "I ain't got any money to pay the man with." (Gumpert was a Philadelphia merchant whom MTL left Tad with during her out-of-town shopping sprees.)

October 7, Friday

The rebel commerce raider CSS Florida is captured in a Brazilian port, in violation of Brazilian neutrality. The diplomatic incident later ends when it sinks "accidentally."

❖ AL appoints five additional directors for the Union Pacific Railroad.

❖ AL tells a biographer that he has never used the word "Jacobinism" in relation to Congress.

- ❖ AL confers with Gen. Nathaniel Banks concerning conditions in Louisiana.
- ❖ AL interviews Mrs. Anna Byers-Jennings, who is seeking the release of Daniel Hayden of Missouri. He tells her to return at 8 a.m. tomorrow.
- ❖ Browning visits AL.

October 8, Saturday

- ❖ Mrs. Anna Byers-Jennings returns at 8 a.m. AL grants her request. She dines at the White House that evening.
- ❖ AL, Stanton, and Gen. Halleck attend the funeral of Lt. John Meigs, son of Gen. Meigs. (He was killed on a map-making expedition when he ran into a Confederate patrol in the rain. His grave was later topped with a prone statue depicting him lying dead in the mud trampled by enemy horses.)
- ❖ The owners of the *Baltimore Evening Post* ask AL to rescind Gen. Lew Wallace's order suppressing the newspaper.

October 9, Sunday

- ❖ AL telegraphs Simon Cameron: "Have no alarm on bogus dispatches." (Cameron had heard a rumor of a disaster concerning the Union army at Petersburg, Virginia.)

October 10, Monday

- ❖ AL testifies for an army claims board that during the Confederate raid in July he watched the Union artillery shell houses, and thought it was necessary. (An owner unsuccessfully argued that the shelling was not war damage, but the government taking possession of private property for public use.)
- ❖ AL hails the proposed new Maryland state constitution, which abolishes slavery.
- ❖ AL confers with Welles about enabling sailors to vote, and bounty pay for marines.

October 11, Tuesday

Election day in many states.

❖ AL telegraphs RTL in Cambridge, Massachusetts, inquiring about her health.
❖ AL goes to the War Department in the evening and stays past midnight getting election results. Meanwhile he reads humor by "Petroleum V. Nasby" (David Locke).

October 12, Wednesday

❖ AL withdraws permission for the delivery of a gunboat being built in New York for the Japanese government due to unsettled conditions in Japan.
❖ AL telegraphs Gen. Grant that Indiana and Ohio are "largely for us" but Pennsylvania remains too close to call.

October 13, Thursday

❖ Based on yesterday's elections, AL estimates that in November he will get 120 electoral votes versus 114. (In fact, it would be 212 to 21.)
❖ AL continues visiting the War Department telegraph office for state election results.
❖ Chief Justice Roger Taney died last night. AL tells Hay that he is in no hurry to replace Taney.
❖ AL tells Indiana Gov. Oliver Morton that he is not in a position to ask Gen. Sherman to allow the soldiers who came home to vote in October to stay through the November election, having told Sherman that was not a requirement.

October 15, Saturday

❖ AL attends funeral services of Chief Justice Roger Taney.
❖ AL hears protests against the voting procedures used in Tennessee.

❖ AL hears that the Maryland state constitution is passing only because of the soldier vote.

October 16, Sunday

❖ AL replies to Pennsylvania Rep. James Moorhead: "I do not remember about the Peter Gilner case, and must look it up before I can answer." (AL later commuted the sentence.)

October 17, Monday

Hood moves west into Alabama. Gen. Sherman decides Hood is not worth chasing.

❖ AL writes "Stampeded" on a gloomy letter from Illinois Rep. Elihu Washburne expressing doubt about the upcoming election.
❖ Browning urges AL to appoint Stanton to replace Roger Taney, but AL responds that Bates has already asked for the position.

October 18, Tuesday

❖ AL confers about New York politics and campaign expenses.

October 19, Wednesday

Rebel forces in the Shenandoah Valley make a surprise attack on the main Union camp, overrun it, and commence looting. They are in turn crushed by a counterattack.

❖ AL endorses the plea of a man trying to get his brother-in-law exchanged from a rebel prison. (The authorities declined to act, saying it would be unjust to the prisoners who are not exchanged. Meanwhile, the man escaped.)
❖ Local Marylanders, celebrating the new state constitution, serenade the White House. AL responds: "If I shall live, I

shall remain president until the fourth of next March; and...
in the interval I shall do my utmost that whoever is to
hold the helm for the next voyage, shall start with the best
possible chance to save the ship."

❖ Nicolay reports on the causes of dissension among the
Republicans in Missouri: "personal spite or greed for spoils."

October 20, Thursday

❖ AL proclaims that the last Thursday in November will be a
day of thanksgiving.

October 21, Friday

❖ AL responds to a serenade celebrating the recent Union
victory in the Shenandoah Valley: "How fortunate it was for
the Secesh that Sheridan was a very little man. If he had been
a large man, there is no knowing what he would have done
with them."

October 22, Saturday

❖ AL receives a delegation complaining about the way the
presidential election is being handled in Tennessee. He
refuses to interfere.

❖ AL attends a military review and misses a visit from
Thurlow Weed.

❖ AL issues a permit for two British Quakers to pass through
the lines into the Confederacy.

October 23, Sunday

❖ AL meets with a delegation of Jews from New York City.

October 24, Monday

❖ AL reviews a new regiment organized from the latest call-up.

❖ Browning and a treasury agent confer with AL about trading in cotton.

October 25, Tuesday

❖ AL sends orders to Nashville, Tennessee, to suspend an execution.

October 26, Wednesday

❖ AL responds negatively to a petition from citizens of two counties in Kentucky asking for the refund of money collected from them to compensate Union loyalists for damages suffered from rebel depredations, although the petitioners openly admit that they sympathize with the Confederacy.

❖ AL orders the release of "Big Eagle," an Indian confined in Davenport, Iowa.

October 27, Thursday

Outside Petersburg, Gen. Grant sends three corps to outflank the rebel west flank, but they are driven back. Winter thereafter stifles major operations.

❖ AL orders a general to look into the petition he received yesterday from Kentucky to at least make sure the local authorities are not lining their pockets.

❖ AL meets with Charles Ballance, an old friend and fellow Illinois lawyer.

October 28, Friday

During the night, the ironclad CSS Albemarle is sunk at its dock by a Union lieutenant standing in the front of an open steam launch holding a long pole with a bucket of explosives at the end. The launch also sinks, but the lieutenant survives, steals a skiff, and paddles out to sea to report to the fleet. (He had a brother who won a posthumous Medal of Honor at Gettysburg.)

- ❖ AL attends a Cabinet meeting where they mostly discuss the upcoming election.
- ❖ After a direct appeal from the prisoner's mother, AL endorses the release of a POW.
- ❖ Welles complains to AL about nautical traffic jams tying up ships in two ports.
- ❖ AL, MTL, and Tad move from the Soldiers' Home back to the White House for the winter.

October 29, Saturday

- ❖ AL in the morning receives women's rights campaigner Sojourner Truth, and signs her autograph album.
- ❖ AL confers with Simon Cameron about the upcoming election and its likely aftermath.

October 30, Sunday

Hood begins concentrating his forces at Tuscumbia, Alabama, intending to move north, retake Tennessee and Kentucky, then move east to partner with Lee to finish off the Yankees in Virginia.

- ❖ AL telegraphs newspaper editor Alexander McClure in Harrisburg, Pennsylvania, asking for his thoughts about the upcoming election.

October 31, Monday

- ❖ AL issues a proclamation admitting Nevada into the union.
- ❖ AL confers with Stanton about a suggestion that they defer men from the draft in order to create a border security unit in Pennsylvania.
- ❖ AL thanks a discharged regiment of hundred-day men.

NOVEMBER 1864

Summary: *The turnaround continues as AL hand-ily wins reelection and Gen. Sherman begins marching through Georgia.*

November 1, Tuesday
- ❖ AL hears Seward read a dispatch announcing the passage of the new (abolitionist) Maryland state constitution.
- ❖ Gen. Butler confers with AL prior to taking charge of policing New York polling places for the national election.
- ❖ AL confers with an associate of James Gordon Bennett about appointing Bennett as minister to France.

November 2, Wednesday
- ❖ AL also receives two New York autograph seekers.
- ❖ Emily Todd Helm asks for clearance to go south to sell cotton.

November 3, Thursday
- ❖ AL issues orders to get a furloughed soldier home in time to vote, although he knows the man intends to vote for Gen. McClellan.
- ❖ AL hears a report from his podiatrist, who has been rallying the Jewish vote in New York City.

November 4, Friday
- ❖ AL officially approves the location of the first one hundred miles of the Union Pacific railroad, west of Omaha, Nebraska.

❖ AL confers with a New York treasury official regarding a rumored conspiracy in which certain banks will raise the price of gold on election day.

❖ AL orders that the unindicted prisoners from the May Illinois Copperhead riot be released, and the indicted ones turned over to the local sheriff.

November 5, Saturday

❖ AL loans $260 for five months to M. B. Church, who had worked in the office of Lincoln and Herndon. (It was never repaid. After AL's death MTL directed that it not be collected.)

November 6, Sunday

❖ AL sends a news summary to Seward, who is home in Auburn, New York. Much of it is from Richmond newspapers.

November 7, Monday

The Union high command scratches together an army in Tennessee to confront Hood.

❖ AL advises Gen. Butler to avoid clashes between the army and local militia during the upcoming election in New York.

❖ Probably so he can get home to vote, AL orders a five-day leave, pass, and transportation to and from Philadelphia for a lieutenant.

❖ AL meets in the evening with Quaker minister Elizabeth Comstock, who reads from the Book of Isaiah.

November 8, Tuesday

Union presidential election.

❖ At about 7 p.m. AL goes with Hay to Stanton's office in the War Department to view telegraphed election returns. Welles, Fox, and others come and go. During quiet intervals, AL reads aloud from the humor writings of "Petroleum V. Nasby" (David Locke), to the annoyance of Stanton. An army officer brings takeout food at about midnight: fried oysters.

❖ AL sends another news summary to Seward in Auburn.

November 9, Wednesday

Gen. Sherman tells his army to "forage liberally."

❖ AL is serenaded at about 2 a.m. by a large crowd celebrating his reelection. He makes a short speech.

❖ AL telegraphs the election results to his old friend Dr. Anson Henry in Oregon, but then does not want to sign the message as it sounds boastful. A newspaper reporter signs it and AL has it sent.

November 10, Thursday

❖ AL endorses the appointment of Mrs. Ella Hobart as chaplain of a Wisconsin artillery regiment. But Stanton will not approve, not wishing to start a precedent.

❖ AL responds to another serenade celebrating his reelection: "If the rebellion could force us to forego or postpone a national election, it might fairly claim to have already conquered and ruined us."

November 11, Friday

❖ AL attends a Cabinet meeting where the members see the contents of the memorandum they signed on August 23.

❖ AL confers with Seward about the seizure of the CSS *Florida* in a neutral Brazilian port.

❖ AL confers about a contractor who supplied tents that violated army regulations.

November 12, Saturday

Union forces begin destroying Atlanta, sparing houses and churches.

❖ At the request of former Ohio congressman John Bingham, AL endorses a pass for a woman in Kentucky.

November 13, Sunday

French troops take Mazatlán, Mexico.

❖ AL continues receiving congratulatory telegrams on his reelection.

November 14, Monday

❖ Gen. Burnside meets in the morning with AL.
❖ Browning meets with AL in the evening and finds that he has not yet started his message to Congress.
❖ AL writes to Gen. Stephen Hurlbut in Louisiana asking why the military authorities there appear to be opposed to the new state government. (Hurlbut replied that nothing has been done for the freed slaves there since the passage of the new Louisiana state constitution except for what the military authorities have done.)

November 15, Tuesday

Gen. Sherman's forces, nearly unopposed, move out of Atlanta toward the sea.

❖ AL asks Gen. George Thomas what force Gen. A. C. Gillem had when he was attacked and routed last night near Morristown, Tennessee. (He had about 1,500 men. AL apparently did not hold it against Gillem. This is the same Gillem whose promotion was delayed in July because someone misspelled his name.)

❖ AL sees Shakespeare's *Hamlet* at Grover's Theater.

November 16, Wednesday

❖ AL confers with Thurlow Weed about the election results.
❖ AL refers a refugee from Alabama to Stanton about supplying ammunition to Unionists in northern Alabama.

November 17, Thursday

❖ AL refers to Seward a plan for buying a controlling interest in the thirty-six remaining Confederate newspapers. (Seward diplomatically replied that no funds were available.)
❖ AL receives the Maryland Union Committee, which congratulates him on his reelection. AL replies that the election shows his policy is the best and only one that can save the country.
❖ AL sees two letters forwarded by Gen. John Dix describing an assassination plot against him, but he shows little interest.

November 18, Friday

❖ AL grants a one-week stay of execution for a condemned soldier.
❖ Dinner guests at the White House are the Rev. and Mrs. Phineas Gurley.

November 19, Saturday

❖ AL repeats his October-26 order for the release of the Indian "Big Eagle" imprisoned in Davenport, Iowa. (The Indian's lawyer complained that the previous order was ignored amidst "gross insults" because it was written with pencil and delivered by a civilian.)

November 21, Monday

Hood's force heads north into Tennessee.

❖ AL writes to the widow Lydia Bixby in Boston after learning (incorrectly) that she had lost five sons in the army: "I feel how weak and fruitless must be any words of mine which should attempt to beguile you from the grief of a loss so overwhelming. But I cannot refrain from tendering to you the consolation that may be found in the thanks of the Republic they died to save." (She had lost two sons and claimed the same fate for the other three for graft purposes.)

November 22, Tuesday

Gen. Sherman's force occupy Milledgeville, Georgia's state capital at the time.

❖ The governor of Kentucky asks AL to release the lieutenant governor of Kentucky who has been arrested for making speeches urging armed resistance to the enlistment or enrollment of slaves. AL says he hopes harmony can be restored now that the election is over.
❖ Elizabeth Todd Grimsley (cousin of MTL) seeks an appointment as a postmaster in Springfield, Illinois.

November 23, Wednesday

❖ AL meets with Stanton, Gen. Halleck, and Gen. Grant and his staff.

November 24, Thursday

❖ AL receives a resignation letter from Bates. (Now that the election crisis was over he wanted to return to private life.)

November 25, Friday

❖ AL attends a Cabinet meeting and reads a draft of his annual message to Congress.

❖ AL tells Pennsylvania Gov. Andrew Curtin that rumors that three southern states have offered to return to the Union are false.

November 26, Saturday

Hood's force runs into a Union force at Columbia, Tennessee, which retreats out of reach.

❖ AL decides that Gen. Nathaniel Banks can stay in Washington for the time being to lobby for congressional acceptance of the new civilian government in Louisiana.
❖ AL offers the attorney general Cabinet post to Joseph Holt, the judge advocate general.

November 29, Tuesday

Hood tries to catch the retreating Union force, fails, and is lavish with his blame.

❖ AL issues an order that if John Castleman is convicted and sentenced, execution of the sentence is to be suspended pending AL's review of the case. (Castleman was a Confederate agent who had been sent to Chicago to help instigate an insurrection there, but was quickly caught. After the war, he was released without trial on the condition that he leave the country, and he did for eighteen months. AL's order was apparently a favor to Castleman's brother-in-law.)
❖ AL sends identical letters to nine state governors again asking for aggregate election results.

November 30, Wednesday

Hood catches up with the retreating Union force and impetuously attacks, losing 6,000 men and six generals. The Union force then resumes its retreat.

❖ AL endorses a request by two New Jersey Quakers for the release of three Quakers held as POWs, saying they had been drafted by the Confederates.

❖ Joseph Holt, the judge advocate general, turns down the attorney general Cabinet position and instead recommends James Speed, an old friend of AL.

DECEMBER 1864

Summary: The quixotic rebel invasion of Tennessee is defeated, Gen. Sherman gets to the sea, but an attempt to take the last rebel seaport is fumbled. On the political front, AL gears up for his next initiative: passage of the 13th Amendment.

December 1, Thursday

The retreating Federals reach Nashville, Tennessee, now a Union fortress.

❖ AL telegraphs James Speed in Louisville, Kentucky: "I appoint you to be Attorney General. Please come on at once."
❖ The resignation of Bates becomes effective and he says goodbye to AL.
❖ Two Tennessee women appeal to AL for the release of their POW husbands. One of them says her husband is a religious man. AL orders the release of the two men but then tells the women what he thinks of their pro-slavery religion, writing it down under the title "The President's Last, Shortest, and Best Speech: "Religion that sets men to rebel and fight against their government, because, as they think, that government does not sufficiently help some men to eat their bread on the sweat of other men's faces, is not the sort of religion upon which people can get to heaven!"

December 2, Friday

Hood's forces dig in outside Nashville. They are not strong enough to besiege the city.

- ❖ AL confers with Indiana Rep. Schuyler Colfax, who urges AL to appoint Chase as the new Supreme Court chief justice.

December 3, Saturday

- ❖ AL attends a Cabinet meeting where he reads a draft of his annual message to Congress.
- ❖ AL denies departure permission for a second warship being built for Japan and authorizes Welles to buy it if it seems suitable.
- ❖ AL talks to reporter Noah Brooks about widespread speculation that Chase will be the next Supreme Court chief justice.

December 5, Monday

- ❖ AL confers with an agent being sent to meet with Gen. Sherman when Sherman reaches the coast.
- ❖ AL, MTL, Seward, Nicolay, and Hay attend *Faust* at Grover's Theater.

December 6, Tuesday

Congress convenes.

- ❖ AL attends a Cabinet meeting.
- ❖ AL sends his annual message to Congress: Foreign relations are favorable. Immigration has been encouraged. Nevada has been admitted, and other territories are growing rapidly. The new Agriculture Department is doing well. Louisiana and Arkansas have organized loyal state governments. Public debt has reached 1.7 billion dollars, but resources remain abundant. The war will continue until "it shall have ceased on the part of those who began it." AL recommends the passage of the 13th Amendment.
- ❖ AL nominates Chase as the new chief justice.

❖ AL responds to a serenading crowd, and mentions Gen. Sherman, currently out of touch in Georgia: "We all know where he went in at, but I can't tell where he will come out at."

December 7, Wednesday

❖ AL confers about patronage with New Mexico Territorial Rep. Francisco Perea.
❖ AL consults with party worker Abel Corbin about organizing the House vote for passage of the 13th Amendment.
❖ In the afternoon, AL formally receives the six justices of the U.S. Supreme Court.
❖ AL asks Stanton to look into a Maryland commission that is supposed to investigate loyalty issues but apparently has not done anything.

December 8, Thursday

Winter weather stifles operations around Nashville.

December 9, Friday

❖ AL attends a Cabinet meeting.
❖ Dr. Robert Stone, AL's family physician, asks AL's help sending clothes to his wife's family in Richmond. (AL gave him a pass for a box of clothes.)
❖ AL goes to the theater with Massachusetts Sen. Charles Sumner and a diplomat. Ward Hill Lamon is upset that AL goes without a guard.

December 10, Saturday

Gen. Sherman's army reaches Savannah, Georgia.

❖ AL authorizes a special commission, with subpoena power, to investigate military and civil administration west of the Mississippi.

❖ AL meets *Harper's Weekly* illustrator Thomas Nast, inventor of the modern visualization of Santa Claus.

❖ Congress not being in session today, AL is swarmed by congressman with constituent requests.

❖ Ward Hill Lamon tries to resign over last night's security slackness.

December 12, Monday

❖ At the request of Kentucky Rep. William Randall, AL releases two POWs.

❖ AL sends a long letter to Gen. Edward Canby in Louisiana explaining that the administration is using human greed to drain cotton out of the South (now that it's reached six times the pre-war price) so that the Confederacy cannot use it to fund its operations. As for the new Louisiana civil government, it may not amount to much now, but it has to start somewhere.

December 13, Tuesday

Gen. Sherman's army gains contact with the Union fleet.

❖ AL sends to the Senate for ratification a commerce and extradition treaty with Haiti.

December 14, Wednesday

❖ AL asks Stanton to investigate the case of a man who volunteered for the military and was rejected, but was then drafted.

December 15, Thursday

The sleet having melted, the Union force at Nashville attacks Hood's forces, driving them back two miles.

❖ AL confers with Stanton, Gen. Grant and Gen. Halleck on the question of removing Gen. George Thomas, who keeps delaying an offensive against Hood outside Nashville. AL agrees with Grant's decision to send another general to replace Thomas. If an offensive begins before the replacement arrives, the replacement is to do nothing. (They are unaware that the offensive has already begun.)

❖ That night Stanton brings news to AL about the fighting at Nashville.

December 16, Friday

Outside Nashville, Hood's army resists until midafternoon, then collapses. The retreat doesn't stop until Tupelo, Mississippi, 200 miles and three weeks later.

❖ AL sends congratulations to Gen. George Thomas, whose replacement he authorized yesterday.
❖ AL attends a Cabinet meeting where he introduces James Speed, the new attorney general.
❖ AL receives a delegation from the Freedmen's Aid Society of Baltimore.

December 17, Saturday

❖ AL confers with Fox, who wants AL to meet a lawyer the navy uses to investigate fraud cases.

December 19, Monday

❖ AL calls for 300,000 additional volunteers, to make up for casualties and for shortfalls in the previous call-ups.
❖ AL attends a concert at Ford's Theater.
❖ Browning meets with AL at the White House in the evening.

December 20, Tuesday

The Confederates evacuate Savannah.

❖ AL attends a Cabinet meeting.

❖ AL confers with Gen. Nathaniel Banks about events in New Orleans.

December 21, Wednesday

❖ AL tells Gen. Butler to suspend the election he has reportedly scheduled for the Eastern Shore of Virginia until he can confer with AL about it. (Gen. Butler replied that no such election had been scheduled. The locals had only discussed holding a political meeting.)
❖ AL hears from a delegation who wants the incumbent retained in the Baltimore custom house.
❖ AL telegraphs MTL in Philadelphia: "Do not come on the night train. It is too cold. Come in the morning."

December 22, Thursday

Gen. Sherman presents Savannah to AL as a "Christmas gift."

❖ AL approves the latest Treasury Department regulations regarding commerce with the South.
❖ AL consults with the Commissioner of Internal Revenue regarding errors in various regulations.
❖ AL meets with Kansas Sen. James Lane who is returning to Kansas to run for reelection. (He ran successfully and then killed himself.)
❖ AL forwards recommendations that James Bigelow, U.S. consul in Paris, be named the next minister to France. (He was.)
❖ AL again pardons a fugitive deserter on condition that he return to his unit and serve his enlistment.

December 23, Friday

❖ AL attends a Cabinet meeting.
❖ AL issues a safe-conduct pass for James Harrison of St. Louis, letting him take as many as three steamboats

past Union lines as long as he follows Treasury Department regulations.

December 24, Saturday

❖ AL hears from a representative from Cleveland who emphasizes the importance of establishing a navy yard on the Great Lakes.

❖ Welles has AL commute a death sentence, and also issue a pass for a woman to go to Richmond.

December 25, Sunday

Gen. Butler lands an army outside Fort Fisher, which defends Wilmington, North Carolina, the last Confederate seaport. After some probing, Butler decides the fort is too strong, reembarks the invasion force, and withdraws.

❖ AL asks Illinois Rep. John Farnsworth if he can do anything for an Illinois woman who is trying to get her sick son out of the army.

December 26, Monday

❖ AL sends congratulations to Gen. Sherman, adding: "When you were about leaving Atlanta for the Atlantic coast, I was anxious, if not fearful; but feeling that you were the better judge, and remembering that 'nothing risked, nothing gained' I did not interfere. Now, the undertaking being a success, the honor is all yours; for I believe none of us went farther than to acquiesce."

❖ AL hosts a Christmas reception at the White House.

December 27, Tuesday

❖ At the request of Fessenden, AL nominates Franklin Yeaton to West Point. (He graduated in 1869.)

❖ AL attends a Cabinet meeting.
❖ AL thanks the College of New Jersey (now Princeton University) for conferring on him a Doctor of Laws degree.

December 28, Wednesday

❖ AL telegraphs Gen. Grant asking for his opinion on the abruptly aborted Wilmington, North Carolina, expedition. (Grant immediately replied: "The Wilmington expedition has proven a gross and culpable failure.... Who is to blame I hope will be known.")
❖ Two women lobby AL about a condemned relative and AL suspends his execution for six weeks.
❖ Welles calls on AL and finds a large crowd waiting on him, "chiefly female."

December 29, Thursday

❖ Welles shows AL dispatches concerning the failure of the expedition to Fort Fisher, North Carolina.

December 30, Friday

❖ AL attends a Cabinet meeting where they discuss the failure at Fort Fisher and possible trouble between Gen. Butler and Admiral David Porter.
❖ AL decides to remove Gen. Butler from command.

December 31, Saturday

❖ AL confers with a woman from Philadelphia who is hoping to get her nephew released from a Confederate prison.
❖ Welles delivers dispatches from Admiral David Porter concerning Fort Fisher.
❖ AL reappoints members of the Levy Court (i.e., the board of local magistrates that performed the role of county commissioners).

❧1865 ☙

JANUARY 1
THROUGH APRIL 15

JANUARY 1865

Summary: With the war winding down, AL is able to work toward his personal goal: the permanent, de jure elimination of slavery. Meanwhile, the rebels show interest in a peace conference—but on their terms.

January 2, Monday

- ❖ AL receives a delegation from Kentucky asking that Gen. Butler be put in charge of their state. AL is incredulous: "How long will it be before you…will be howling to me to remove him?"
- ❖ AL and MTL hold a crowded New Year's reception at the White House.

January 3, Tuesday

- ❖ AL attends a Cabinet meeting with only three members present.
- ❖ AL asks Seward to find a diplomatic post for Col. Philip Figyelmessy, a Hungarian who had been on the staff of fellow Hungarian Gen. Julius Stahel. (He was later made U.S. consul at Demerara, of province of British Guiana, modern Guiana, in South America).

January 4, Wednesday

- ❖ AL grants permission to Fergus Peniston to transport from outside Union lines 23,640 bales of cotton and 17,300 barrels of naval stores that he already owned (i.e., he is not paying the enemy for them.) to New Orleans.

❖ AL tells Stanton that he favors unrestricted trade from Kentucky across the Ohio River.

January 5, Thursday

❖ AL receives a delegation from Maryland asking that state Senator-elect Levin Waters be released from military custody.
❖ Browning visits AL, who talks about Emily Todd Helm and Martha Todd White, both of whom have cotton to sell.
❖ AL directs Gen. Grant to issue a pass to Richard Jacob, lieutenant governor of Kentucky, who is in Richmond, so he can come to AL in Washington.
❖ AL returns to the House a joint resolution containing the cumulative corrections to the Internal Revenue Act.

January 6, Friday

Sometimes heated debate begins in the House on the 13th Amendment. It has already passed the Senate.

❖ AL attends a Cabinet meeting.
❖ Gen. Grant telegraphs AL requesting the prompt removal of Gen. Butler.
❖ AL meets with Horace Greeley.
❖ AL asks Gen. Napoleon Dana in Memphis, Tennessee, why he is imposing conditions on trade over and above those of the Treasury Department. (Dana replied with a fawning apology.)

January 7, Saturday

Gen. Butler is removed.

❖ AL consults with Welles and Admiral David Farragut about the capture of Mobile, Alabama.

❖ AL, MTL, and Tad see *Leah, The Forsaken* starring Avonia Jones at Grover's Theater.

January 8, Sunday

❖ AL again meets with Shakespearean actor James Hackett, who says he would like to see Hackett play Shakespeare's "Falstaff" character. He also complains of being consistently oppressed by cares of state and having little time for socializing or recreation.

January 9, Monday

❖ AL asks Illinois Sen. Lyman Trumbull about seating the proposed senators from the Louisiana reconstruction state government: "Can Louisiana be brought into proper practical relations with the Union, sooner, by admitting or by rejecting the proposed senators?" (Regardless, they weren't seated, as congressman either thought the new state constitution wasn't radical enough, or that the enabling elections were a facade.)

❖ AL hosts the first White House evening reception of the season.

January 10, Tuesday

❖ AL attends a Cabinet meeting.

❖ AL tells the head of the Baltimore and Ohio Railroad, that coal (used to make gas for the gaslight utility) must be gotten to Washington, if necessary at the expense of other freight priorities.

January 12, Thursday

Francis Blair Sr., carrying a pass from AL, meets with Jefferson Davis, who agrees to peace negotiations "between our two countries."

❖ AL pardons David Levy for desertion on condition that he serve out his enlistment. (Levy used AL's note in 1902 to prove that he qualified for a pension.)

January 13, Friday

The force that landed at Fort Fisher, North Carolina, last month lands there again, under new management. In Mississippi, Hood resigns.

❖ AL grants Gen. Butler permission to come to Washington, as he has been summoned to a meeting of the Joint Committee on the Conduct of the War.

January 14, Saturday

❖ AL writes to Gen. Grant asking about the fate of Henry Foote, a former Tennessee member of the Confederate Congress whom the Confederates arrested as he tried to leave Richmond for Washington. (Grant didn't know anything. Foote later managed to make it to in England and then to New York, where he was arrested in turn by Union authorities.)
❖ MTL hosts her first Saturday reception of the season, attended also by AL and RTL.

January 15, Sunday

Fort Fisher falls to a determined assault, closing the last rebel seaport.

❖ AL telegraphs Gen. Grenville Dodge in St. Louis that it might be possible to bring calm to northern Missouri by withdrawing Union troops from there. (Dodge responded that loyal residents would hate the idea and disloyal residents would love it.)

❖ Seward directs government offices to honor the memory of Edward Everett, who died at 4 a.m.

❖ AL meets with Prof. Lewis Agassiz, geologist.

January 16, Monday

❖ AL writes a pass for Harriet Bledsoe, the wife of former acting assistant Confederate Secretary of War Albert Bledsoe. A friend of AL and MTL from her younger days in Springfield, Illinois, she had gone North to get clothing for her children.

❖ Francis Blair Sr. returns from his interview with Jefferson Davis and reports to AL.

❖ AL confers with New Mexico Territorial Rep. Francisco Perea about patronage in New Mexico.

January 17, Tuesday

❖ AL attends a Cabinet meeting where they discuss the recent capture of Fort Fisher.

❖ At the request of Kentucky Sen. Lazarus Powell, AL issues the following "safeguard": "Let no depredation be committed upon the property or possessions of the 'Sisters of Charity' at Nazareth Academy, near Bardstown, Kentucky."

January 18, Wednesday

❖ AL again confers with Francis Blair Sr. regarding Blair's talks with Jefferson Davis.

❖ AL confers with Ohio Rep. James Ashley about passage of the 13th Amendment in the House.

January 19, Thursday

❖ AL writes to Gen. Grant about getting a job for RTL. (Grant made RTL a captain on his staff.)

- ❖ AL writes to Gen. Edward Ord regarding Frank Judd, son of Norman Judd who managed AL's 1860 presidential campaign and who is now minister to Prussia. Frank Judd had been nominated to West Point, skipped the entrance exam, deserted from two regiments, and was facing execution. "He is the son of so close a friend of mine that I must not let him be executed." (He was not executed.)
- ❖ AL confers with an Indiana official about possible prisoner exchanges.

January 20, Friday

- ❖ AL attends a Cabinet meeting where Stanton reports on his recent trip to Savannah, Georgia.
- ❖ AL directs Gen. Joseph Reynolds in Arkansas to look into the case of a woman whose house and furniture were taken by the military.

January 21, Saturday

- ❖ AL attends a brief conference with Gen. Grant, Gen. Sheridan, and Stanton.
- ❖ MTL's Saturday reception is well attended despite poor weather.

January 22, Sunday

- ❖ AL confers with New York Gov. Reuben Fenton about the calculation of local draft quotas.

January 23, Monday

- ❖ AL spends the day reviewing forty-five court-martial cases.
- ❖ AL attends the White House evening reception.

January 24, Tuesday

Regular prisoner exchanges resume.

❖ AL informs Johnson that he must be in Washington for the inauguration on March 4. (Johnson, currently military governor of Tennessee, wanted to remain in Tennessee until April 3 when the state would formally reenter the Union.)
❖ AL, Welles, Stanton, and Admiral Farragut confer about navy personnel matters.

January 25, Wednesday

❖ AL sends a memo to Stanton titled "About Jews." First, he asks that his celebrity podiatrist, Dr. Isachar Zacharie, be allowed into Savannah to bring back certain relatives now that the port is under Union control. Second, he is concerned that Major Leopold Blumenburg, a Baltimore Unionist, has been dismissed from the army without a hearing. (Wounded at Antietam, Blumenburg had been made a provost-marshal but was later accused of using enhanced interrogation methods on suspected deserters. AL gave him a civilian job.)
❖ AL reviews thirty court-martial cases.

January 26, Thursday

❖ AL meets with the mayor of Cleveland and with Ohio congressman regarding naval defenses on the Great Lakes.
❖ AL meets with a delegation of working women from the Philadelphia Arsenal.

January 27, Friday

❖ AL sends the Senate a list of Federal district attorney nominations and vacancies.
❖ Several hundred members of the U.S. Christian Commission call on AL to thank him for his help, and he responds that he and they are both working for the same cause.

January 28, Saturday

❖ AL again confers with Francis Blair Sr. about Blair's meeting with Jefferson Davis.

❖ At the request of a Kentucky congressman and others, AL issues a pass to Mrs. Lallie Holliday of Kentucky to visit her husband in the Union POW camp on Lake Erie.

❖ AL is not able to attend MTL's afternoon reception due to official engagements.

January 29, Sunday

❖ AL attends the third anniversary meeting of the U.S. Sanitary Commission held at night in the House chamber.

January 30, Monday

❖ AL sends a letter to be handed to the three Confederate commissioners scheduled to come to Fortress Monroe: "That if you pass through the U.S. Military lines it will be understood that you do so for the purpose of an informal conference, on the basis of the letter, a copy of which is on the reverse side of this sheet." The letter on the reverse side is a copy of the letter that AL gave to Francis Blair Sr. to give to Jefferson Davis, saying AL was agreeable to a peace conference "with the view of securing peace to the people of our one common country."

January 31, Tuesday

The 13th Amendment passes the House by the necessary two-thirds majority. (It became effective December 18, 1865, when ratified by enough states.)

❖ AL sends Seward to Fortress Monroe to confer informally with the three Confederate commissioners. AL says he will respond to any proposals that are not inconsistent with the restoration of peace and national authority, and with the abolition of slavery.

FEBRUARY 1865

Summary: *The peace conference immediately deadlocks—and the Confederate military position begins to collapse.*

February 1, Wednesday

In Georgia, Gen. Sherman's army moves north, troubled more by the weather than by the enemy.

❖ Referring to the peace conference, AL telegraphs Gen. Grant: "Let nothing which is transpiring, change, hinder, or delay your military movements, or plans."

❖ AL talks to Henry Ward Beecher about the prospects for peace, not mentioning the pending peace conference.

❖ AL confers with Illinois Democrat legislator James W. Singleton, whose reputation as a Copperhead recently got him an interview with Jefferson Davis.

❖ A crowd celebrating the 13th Amendment serenades AL, who responds: "This amendment is a King's cure for all the evils. It winds the whole thing up."

February 2, Thursday

❖ AL telegraphs Gen. Grant: "Say to the gentlemen I will meet them personally at Fortress Monroe as soon as I can get there."

❖ AL leaves surreptitiously at 11 a.m. on a special train to Annapolis, Maryland, where he boards a steamer which reaches Fortress Monroe in the evening. There he boards the steamer *River Queen* anchored in Hampton Roads.

February 3, Friday

- ❖ AL spends four hours with the Confederate peace commissioners. These include Alexander Stephens, AL's former political ally.
- ❖ The Confederates treat AL's precondition of reunion as a demand for unconditional surrender and the talks stall. But they agree to proceed with prisoner exchanges, including the exchange of Stephens' nephew.
- ❖ AL leaves of the area at about 5 p.m.

February 4, Saturday

- ❖ AL arrives in Washington at about 9 a.m., passing through Annapolis, Maryland.
- ❖ AL directs that the nephew of Alexander Stephens (John Stephens, a rebel lieutenant) be released from a POW camp and report to him at the White House.
- ❖ AL transmits to the Senate Seward's report on conditions in Mexico and correspondence on the case of the French military steamer *Rhine*. (Thanks to deceptive paperwork, the ship had carried provisions from San Francisco to French troops in Acapulco in August, violating U.S. neutrality.)
- ❖ AL meets with the Cabinet to report on what happened at Hampton Roads.
- ❖ AL attends MTL's Saturday reception at 1 p.m.

February 5, Sunday

Outside Petersburg, Virginia, the Union army resumes operations, pushing the trench line farther west.

- ❖ AL calls a special Cabinet meeting and reads his proposal to distribute $400 million among the slave states, in proportion to their slave populations, in return for an end of hostilities by April 1. The members unanimously oppose the idea. (It was never presented to Congress.)

February 6, Monday

- ❖ AL confers with a delegation from New York City regarding draft quotas.
- ❖ AL sets up a committee to examine the state draft quotas and credits for volunteers.
- ❖ The Tuesday evening reception has the largest attendance this season.

February 7, Tuesday

- ❖ AL attends a Cabinet meeting.
- ❖ AL authorizes a man living behind rebel lines to collect rent on property inside Washington, as he is known to be loyal.
- ❖ AL confers with Indiana Rep. Schuyler Colfax about the Hampton Roads conference.
- ❖ AL tells Gen. Grant that he can disregard trade permits at will. (Grant had turned back a steamboat with a permit to carry a cargo of sugar and coffee into the rebel lines and return with bales of cotton. Grant thought it would serve to feed the enemy.)
- ❖ AL telegraphs an officer in Kentucky: "Complaint is made to me that you are forcing negroes into the military service…. You must not force negroes any more than white men."

February 8, Wednesday

- ❖ AL interviews a delegation from west Tennessee about the hardships facing the people there.
- ❖ AL responds to a complaint from the governor of Vermont concerning the state's quota in the recent call-up: "The pending call is not for 300,000 men subject to fair credits, but is for 300,000 remaining after all fair credits have been deducted."
- ❖ AL and MTL host a dinner party at the White House for a dozen guests, including Dennison, Speed, and Admiral David Farragut.

February 9, Thursday

French troops take Oaxaca, Mexico.

❖ AL receives a delegation from the New York Young Men's Republican Union.

❖ Browning visits AL at night. AL gives him a letter to take to Gen. Grant about the activities of James W. Singleton (the self-appointed go-between with the Confederate government).

February 10, Friday

❖ AL sends documents to Congress concerning the Hampton Roads conference.

❖ AL attends a cabinet meeting.

❖ AL endorses the release of certain POWs at the request of Kentucky Sen. Garrett Davis, who assures AL that he is not charging money to make the request.

❖ AL sends the nephew of an Alexander Stephens to the South, with instructions for Stephens to send North an officer of the same rank, "imprisoned at Richmond, whose physical condition most urgently requires his release."

❖ AL, Gen. Grant, and Gen. Burnside attend Ford's Theater in the evening.

February 11, Saturday

❖ AL asks Stanton to see if he could help a group of Quakers from Illinois who are unable to pay the draft commutation fee.

❖ AL assists MTL in welcoming guests to the afternoon reception. These included Gen. and Mrs. Grant and Admiral and Mrs. David Farragut.

February 12, Sunday

❖ AL writes to Gen. John Pope in Missouri to tell him that provost-marshals cannot decide themselves when conditions of bonds have been violated and thereupon seize property and sell it. Courts do that.

❖ After consulting with a physician, AL is told a particular prisoner is "partially insane" and should be released on those grounds.

February 13, Monday

❖ Responding to an appeal from the prisoner's brother (a Baltimore resident) AL orders the parole of a Confederate lieutenant who is only fifteen.

❖ AL endorses a list of demands to the military commanders of western Tennessee, presented by the delegation he saw last Wednesday, mostly concerning limitations to military service for local officials and veterans.

❖ AL and MTL host a state dinner for sixteen senators and their wives. RTL also attends.

February 14, Tuesday

❖ AL approves a resolution providing for a "Congressional Directory."

❖ AL confers with a delegation from Philadelphia presenting recommendations for the relief of military orphans.

❖ AL confers about the appointment of James Gordon Bennett as minister to France.

❖ AL makes William Stoddard, formerly one of his secretaries, a marshal in the eastern district of Arkansas.

February 15, Wednesday

❖ AL attends the afternoon funeral of Maryland Sen. Thomas Hicks, held in the Senate chamber.

February 16, Thursday

❖ AL, apparently at one sitting, suspends two death sentences, paroles a POW so he can testify at a murder trial, and issues a pass for a Southern woman who had come North to get medical treatment for her child and wants to return to the South.

❖ AL, MTL, and RTL host a state dinner for twenty senators whose wives are not in the capital.

February 17, Friday

Gen. Sherman's troops enter Columbia, the capital of South Carolina, where the rebellion began. That night it burns to the ground. On the coast, the rebels evacuate Charleston, South Carolina, where the war began.

❖ Responding to a plea from Horace Greeley, AL agrees to the exchange of Roger Pryor, a Confederate general. (Pryor had been a firebrand secessionist Virginia newspaper editor before the war. After the war, he moved to New York City and became Ben Butler's law partner.)

❖ AL confers with Browning about the case of John Beall, condemned as a spy after trying to become a privateer on Lake Erie, sinking two ships in the process.

❖ AL issues a proclamation convening the Senate for a special session on March 4, 1865 (for the inauguration).

❖ AL commutes the sentence of several clothing merchants in Washington and Baltimore convicted by the testimony of a witness who AL distrusted.

❖ AL signs the commission of Capt. Robert T. Lincoln, U.S. Army.

February 18, Saturday

❖ AL confers with several people about the case of Norman King, whose death sentence AL had suspended but had not commuted. (He later pardoned King.)

❖ AL hears from a delegation from the Massachusetts legislature urging a Cabinet position for Massachusetts Gov. John Andrew.

❖ MTL hosts the regular Saturday-afternoon reception, assisted by AL.

February 20, Monday

❖ AL officially offers newspaper mogul James Gordon Bennett the position of minister to France.
❖ AL suspends White House public receptions "for the present."
❖ AL writes to Missouri Gov. Thomas Fletcher that while there is no organized enemy military force in the state, violence remains rampant. He suggests holding mass meetings where residents swear off violence.

February 21, Tuesday

❖ AL confers with Speed, Chase, and Welles concerning the suspension of habeas corpus.

February 22, Wednesday

❖ AL asks Stanton about how to respond to an appeal from officials in Philadelphia, who say they can raise one hundred volunteers a day if only the draft is put off for week, since they can't use their $400 bounty when the draft is in effect. (Stanton advised, "I am respectfully constrained to advise most earnestly against your interference with the draft in Philadelphia unless you are prepared to give it up altogether.")
❖ AL authorizes the release of POW Horace Lurton, reportedly ill, on the direct appeal of the soldier's mother. (At least that was story Lurton would tell after he became a Supreme Court justice.)
❖ Welles goes to the White House to report the taking of Fort Anderson, North Carolina (part of the defenses of Wilmington, North Carolina).

February 23, Thursday

❖ AL hears from numerous parties about the case of John Beall, scheduled to be executed tomorrow. (One of these may have been John Wilkes Booth.)

❖ Browning sees AL about the Beall case in the evening and finds AL undecided, as well as looking and feeling bad.

❖ AL tells various parties as they arrive at the White House that if their visit concerns Beall they will not get an audience.

February 24, Friday

❖ AL refuses to see a delegation about the John Beall case, saying his mind is made up. (Beall was hanged later that day.)

❖ AL pardons another deserter who appeals directly to him, on condition that the man returns to his unit and serves his enlistment.

February 25, Saturday

❖ MTL and AL greet guests at the Saturday afternoon reception.

❖ French diplomat Charles Adolphe de Pineton, the Marquis de Chambrun, attends the reception and meets AL. Later he writes: "He dominates everyone present and maintains his exalted position without the slightest effort."

February 26, Sunday

❖ AL sees painter Francis Carpenter in his office.

February 27, Monday

❖ AL sends a note to the commander of a particular fire engine asking him to pump out a particular well, "which Tad will show."

❖ Illinois Rep. Isaac Arnold confers with AL, asking for a job. (Arnold introduced the 13th Amendment in the House but decided not to run for reelection.)

MARCH 1865

Summary: After the Second Inauguration AL visits Gen. Grant's headquarters, as MTL's public behavior becomes increasingly problematic.

March 1, Wednesday

- ❖ AL responds to the official notification of his reelection: "I accept the renewed trust, with its yet onerous and perplexing duties and responsibilities."
- ❖ AL hails the establishment of a new bureau of the U.S. Sanitary Commission aimed at finding employment for disabled soldiers. (Sponsors included Theodore Roosevelt Sr.)

March 2, Thursday

The last Confederate force in the Shenandoah Valley is routed by Gen. Philip Sheridan, who then takes his force south to the Petersburg, Virginia, area.

- ❖ AL telegraphs Gen. Grant asking if the Richmond newspapers have said anything about Gen. Sherman, out of touch in the Carolinas. (Gen. Grant replied reassuringly: "There is every indication that Genl Sherman is perfectly safe.")

March 3, Friday

Congress holds its last meeting of the session, not adjourning until tomorrow morning.

- ❖ AL signs legislation establishing the Freedmen's Bureau.
- ❖ AL attends a Cabinet meeting.

- ❖ AL is at the Capitol signing bills late into the night.
- ❖ A delegation of New Yorkers serenades AL, who responds: "Sherman went in at Atlanta and came out right. He has gone in again at Savannah, and I propose three cheers for his coming out gloriously."

March 4, Saturday

Second Inauguration

Lincoln, center, delivers his second inaugural address, while his eventual assassin stands in the balcony above him.

- ❖ AL is at the Capitol early to sign bills.
- ❖ The weather is dark and rainy.

- ❖ MTL, RTL, and a friend in the family carriage approach the Capitol in the inaugural procession at about 10 a.m. MTL thinks the procession is too slow and cuts through.
- ❖ Ceremonies start in the Senate chamber at about noon.
- ❖ Johnson makes his inaugural address. Having self-medicated with whiskey due for a bout with typhoid, his address is a drunken, boorish tirade that drags on for an excruciating twenty minutes until Hamlin gets his attention.
- ❖ Johnson takes the oath of office with lengthy digressions, and sloppily kisses the Bible.
- ❖ The presidential party moves out to the speaker's platform erected on the outside of the Capitol. The crowd follows, pressing into every vantage point.
- ❖ The clouds part. A shaft of sunlight descends on the speaker's platform.
- ❖ AL delivers his Second Inaugural Address. There is no discussion of public policy or plans. He barely alludes to the "satisfactory" course of the war and tersely describes how the war began (brinksmanship) and its cause (slavery). He notes that both sides invoke God. While he doesn't see that the pro-slavery enemy has much grounds for expecting divine favor, "let us judge not, that we be not judged." Meanwhile the war has become a bloodbath that neither side wanted, indicating that the Almighty has His own purposes. Perhaps that the war must continue until the wealth accumulated by slavery is gone, and blood drawn by the sword equals blood drawn by the lash. With no hint of triumph he then calls for mercy in victory: "With malice toward none, with charity for all, with firmness in the right as God gives us to see the right, let us strive on to finish the work we are in, to bind up the nation's wounds, to care for him who shall have borne the battle and for his widow and his orphan, to do all which may achieve and cherish a just and lasting peace among ourselves and with all nations."
- ❖ Supreme Court Chief Justice Salmon Chase delivers the oath of office.

❖ The presidential party moves to the White House for the traditional post-inaugural reception.

❖ Frederick Douglass has trouble getting in. Inside, AL comes over to him and asks Douglass' opinion of his speech. "A sacred effort," Douglass calls it.

March 5, Sunday

❖ AL attends religious services in the morning with MTL at the Capitol.

❖ AL confers with Thurlow Weed about Fessenden's pending departure from the Cabinet. (He was elected to the Senate.)

❖ AL asks Comptroller of Currency Hugh McCulloch to become Secretary of the Treasury.

March 6, Monday

❖ Fessenden officially resigns as Secretary of the Treasury. AL nominates McCulloch to replace him.

❖ The Senate convenes for a special session.

❖ AL hosts a reception for the diplomatic corps at noon.

❖ AL poses for photographs.

❖ Supreme Court Chief Justice Salmon Chase confers with AL about exempting counties in Eastern Virginia from insurrectionary status.

❖ AL and MTL arrived at the Inaugural Ball (attended by about 4,000 people) after 10 p.m. Dinner is held shortly after midnight. The couple withdraws at about 1 a.m.

March 7, Tuesday

Gen. Sherman's forces reach North Carolina.

❖ AL spends considerable time issuing permits for people with products inside rebel lines to bring them into Union lines for sale to government agents.

❖ AL sees the editor of French-language newspaper in New York, and sends him to Welles with a suggestion that Welles place government advertisements in the newspaper. (There is no record that he ever did.)

❖ The Senate confirms McCullough as Secretary of the Treasury.

❖ AL attends a Cabinet meeting.

❖ AL sends Gen. Grant the gold medal bestowed on him by Congress in 1863.

❖ AL and MTL attend Friedrich von Flotow's *Martha* at Grover's Theater. The crowd applauds AL after they finally notice he has entered his box.

March 8, Wednesday

❖ AL receives the resignation of Usher as Secretary of the Interior. (He continued to serve for two months. AL did not think there should be two Cabinet members from the same state, and Usher and McCullough were both from Indiana.)

❖ AL offers Blair the position of minister to either Spain or Austria.

❖ AL receives a delegation from Pennsylvania concerned about the way the draft is being applied.

❖ AL nominates a naval officer on the reserve list for promotion, as the man had missed his last promotion due to a service-related physical disability.

March 9, Thursday

❖ Maryland Gov. Thomas Swann and a delegation calls on AL to complain about certain of AL's recent appointments in Maryland. (These included Leopold Blumenberg, now superintendent of warehouses in the Baltimore customhouse, whom AL had inquired about on January 25, 1865.)

❖ AL discovers that the messenger carrying James Gordon Bennet's reply to AL's offer of the position as minister to France is stuck in Philadelphia by bad weather, but the

Senate will adjourn Saturday, so it will soon be too late for a confirmation hearing. (When the messenger finally got through, AL found that Bennet had declined the position, citing his age, sixty-nine.)

March 10, Friday

* AL confers with Maine railroad and credit reporting magnate John Poor about offering a Cabinet position to Hamlin, who is also from Maine.
* AL attends a Cabinet meeting.

March 11, Saturday

* AL proclaims amnesty for all deserters who return by May 10, 1865, and serve their original enlistments.
* MTL hosts her last Saturday reception for the season.
* AL nominates Nicolay as consul at Paris. He is immediately confirmed by the Senate.
* The Senate adjourns.
* Browning and others confer with AL about James W. Singleton and his schemes to make millions through trade with the South.

March 12, Sunday

* AL offers Illinois Rep. Isaac Arnold a position as a Treasury Department auditor.
* AL meets with his old friend Dr. Anson Henry—who suddenly asks to be made head of the Bureau of Indian Affairs. AL notes that the job is already filled, and Henry is satisfied.

March 13, Monday

The Confederacy begins enlisting black soldiers.

* AL asks Gen. Grant to look into the case of 200,000 pounds of tobacco destroyed by Union troops in Fredericksburg,

Virginia, that was supposed to be connected to the schemes of James W. Singleton.

❖ AL, sick, is not seeing visitors.

March 14, Tuesday

❖ AL is confined to his bed with influenza. The Cabinet meets in his room.

March 15, Wednesday

❖ AL is recovering from influenza and able to conduct a limited amount of business.
❖ AL responds to Thurlow Weed, who had written AL to praise his speech given in response to his official notification of reelection. AL thanks him, and then critiques his own Second Inaugural Address: "Perhaps better than anything I have produced; but I believe it is not immediately popular. Men are not flattered by being shown that there has been a difference of purpose between the Almighty and them."
❖ AL confers at length with a delegation from Louisiana about the organization of civil government there.
❖ Welsh writer Samuel Roberts, who covers America for newspapers in England and Wales, meets with AL.
❖ AL and MTL see Mozart's *The Magic Flute* at Grover's Theater, accompanied by Gen. James Wilson and by Clara Harris, daughter of New York Sen. Ira Harris.

March 16, Thursday

The Confederates unsuccessfully try to stop Gen. Sherman's army at the Battle of Averasborough.

❖ AL still feels feeble and takes a carriage ride with Tad.
❖ AL tells Browning that Stanton has gone to see Gen. Grant about the operations of James W. Singleton.

March 17, Friday

❖ AL issues a "Proclamation Concerning Trade with Indians" calling for a court-martial for anyone supplying arms to hostile Indians.

❖ At a ceremony on a National Hotel balcony, AL presents a rebel flag to Indiana Gov. Oliver Morton that was captured by an Indiana regiment.

❖ AL then speaks, expressing amazement that the Confederacy would enlist black soldiers, and especially that black men would fight for the Confederacy, saying that such men might prefer slavery. "I would allow those colored persons to be slaves who want to be; and next to them those white persons who argue in favor of making other people slaves."

March 18, Saturday

❖ AL discharges draftee Charles Dorsett, as he is married and has a brother in a rebel prison.

❖ AL dismisses the fraud conviction against the Smith brothers, in Boston, saying it is "beyond the power of rational belief" that they would commit a $100 fraud as part of a million-dollar contract.

March 19, Sunday

Gen. Sherman's forces encounter a Confederate force at Bentonville, North Carolina, triggering three days of fighting.

❖ AL approves the plans of Gen. John Pope in St. Louis to gradually demilitarize Missouri and return control of civil life to the civil authorities.

March 20, Monday

❖ AL meets with Russian minister Baron de Stoeckl and predicts that the war will be over by the end of the year.

- ❖ AL accepts an invitation to visit Gen. Grant's headquarters at City Point, Virginia, "after the next rain."
- ❖ At the request of New York. Rep. Thomas Davis, AL releases a POW.
- ❖ AL confers about patronage with Maryland Gov. Thomas Swann and Maryland Sen. John Creswell.
- ❖ AL confers with Washington Territory Gov. William Pickering concerning Pickering's reappointment.

March 21, Tuesday

The Confederates retreat from Bentonville, ending serious efforts to stop Gen. Sherman.

- ❖ AL offers to make Gen. Walter Scates (former Illinois chief justice) chief justice of New Mexico Territory if he chooses to reside there. (He chose not to.)
- ❖ AL attends a Cabinet meeting.
- ❖ AL and MTL see Francois-Adrien Boieldieu's "La Dame Blanche" at Grover's Theater.

March 22, Wednesday

- ❖ Massachusetts Sen. Charles Sumner shows AL a letter from the Duchess of Argyll, who expresses a belief that "the speech at the Gettysburg Cemetery must live."
- ❖ Hay is appointed secretary of legation at Paris, to leave in a month.

March 23, Thursday

- ❖ AL and party, including MTL and Tad, leave Washington at about 1 p.m. aboard the River Queen.

March 24, Friday

- ❖ AL arrives at City Point, Virginia, at about 9 p.m. and meets with Gen. Grant.

- ❖ Mrs. Grant has a separate meeting with MTL, who is annoyed when Mrs. Grant sits down before MTL invites her to.
- ❖ The River Queen is moored outbound of Gen. Grant's headquarters boat, but MTL will not cross "Mrs. Grant's boat," so the vessels must be switched whenever MTL goes ashore.

March 25, Saturday

During the night, the Confederates storm the Union trenches outside Petersburg, Virginia, at Fort Stedman, hoping to relieve the pressure on Richmond. It is a bloody failure.

- ❖ Capt. Robert Lincoln arrives for breakfast and tells of the fighting.
- ❖ AL visits Gen. Grant's headquarters and asks to visit the battleground.
- ❖ At noon, AL boards the military railroad and goes seven miles to the front. They mount horses to reach the Fort Stedman area.
- ❖ The dead and wounded are still being brought in. AL sees 1,600 forlorn, ragged prisoners march by.
- ❖ AL keeps remarking that he hopes no further bloodshed will be necessary.
- ❖ They return to the train. Cars carrying wounded men are attached. AL seeks to comfort some of them. A young Confederate with a head wound dies calling for his mother. AL weeps.
- ❖ Back at City Point, AL joins Gen. Grant and others around a campfire and says little at first. Then he reminiscences about the difficulties encountered in the war, but says he never doubted the Union could prevail.
- ❖ AL goes to bed early.

March 26, Sunday

- ❖ AL approves Stanton's plans for a commemorative flag-raising at Fort Sumter on the anniversary of its surrender.

- ❖ AL finds and adopts three stray kittens.
- ❖ AL's ship moves down the James River where AL can view the forces of Gen. Philip Sheridan as they cross, having arrived overland from the Shenandoah Valley.
- ❖ AL then reviews the naval squadron.
- ❖ The presidential party then proceeds to a campground to review an army unit. Hear that the troops have been waiting for hours and missed lunch, AL presses ahead to start immediately.
- ❖ The troops cheer AL enthusiastically as he rides down the lines.
- ❖ Trailing behind in her carriage, MTL is enraged to hear that the wife of a general got permission to remain at the front. She is mollified when told that Stanton gave the permission.
- ❖ MTL arrives and finds another woman on horseback near AL. She is enraged, saying the woman is trying to act like the president's wife, and lashes out of Mrs. Grant and others who try to argue with her.
- ❖ At dinner, MTL insists that AL fire the woman's husband, a general.
- ❖ After dark, AL calls another officer, who witnessed the scene, to his bedroom and has the officer recount what he saw, and MTL tries to get the officer to see it her way. He remains neutral.

March 27, Monday

- ❖ AL announces that MTL is unwell.
- ❖ AL visits Gen. Grant's headquarters in the morning and returns for lunch.
- ❖ After lunch, the presidential party takes a sightseeing excursion on the Appomattox River.
- ❖ Gen. Sherman arrives in the evening and AL has a meeting with him, Gen. Grant, and Admiral David Porter. They explain that the biggest danger is that Lee's army will escape before Gen. Sherman's army arrives.

❖ AL repeatedly asks if it will be possible to end the war without another bloody battle. The generals respond that it is up to the Confederates.

March 28, Tuesday

❖ AL meets again in the morning with Gen. Grant, Gen. Sherman, Admiral David Porter, and several other generals.
❖ Gen. Sherman leaves at about noon to return to his army in North Carolina.
❖ MTL remains in seclusion.

March 29, Wednesday

Union forces outside Petersburg, advance around the west end of the trench lines.

French troops take Guaymas, Mexico.

❖ AL stays aboard the River Queen but sends telegrams inquiring about the various actions going on along the front.
❖ MTL remains in seclusion.

March 30, Thursday

Operations around Petersburg, are slowed by torrential rains.

❖ AL stays aboard the *River Queen*. Seward joins him.
❖ MTL remains in seclusion.

March 31, Friday

West of Petersburg, the Union offensive is stopped by a Confederate counterattack.

- ❖ AL stays aboard the *River Queen* and gets regular reports of the fighting from Gen. Grant's headquarters.
- ❖ AL is depressed to realize that there will be a general attack on Petersburg, triggering another bloody battle.
- ❖ Stanton urges AL to remain a few more days at the front: "A pause by the army now would do harm; if you are on the ground there will be no pause."
- ❖ MTL remains in seclusion.

APRIL 1865

Summary: With victory almost at hand, AL glimpses a future of peace and prosperity, albeit not without further struggles for justice and equality. It is only a glimpse.

April 1, Saturday

> West of Petersburg, Virginia, reinforced Federals launch another attack—and the defense crumbles.

❖ AL spends much of the day ashore going over telegrams and updating situation maps.

❖ AL is shown Confederate battle flags captured earlier in the day.

❖ MTL leaves at about noon with Seward and Carl Schurz to return to the White House. MTL spends the trip telling Schurz gossip.

❖ Tad remains with AL.

❖ AL returns to the River Queen in the evening and is seen walking the deck most of the night.

April 2, Sunday

> A Union predawn attack shatters the rebel front outside Petersburg. Lee orders a full retreat. Richmond evacuates.

❖ AL spends much of the day sending and receiving telegrams.

❖ He informs MTL of the situation.

❖ He rides out to Petersburg to view the fighting from a distance.

April 3, Monday

Union troops occupy Richmond. Lee's hotly pursued army struggles over multiple roads to the west.

❖ AL and Tad visit Gen. Grant in Petersburg, which is now Union-occupied. They are also joined by Capt. Robert Lincoln and Admiral David Porter.

❖ Their train stops while thousands of rebel prisoners—ragged, barefoot boys—are marched across the track. AL reacts: "Poor boys! Poor boys! If only they knew what we were trying to do for them they would not have fought us, and they would not look as they do."

❖ AL beams while he shakes Gen. Grant's hand: "I had a sort of sneaking idea all along that you intended to do something like this."

❖ They talk for about ninety minutes about post-war policy. AL emphasizes that he wants leniency.

❖ Back at City Point, Virginia, AL looks refreshed and energized.

❖ In the evening, AL telegraphs MTL: "Petersburg and Richmond are both in our hands; and Tad and I have been to the former and been with Bob four or five hours. He is well and in good spirits. Come down as you proposed." (MTL had announced a plan to return to City Point.)

❖ AL also telegraphed Stanton: "Yours received. Thanks for your caution…. I will take care of myself."

April 4, Tuesday

Tad's 12th birthday.

❖ AL and Tad move up the James River in the River Queen, switching to a warship and then to a rowed gig.

❖ They land at Richmond at about 3 p.m., accompanied by four officers and a dozen armed sailors, and head into the city through ecstatic crowds of mostly black people.

- ❖ When individuals kneel to AL and kiss his feet, he tells them to stop. They are free citizens of a republic. They should kneel only to God.
- ❖ They soon attract a larger escort, and ask to be taken to the Confederate White House. AL sits in Jefferson Davis's chair, asks for a drink, and looks weary.
- ❖ AL meets privately with some Confederate officials who show up, led by John Campbell, who had been one of the Confederate commissioners at the Hampton Roads conference. They agree to meet again tomorrow to discuss peace arrangements.
- ❖ AL is given a tour of the city in an ordinary buggy.
- ❖ The presidential party spends the night in a warship on the river.
- ❖ Southern manufacturing and railroad magnate Duff Green comes aboard the ship to meet AL, who greets him as a friend. Green then calls AL a tyrant and murderer who started the war and accuses of AL of coming to Virginia to gloat. AL, for once, responds in kind, saying (among other things, as rendered by a naval officer): "You talk of the North cutting the throats of the Southern people. You have all cut your own throats, and, unfortunately, have cut many of those of the North. Miserable impostor, vile intruder!" Green simply leaves.

April 5, Wednesday

- ❖ AL again goes ashore at Richmond and meets with Confederate official John Campbell.
- ❖ AL lists his preconditions: reunion, the end of hostilities, and the end of slavery. Those who persist in fighting can expect confiscations. Campbell spells out possible peacemaking procedures based on negotiations with Confederate officials. There is discussion of convening the Virginia legislature to vote the state, and its troops, out of the Confederacy. AL says he will think about it.

- ❖ AL then meets with the occupation commander. As for treating the locals, AL advises, "I'd let 'em up easy."
- ❖ AL returns to City Point. A captured Confederate general asks to see AL. The man turns out to be Rufus Barringer of North Carolina, younger brother of Daniel M. Barringer, a fellow Whig whom AL had been friends with when AL was in Congress. They talk about old times. At the end of their conversation, AL gives him a note for Stanton asking for comfortable detention for Barringer, who steps outside, breaks down, and weeps.
- ❖ In the morning, MTL leaves Washington to return to City Point. She is accompanied by freedwoman dress designer Elizabeth Keckly; Massachusetts Sen. Charles Sumner; his friend the Marquis de Chambrun; Iowa Sen. and Mrs. James Harlan and their daughter Mary (whom RTL would marry in 1868); Speed, and others.
- ❖ At 6 p.m., AL learns that Seward was seriously injured in a carriage accident.

April 6, Thursday

- ❖ AL directs that "the gentlemen who have acted as the Legislature of Virginia, in support of the rebellion" can assemble in Richmond to withdraw from the war. If they do anything hostile they are to be dispersed.
- ❖ AL visits headquarters seeking news on Gen. Grant's operations. Meanwhile he reads aloud from the works of humorist Artemus Ward (Charles Farrar Browne).
- ❖ MTL and party arrive at noon. Relaying news of victories, AL looks serene.

April 7, Friday

Gen. Grant opens correspondence with Lee, who asks what terms Gen. Grant has in mind.

- ❖ AL reviews telegraph traffic and forwards reports of victories to Stanton.

- ❖ MTL and party visit Richmond.
- ❖ AL telegraphs Gen. Grant: "Gen. Sheridan says, 'If the thing is pressed I think that Lee will surrender.' Let the thing be pressed."
- ❖ AL remarks to one official that, "Sheridan seemed to be getting Virginia soldiers out of the war faster than this legislature could think."
- ❖ AL reviews troops and shakes hands.
- ❖ Maine Rep. James Blaine and Illinois Rep. Elihu Washburne, also visiting the front, visit AL in the evening aboard the *River Queen*, with Mrs. Grant. They discuss the desirability of arresting and hanging Jefferson Davis, but AL will not endorse the idea.
- ❖ Someone mentions seeing women kiss AL's hand during his Tuesday visit to Richmond, triggering a tantrum by MTL.

April 8, Saturday

Gen. Grant states his terms to Lee: parole until exchanged.

- ❖ AL takes his guests up the military railroad and then by carriage to visit Petersburg.
- ❖ MTL snaps at Mrs. Grant and Mrs. Harlan for sitting next to her without permission and rolls on the ground tearing her hair when she finds that other women have been invited.
- ❖ A black boy offers to "tote" something for AL, who has never heard the word. Massachusetts Sen. Charles Sumner fills him in, at length.
- ❖ Some of the black servants on the *River Queen* ask to come along. AL has them sit with him on the train, to the amazement of the Marquis de Chambrun.
- ❖ On the way back, AL stops to admire a tree.
- ❖ Then he stops to admire a rural graveyard and tells MTL he would prefer being buried in such a place.
- ❖ On the military railroad, he stops the train to retrieve a turtle by the roadside that amuses him and Tad.

❖ In the afternoon, AL spends five hours touring military hospitals and shaking hands. One man dies shortly after greeting him.

❖ AL also goes to the tent of the Confederate prisoners, who (although surprised) also shake hands.

❖ Back on the steamboat AL tells the Marquis de Chambrun that there will be no war with France over Mexico. He has the band play "La Marseillaise." The marquis has not heard it, as the revolutionary song is banned in France.

❖ The *River Queen* leaves for Washington at 10 p.m. AL stands silently at the rail, watching the landscape.

April 9, Sunday, Palm Sunday

Lee surrenders.

❖ AL reads aloud from Shakespeare to his guests on the *River Queen.*

❖ The Marquis de Chambrun describes AL's mood as cycling from open and generous to deep, silent sadness, which he would fight off before returning to apparent good humor. He sees AL repeat the cycle twenty times in an evening.

❖ AL arrives in Washington at about 6 p.m. Bonfires celebrate rumors of Lee's surrender.

❖ AL visits the injured Seward and tells him about the trip and of shaking 7,000 hands, leaving when Seward falls asleep.

❖ AL returns to the White House exhausted. He revives when Stanton arrives with a telegram from Gen. Grant. "Gen. Lee surrendered."

❖ A crowd calls for AL to speak, but he only responds "pleasantly."

April 10, Monday

❖ AL is repeatedly serenaded by celebratory throngs and repeatedly tells them that he'll have a speech written tomorrow. The Marine band is leading one of the crowds and AL has them play "Dixie" as the Union has "fairly captured it."

❖ AL attends a Cabinet meeting.
❖ AL confers with Browning on various topics.
❖ AL poses for photographs.

Comparing what is traditionally called the "last photograph of Lincoln from life," at right, to his first official photo with a full beard, we can see the toll that the presidency had taken on him.

April 11, Tuesday

French troops are defeated at Tacambaro, Mexico.

❖ AL attends a Cabinet meeting where they discuss cotton trading regulations.
❖ AL consults with Gen. Butler on problems involving freed slaves.

❖ AL sends Ward Hill Lamon to Richmond to consult about reconstruction. (That made him unavailable for security Friday.)

❖ As promised yesterday, AL delivers a speech (his last public address) from a White House window to a celebratory throng. He thanks God and the military for the recent victories, and then delivers a lengthy defense of his reconstruction policy in Louisiana. He mentions that he would prefer that black veterans and "very intelligent" blacks be given the vote—enraging John Wilkes Booth in the crowd.

April 12, Wednesday

❖ AL has breakfast with Browning, who introduces AL to Alabama unionist William Bibb, and they discuss reconstruction.

❖ AL cancels permission for the Virginia Confederate legislature to convene, as they view the permission as recognition of the rebel government's legitimacy. (Stanton also objected to the permission on those grounds.)

❖ AL discusses patronage in Nebraska with Iowa Sen. James Harlan and with William Kellogg, the former chief justice of the Nebraska Territory.

❖ AL discusses reconstruction with the Marquis de Chambrun, and says he intends to insist on clemency for the Confederates.

❖ AL endorses the decision of the commander of the Union occupation force in Richmond to not require prayers for AL on Sunday in churches.

April 13, Thursday

❖ AL visits the telegraph office early in the morning looking for news.

❖ AL confers with Stanton, Welles, and Gen. Grant of the military situation.

- ❖ AL issues passes to people wanting to go into the South, including James W. Singleton.
- ❖ AL writes to his old friend, Supreme Court Chief Justice David Davis, asking him not to argue with Speed, also his old friend. (They had disagreed about a judge in Idaho Territory.)
- ❖ AL has a headache and declines to accompany MTL on a tour of the various celebratory illuminations around town.
- ❖ MTL gets Gen. Grant to accompany her instead. Repeatedly the crowds chant "Grant!" and she feels slighted and moves to get out, and then changes her mind when the crowds also chant "Lincoln!"

April 14, Friday, Good Friday

- ❖ AL has breakfast with Capt. Robert Lincoln, who tells him of what he saw of Lee's surrender. AL urges him to leave the army and finish law school.
- ❖ Discovering they are expected to accompany AL and MTL to the theater that night, Gen. and Mrs. Grant decide to visit their children in New Jersey, and leave town on a train.
- ❖ AL confers with Indiana Rep. Schuyler Colfax, on his way to the West Coast. Rep. Colfax also declines the theater invitation.
- ❖ Mr. and Mrs. Stanton also decline the theater invitation, as does Stanton's assistant.
- ❖ AL confers with New Hampshire Sen. John Hale, who has been appointed minister to Spain.
- ❖ Numerous congressmen drop by to congratulate AL on the end of the war.
- ❖ In the telegraph office, AL invites the manager to the theater that evening. Stanton will not let him off, however. (AL had a standing joke about using the manager as a bodyguard, due to his outstanding strength.)
- ❖ AL confers with Maryland Gov. Thomas Swann and Maryland Sen. John Creswell on patronage in Maryland.

- ❖ For once looking crisp rather than rumpled, AL attends a Cabinet meeting where Gen. Grant reports on Lee's surrender, and Stanton discusses plans to reestablish Federal authority in the South.
- ❖ AL mentions a recurring dream to the Cabinet. He is on a "singular, indescribable vessel" moving rapidly toward a dark and indefinite shore. He had the dream before receiving other pieces of momentous news, so he assumes that important news will soon arrive, presumably of the final Confederate surrenders.
- ❖ AL and MTL have late lunch together.
- ❖ AL meets with Johnson (possibly for the first time since the inauguration).
- ❖ A black woman pushes into the room to see AL about her husband's pay.
- ❖ Ohio Rep. Samuel Shellabarger confers with AL about patronage.
- ❖ Informed that a Confederate agent in Canada has entered the U.S. on his way to Europe, AL says to let him go.
- ❖ McCulloch and New Hampshire Rep. Edward Rollins call on AL.
- ❖ AL and MTL go for a carriage ride. At the Navy Yard, they see three monitors damaged at Fort Fisher, North Carolina. AL talks of returning to private life after he finishes his term. She remarks at how cheerful AL seems.
- ❖ On returning they find Illinois Gov. Richard Oglesby and other Illinois friends at the White House. AL reads aloud from the works of humorist Petroleum V. Nasby (David Locke).
- ❖ Massachusetts Rep. George Ashmun asks to see AL about a claims matter, and AL agrees to see him at 9 a.m. tomorrow.
- ❖ AL exchanges some remarks with former Illinois congressman Isaac Arnold, his ally in the 13th Amendment passage, while getting in his carriage.
- ❖ Tad attends a children's production at Grover's Theater.
- ❖ The presidential party (including AL, MTL, her young friend Clara Harris, and Miss Harris' fiancé/stepbrother Major

Henry Rathbone) arrive at Ford's Theater at 8:30 p.m., about half an hour into the production of *Our American Cousin*, starring Laura Keene.

❖ AL tells his bodyguard to go watch the play. He heads to a nearby tavern instead.

❖ John Wilkes Booth shoots AL at 10:13 p.m. and then flees.

❖ At about the same time, as part of the same plot, Seward is stabbed by a home invader, as are several other people in his house. All survive.

❖ AL never regains consciousness. He is moved to a house across the street and placed on a bed in a first-floor room.

❖ Capt. Robert Lincoln arrives with Hay and is told there is no hope. He summons some friends of MTL, who sit with her in the next room.

April 15, Saturday

❖ Various officials come and go during the night. Stanton sets up an emergency headquarters.

❖ The pulse of AL ceases at 7:22:10 a.m.

❖ Stanton breaks the silence: "Now he belongs to the ages."

ᏝAFTERWORDᏟ

Well did Abraham Lincoln, in his Second Inaugural Address, marvel at the unexpected length and severity of the war. Had the eastern armies advanced at the same rate as the western armies, Richmond would have fallen by the end of summer 1862. Judging by what happened in 1865, the insurgency would have disintegrated soon thereafter.

But the issue of slavery would not have been resolved. Only by passing the 13th Amendment was the root cause of the war removed. Lincoln was able to get it passed only in early 1865, after years of horror had sufficiently altered Northern public opinion about the issue.

Meanwhile, an earlier end to the war would have meant that the South was not convincingly defeated. The result would likely have been guerrilla war, capable of re-igniting a full-scale war at some point.

But even with the slavery issue resolved, Lincoln was obviously not satisfied, and was aiming at full voting rights and civil rights for all citizens (or at least adult males). But his assassination removed him from the picture, and it was almost exactly a century before the issues were directly addressed in a manner that Lincoln would doubtlessly have preferred, with the Civil Rights Act of 1964 and the Voting Rights Act of 1965.

But to say that Lincoln embodied some kind of factor-of-twenty-five moral superiority is too parochial, as it only examines a few decades of the history of a single nation. Lincoln's impact may surpass that by yet another factor of twenty-five.

Russian novelist Count Leo Tolstoy, known worldwide as the author of *War and Peace* and *Anna Karenina,* and for his late-life quest for meaning in human existence, was asked in 1908 or early 1909 to write something for the upcoming centennial of Lincoln's birth. He was not able to do it. (He died in 1910.) But he did give an interview, telling of a Lincoln-related experience he once had.

He had been traveling the Caucasus Mountains and was the dinner guest of a Circassian chieftain. (Circassians lived in the northwest Caucasus, near the Black Sea.) After dinner, the chieftain began asking Tolstoy about the outside world.

Tolstoy told him about the latest developments in technology, and the man was uninterested. But when Tolstoy started talking about military and political events, the chieftain not only perked up but sent for his sons and neighbors, who sat around Tolstoy on the floor, listening raptly.

So he began with events in Russia and moved out to the rest of the world. When he spoke of Napoleon they wanted to hear every possible detail, down to the color of his horse. After Napoleon, Tolstoy thought he was done, but his host still had questions.

The chieftain said there was someone else they had heard about, a hero, said to be the greatest ruler of the world. He was so great that he forgave his mortal enemies and shook hands with those who plotted against his life. A man named Lincoln...

&BIBLIOGRAPHY&

The principal source was *Lincoln Day-by-Day: A Chronology*, compiled by the Lincoln Sesquicentennial Commission and the Abraham Lincoln Association, and published by the U.S. Government Printing Office in 1960. It is available online at http://www.thelincolnlog.org/ (and elsewhere) under the title "The Lincoln Log: A Daily Chronology of the Life of Abraham Lincoln." The online version also includes ongoing corrections and additions from the "Papers of Abraham Lincoln" project of the Illinois Historic Preservation Agency and the Abraham Lincoln Presidential Library and Museum. Also included are entries from third-party published memoirs, plus newspaper articles.

Other works consulted throughout include:

Burlingame, Michael. *Abraham Lincoln: A Life*. Baltimore: Johns Hopkins University Press, 2008 (2 volumes).

Goodwin, Doris Kearns. *Team of Rivals: The Political Genius of Abraham Lincoln*. New York: Simon & Schuster, 2005.

Long, E. B. *The Civil War Day by Day: An Almanac, 1861-1865*. New York: Doubleday & Co., 1971.

Keckley, Elizabeth. *Behind the Scenes, or, Thirty Years a Slave and Four Years in the White House*. New York: G. W. Carleton & Co., 1868.

Symonds, Craig L. *A Battlefield Atlas of the Civil War*. Baltimore: The Nautical and Aviation Publishing Company of America, 1983.

Esposito, Brig. Gen. Vincent J. *The West Point Atlas of American Wars, Volume 1, 1689-1900*. New York: Praeger Publishers, 1959.

Century Magazine staff. "Battles and Leaders of the Civil War." New York: Castle Books, 1956 (4 volumes, reprint of the 1887 original).

War Department. *The Ordnance Manual for the Use of Officers of the United States Army*. Philadelphia: J. B. Lippincott & Co., 1861.

Kautz, Brevet Major Gen. August V. *Customs of Service for Officers of the Army*. Philadelphia: J. B. Lippincott & Co., 1866.

War Department. *Official Army Records of the War of the Rebellion.* Washington, D.C.: War Department, 1901.

Bruce, Robert V. *Lincoln and the Tools of War.* Pickle Partners Publishing, 2017 (Reprint from 1956).

Haupt, Herman. *Reminiscences of General Herman Haupt,* Milwaukee: Wright & Joys, 1901.

Zurski, Ken. *Peoria Stories: Tales from the Illinois Heartland.* Chicago: Amika Press, 2014.

Brewer, James D. *Tom Worthington's Civil War: Shiloh, Sherman, and the Search for Vindication.* Jefferson, North Carolina: McFarland & Co., 2001.

Online material:
  New York Times
  The Library of Virginia
  Richmond Times Dispatch
  Chicago Tribune
  Everything Lincoln
  Naval Historical Center
  Find a Grave
  The Civil War Project
  Antietam on the Web
  Mr. Lincoln & Friends
  New York World
  Wikipedia

ଃ ABOUT ଞ THE AUTHOR

Lamont Wood is a journalist and history writer. He has been freelancing for more than three decades in the history, high-tech, and industrial fields. He has sold more than six hundred magazine feature articles and twelve books. He and his wife, Dr. Louise O'Donnell, reside in San Antonio, TX.